AN ARMY IN CRISIS

AN ARMY
IN CRISIS

SOCIAL CONFLICT AND THE

U.S. ARMY IN GERMANY, 1968–1975

ALEXANDER VAZANSKY

University of Nebraska Press   Lincoln

Library of Congress Cataloging-in-Publication Data
Names: Vazansky, Alexander.
Title: An army in crisis: social conflict in the U.S.
Army in Germany, 1968–1975 / Alexander Vazansky.
Description: Lincoln NE: University of Nebraska Press,
[2019] | Includes bibliographical references and index.
Identifiers: LCCN 2019003993
ISBN 9781496215192 (cloth: alk. paper)
ISBN 9781496217394 (epub)
ISBN 9781496217400 (mobi)
ISBN 9781496217417 (pdf)
Subjects: LCSH: United States. Army—Foreign
service—Germany (West)—History. | Soldiers—
Germany (West)—Social conditions. | Soldiers—United
States—Social conditions—20th century. | United
States—Race relations—History—20th century.
| Drug abuse—United States—History—20th
century. | Drug abuse—Germany (West)—History.
| Vietnam War, 1961–1975—Protest movements. |
Sociology, Military—Germany (West) | Sociology,
Military—United States—History—20th century.
Classification: LCC UA26.G3 V39 2019 |
DDC 355.1/23094309047—dc23
LC record available at https://lccn.loc.gov/2019003993

Set in Adobe Text by Mikala R. Kolander.
Designed by N. Putens.

CONTENTS

ACKNOWLEDGMENTS

It has been a long road from my original idea of exploring the GI experience in West Germany during the later phases of the Vietnam War. On the way I have received inspiration and support from many people. Allan Winkler encouraged me to pursue an academic career. After returning to Heidelberg Detlef Junker took a chance on a student he had never met and hired me as a graduate assistant. He suggested that I look into GIs in Germany as a focus for my research and graciously agreed to be my advisor. Over the years he has provided me with unique opportunities to grow as a scholar, teacher, and administrator. I owe him a debt that cannot be properly repaid. Philipp Gassert, who was then an assistant professor at Heidelberg, has also been a valuable source of advice and feedback through the years. There are few people I know who are not only great scholars but have a clear understanding of the workings of academia. Over the years Professor Junker has created an impressive network of scholars, many former students like Philipp, who have served as an inspiration and a resource for the younger generation of scholars like me. The current Curt Engelhorn Chair of American History at Heidelberg University, Manfred Berg, has been a friend and inspiration to me. Egbert Klautke, who I met long before becoming a graduate student, has nudged me in the right direction at crucial points in my academic career. Thomas Maulucci had just recently completed his degree at Yale when we started working together for Professor Junker. Over the years he has been a great friend, collaborator, and editor. I was fortunate to meet the great trailblazer regarding the history of GIs in Germany, Maria Höhn, early in my journey. She has been a source of inspiration and feedback, without which I would have never gotten to this place.

As I was based in Heidelberg, traveling to the relevant archives in the United States required considerable funding and support. I want to thank the German Historical Institute in Washington DC for providing me with a three-month doctoral fellowship and for accepting me into its Young Scholars Forum in 2003. Thanks to the generosity of the Jacob Gould Schurman Foundation, I was able to focus on my research and writing for a whole year in 2003.

The staff of multiple archives provided crucial support in letting me search their collections. Dieter Brünn and Dave Harris, who passed away a few years ago, granted me access to their Archiv für Soldatenrechte in Berlin. This collection is now housed at the International Institute of Social History (IISH) in Amsterdam and has been named the Brünn-Harris-Watts Collection. I want to thank the staff at the Library of the Army War College and at the U.S. Army Military History Institute, both in Carlisle, Pennsylvania, for their support, as well as the U.S. Army Military History Center at Fort McNair in Washington DC. I would also like to thank the staff at the Bundesarchiv in Freiburg.

I was fortunate to spent my graduate school years in Heidelberg among a cohort of brilliant students. Martin Klimke's sheer volume of activity was awe-inspiring. I am grateful for the opportunities he gave me to present at various conferences he co-organized and for his feedback on parts of my work. I want to thank Holger Klitzing, Mischa Honeck, and Thomas Gijswijt for the many interesting discussions we had regarding our scholarship. I am particularly grateful to Christiane Rösch, who as a friend, fellow graduate student, and administrator was a constant source of intellectual, moral, and professional support. My friend Alex Emmerich was an important presence in my life during some of the more difficult periods of completing my research.

I am grateful to Professor Junker, Philipp Gassert, Chris, and Alex for giving me the opportunity to teach and work at the newly created Heidelberg Center for American Studies at Heidelberg University in 2004. The experience I gained as a teacher and administrator have been invaluable in my academic career. Working at the HCA allowed me to complete my writing. It also brought me into contact with so many inspirational scholars, students, and colleagues. Bill Funk was the

HCA's first Fulbright fellow. He took the time to read my chapter on political dissent in USAREUR and provided me with invaluable feedback. Dietmar Schloss and Dorothea Fischer-Hornung were important academic influences even before my time at the HCA. I want to thank James Sparks, Ole Wangerin, Rebekka Weinel, Noemi Huber, Sebastian Werner, Claudia Müller, Sophie Lorentz, Elena Matveeva, Holly Uhl, Jana Freihöfer, Michael Tröger, and Anja Schüler for their warm collegiality and friendship. The HCA was one of the most entertaining and supportive places I have ever worked. I also wanted to thank Dani Albrecht and Simon Wendt, who worked at the Curt Engelhorn Chair during the same period, for their friendship. I was fortunate to encounter some extremely talented students at the HCA. Anthony Santoro and his wife, Iris Hahn-Santoro, as well as Amy Foster-Parish and her husband, Matt Parish, have become lifelong friends. I particularly want to thank my friend and co-MAS coordinator Anne Sommer (née Lübbers) for a great time sharing our responsibilities and an office. A very special thanks also goes to Wilfried Mausbach, the executive director at the HCA, who was a great boss and continues to be my friend.

After completing my studies in Heidelberg in 2009, I was fortunate to find a position as a lecturer in history at the University of Nebraska–Lincoln. I want to thank Ken Winkle, who was then the chair of the History Department, for giving me that opportunity. I want to thank Doug Seefeld and his wife, Tara Wood, for their friendship and early career advice. I will be forever grateful to Pete Maslowski for reading my work and suggesting that I submit the manuscript to the University of Nebraska Press. His feedback has been invaluable. Vanessa Gorman has been an inspiration as a teacher. Gerald Steinacher, Bedross Der Matossian, Katrina Jagodinski, and Sean Trundle have been great colleagues and friends. I am grateful to the entire history faculty and the College of Arts and Sciences for hiring me as an assistant professor in 2013. In completing this book I have relied heavily on the feedback of three colleagues. I am grateful to Will Thomas, for guiding me through my years as a visiting assistant and assistant professor as chair of the department, as well as his feedback on my manuscript.

Tim Mahoney has been an invaluable source of guidance and advice in completing this manuscript. James Garza has been a great mentor both as a teacher and writer. Our current chair, James LeSueur, has been a great source of support in these final stages of completing the manuscript. Outside the Department of History, Marco Abel, professor of English, has provided me with invaluable professional advice and scholarly opportunities. I am grateful for his friendship.

Neither my career as an academic nor the publication of this book would have been possible without the love and support of my family. I am deeply grateful to my late uncle Steve Davidson, my aunt, Sylvie Davidson, and my cousins Sarah and Sophie Davidson for their advice and support in seeking an academic career. They have hosted me in Carlisle and Washington during my many research trips. I never could have completed this work without them. My late uncle Ernst Vazansky provided me with financial and moral support during my student years. When I got married in 2009 I gained a new family. I want to thank my parents-in-law, Joseph and Frances Jones, my siblings-in-law, Antoinette, Stephanie, and Jelani Jones, my niece, Shianna, my nephew, Ian, and finally my great-niece, Chloé, for welcoming me into their family. I will be eternally grateful to my parents for allowing me to develop and pursue my interests wherever they led. My father, Peter Vazansky, imbued me with a deep love of history. The intellectual curiosity and quest for self-knowledge of my mother, Margaret, have been a profound inspiration. My brother, Christopher, and sister, Lisa, have been a bedrock of emotional support and stability in this often-difficult journey. Christopher's partner, Ariane, and the next generation of Vazanskys—Mathilda, Wanda, and Samuel—are a comfort and an inspiration. Finally, I want to thank my wife, Jeannette Eileen Jones. If we had not met and fallen in love in 2007 I might never have completed this project. She is my inspiration as a scholar, writer, activist, and partner. I love you!

In the summer of 1971 two *Washington Post* reporters, Haynes Johnson and George C. Wilson, visited bases of the U.S. Army all over the world talking to military and civilian officials stationed there. Among the bases visited were ten locations in Germany. The reporters wrote a series of articles entitled "Army in Anguish" that the *Post* published in September 1971. For their introductory article, the reporters chose to describe Merrell Barracks in Nuremberg. The predominant image evoked was one of decay; plaster fell from the walls and ceilings, windows were broken, and the halls were dimly lit. But the physical decay was not as significant as the breakdown in morale that accompanied it. Soldiers testified "to something more than physical neglect and disintegration." They spoke "of a breakdown in spirit, in ethics and in discipline." Soldiers were afraid to walk around the barracks at night because drug abuse, burglaries, acts of violence, and racial conflict had become a part of daily life.[1]

What the reporters observed among American troops in 1971 stood in stark contrast to what the reporters imagined the previous inhabitants of these barracks, the members of the German SS, must have looked like: "Outside the barracks young soldiers in floppy hats, wide dark glasses, t-shirts, and long hair stroll across cobblestones which 27 years ago resounded with the rhythmic stomp of storm trooper boots. The young American GIs on work detail carry out garbage cans whose metal sides are brightly painted with peace symbols."

In unfavorably comparing the current conditions with those of the past, the authors contrasted the disciplined and awe-inspiring military machine of the Third Reich with the run-down barracks and shabby looking GIs they saw now. The article evokes dismay at how far the army had fallen from its more glorious past when it had beaten

Germany's military might and marched into Nuremberg victorious. Now twenty-six years later, the reporters argued, Nuremberg had become the symbol of the army's greatest crisis, a crisis that threatened the army's very existence. The symptoms of this crisis were "crime, drugs, racial conflict, rebellion against officers, boredom, and attitudes that always have been anathema to armies."

About the same time, other observers reported on the broader problems of the U.S. Army as a whole. In an article written for the *Armed Forces Journal*, Col. Robert Heinl claimed that the morale, discipline, and battle worthiness of the U.S. armed forces was "lower and worse than at any time in this century and possibly in the history of the United States."[2] While Heinl wrote about all four armed services, the army was the primary concern. The greatest problem the armed forces were facing, Heinl believed, was political dissent within their ranks, reflected by the formation of dissent organizations and publishing of numerous underground newspapers. According to Heinl, the federal government and federal courts were uninterested in the matter or they shared the dissenters' antimilitary views. Other army officers shared Heinl's concerns. Lt. Col. William L. Hauser concurred that the army was "going through its most trying time" due to the aftermath of an "unwon" war in Vietnam, a crisis of conscience rooted in atrocities and criminality among the troops, and a general failure to "come to terms with the Age of Aquarius."[3] Even Gen. William Westmoreland, chief of staff and former commander of the forces in Vietnam, acknowledged that the U.S. Army was experiencing a "social crisis" due to increasing drug usage and racial tensions.[4]

How had it come to this? The conditions at Nuremberg that the *Washington Post* reported on in 1971 were especially shocking because they described a breakdown of order and discipline in West Germany. Since its vaunted military victory in 1945 and the United States' decision to maintain 250,000 troops in Germany after the war, the U.S. Army had for the most part been a model of what a peacetime occupying army stationed in an ally's country should be. The army had benefited for twenty-five years from the positive results of U.S. foreign policy toward West Germany and the deference of the Federal Republic toward it, and it established cordial and even friendly relations with German society. As an occupying army, which had brought as many as 16 million Americans, both service members and their dependents, to Germany at one time or another between 1945 and 1990, the U.S. Army was, for many Germans, the face of U.S. society. And the way the Germans interacted with the U.S. Army among them formulated the general image that Americans had of postwar Germany. Thousands of U.S. Army personnel married Germans and had children, thus creating transnational families who lived within a transnational German and American society. As a result, the U.S. Army, occupying a former military adversary, now a trusted ally in Cold War Europe, was as much a social entity as a military and diplomatic entity.

The history of long-term occupations has received increased scholarly attention as U.S. forces have been deployed in postconflict roles in more and more places.[5] Political scientists have used the comparisons to the U.S. occupation of Germany and Japan to determine the viability and chances of success of future occupations. Historians such as Gregory P. Downs have studied the political and social impact of the army's Reconstruction era occupation of the southern states.[6] Anni Baker has written a study examining the social, economic, and political impact of U.S. military forces around the world.[7] While the western occupation of the Federal Republic formally ended with its entry into NATO on May 5, 1955, West Germany's sovereignty remained incomplete. The Allies retained the right to station troops on German territory and ensure the security of those forces.[8] The U.S. Army in Europe became one of the largest and longest serving occupation forces in U.S. history.

Recognizing the particularly complicated context in which any occupying army exists, this study is a social and cultural history of how the "social crisis" among the U.S. Army forces stationed in Germany unfolded between 1968 and 1975. I argue that the social crisis was caused by an intersection of three major developments. The shifting deployment of the U.S. Army across the world during the years of the Vietnam War had a dramatic impact on the position and experiences of the U.S. Army personnel in Germany. Likewise, the changing social and political realities of life in postwar Germany and Europe began to shift the interactions between the U.S. Army and its host society. And finally, and perhaps most important, the dramatic political and social transformations happening in American society caused by the civil rights movement, the Vietnam War, and the youth movement in the 1960s and early 1970s resulted in a dramatic rise in racial tensions, drug use, dissent, and even insubordination within the U.S. Army in Germany in the late 1960s.

The entire fifty-year postwar period during which an estimated 16 million Americans lived in Germany as a result of the U.S. military presence has elicited relatively few historical accounts. When more than 2.6 million soldiers occupied Germany in the final days of World War II in 1945, nobody believed that there would still be American troops stationed in Germany twenty years later, nor that the history of the U.S. presence in Germany would span more than fifty years.[9] The initial occupation period between 1945 and 1949 has received increased attention from historians.[10]

During this early period, German deference to the U.S. forces was highest. Despite the ban on fraternization, relations between the U.S. occupiers and Germans became increasingly cordial. As GIs began to see Germans as victims, they adopted the role of their providers and protectors.[11]

The conventional narrative for the 1950s regarding U.S. troop presence in Germany is one of growing familiarity and trust between the Germans and the Americans. The Berlin Crisis and the emerging Cold War polarization of 1949 brought a mutual perception of each other as allies in the confrontation with the Soviet Union. The signing of the North Atlantic Treaty in April 1949 and the invasion of South Korea in June 1950 led to the realization that a more permanent U.S. presence on the European frontline of the Cold War would be necessary. The Truman and Eisenhower administrations reinforced the strength of the U.S. forces in Germany to more than 300,000 by 1954. The largest contingent was that of the army.[12] The reactivation of the Seventh Army in Stuttgart breathed new life into U.S. Army, Europe (USAREUR). By the end of 1951, the United States had more than 230,000 soldiers stationed in Germany. The number would hover around a quarter of a million throughout the 1950s and well into the 1960s.[13]

The strategic and operational outlook for USAREUR shifted considerably. During the Eisenhower era, the army struggled to define its role within a strategic outlook predicated heavily on nuclear deterrence. USAREUR reorganized units into pentomic divisions emphasizing the use of tactical nuclear weapons in any future military confrontation with the Warsaw Pact. This reorganization proved difficult and was deemed operationally flawed, but it allowed the army to justify the presence of a large conventional force in West Germany.[14]

The fact that such an extensive military presence became a permanent institution in Germany had a profound impact on the lives of the large number of U.S. soldiers stationed there as well as on the lives of their German hosts.[15] A significant development leading to differences between the early occupation period of the late 1940s and the military presence in the 1950s was the influx of dependents. By 1953, more than 78,000 dependents were living in Europe. The rising number of U.S. personnel and civilians led to the establishment of entire American communities within Germany.[16]

Maria Höhn's work provides the most groundbreaking and insightful analysis of the impact of these communities in Germany. To a certain degree Höhn's study reinforces and verifies the common narrative of the 1950s as the "golden years" of German-American relations where the efforts of military commanders to portray the U.S. presence in terms of friendship and common political and cultural interests was largely successful. However, Höhn also complicates this predominantly positive narrative of the 1950s by inserting race and gender into her analysis. She shows that despite overall goodwill, at times cultural differences made relations tense.

The complications and ambivalences that Höhn reveals in contrast to the overall positive view of the U.S. presence during the 1950s are important in setting the stage for what occurred a decade later. There have been no similar historical analyses of the 1960s or 1970s.[17] The book will analyze the social conflicts afflicting the U.S. troops in USA-REUR between 1968 and 1975, factoring in the German environment in which these conflicts emerged.

The study begins in 1968, which was a momentous year in both countries. It represented the culmination and turning point for the 1960s protest movements. However, the main focus is on the early 1970s, ending with Gen. Michael S. Davison's retirement in 1975. During this period the U.S. Army in Germany became a site of the mainstreaming and co-optation of 1960s issues, particularly regarding racial equality and the treatment of drug users. But it became equally exemplary for the fragmentation of the protest movements and the failure of the more radical elements to foment revolution or insurrection.

In his book *Decade of Nightmares* Philip Jenkins argues that rather than seeing the 1970s as a distinct era, the early 1970s should be interpreted as an extension of the long 1960s that came to an end with the resignation of Richard Nixon. The years 1974 and 1975 represent a sharp break in U.S. history and culture that make it "difficult to think of 'the Seventies' as a meaningful period." The years after 1975 mark the beginning of the 1980s. Accordingly, the early years of the decade saw the mainstreaming of the 1960s. Political conflicts and social changes were affecting institutions and communities "beyond the political elites and the major cities." The situation in USAREUR and the U.S. armed services very much reflected this idea. As an institution that had officially integrated in the early 1950s, the U.S. Army had not been a major focal point of early 1960s civil rights activism. However, the shift toward black power and cultural nationalism and the concurrent exposure of structural and cultural racism outside the segregationist South had major implications for the armed forces as well. Similarly, antiwar activism within the army lost its impetus as the Vietnam War receded in importance in the public mind. Drug abuse policies still strongly focused on rehabilitation, another marker of the 1960s, rather than criminalization despite Nixon's "War on Drugs" rhetoric. The retirement of the USAREUR commander in chief, General Davison, in 1975 also marked the end of the social crisis or at least the perception thereof.

Up until the escalation of U.S. involvement in Vietnam in 1964, West Germany had been the most essential American outpost. Once the Kennedy administration placed greater emphasis on the concept of "flexible response," the justification for a strong conventional force in Europe became less strained. Thus much of the military resources in both men and material were concentrated in Germany. Officers sought out assignments in Germany to advance their careers. This had changed by 1970. Just as "flexible response" became the guiding concept placing central importance on USAREUR and Seventh Army in U.S. and NATO's strategic planning, the U.S. engagement in Vietnam threatened the readiness and operational transformation of the forces in Germany.[18] Because of the intensified engagement of the United States in Southeast Asia after the Tonkin Gulf Resolution of 1964, resources shifted away from Europe to Vietnam. By 1969, many officers and noncommissioned officers in the senior ranks had been relocated to Vietnam, leaving a serious shortage of experienced personnel in Germany. Funding and equipment were also in short supply. As a result, training exercises became increasingly hard to conduct. The barracks, most of which had been taken over from the German army in 1945, were in bad condition, but USAREUR did not have sufficient funds for building renovations.[19] Commanders in Germany were left with the unenviable task of maintaining U.S. readiness in Germany. Even though Germany was becoming once again the army's premier military outpost as the involvement in Vietnam was coming to a close, officers no longer sought out duty in Germany. Instead, it had become an assignment to avoid. Thus developments in USAREUR as the scene of the army's most dramatic social crises both before and after the Vietnam War make it the most interesting focus for study and analysis.

In West Germany, three major problem areas surfaced consistently: race relations, drug abuse, and dissent. They will form the major focus of this analysis. The term "dissent" normally referred to opposition among enlisted men to the hardships of army life, to the perceived arbitrariness of army regulations, and to the officers and noncommissioned officers enforcing them, as well as to the war in Vietnam. Although I will describe each problem area separately, the interrelationships among these three areas were apparent to most contemporaries. While reporters, soldiers, and other contemporaries in Germany normally referred to political opposition and resistance as a problem separate from race relations and drug abuse, the term actually encompassed all three areas.

In 1977 sociologist Lawrence B. Radine published an analysis of social control in the U.S. Army. The army's approaches to social control, he found, ranged from suppression of dissidence and coercive control to professional paternalistic control and to what he termed co-optive rational control using behavioral science and management.[20] The approaches introduced by Radine are useful in exploring the leadership's handling of the situation in Germany between 1968 and 1975. The two generals who successively served as commander in-chief of the U.S. Army, Europe (CINCUSAREUR) in Germany varied in their priorities and the emphasis they placed on employing these different approaches. These variations in emphasis influenced their success in containing the social crisis. Only by placing more priority on open communications and responsible leadership or, to put it in Lawrence's frame of reference, by emphasizing co-optive strategies and professional paternalism did they succeed in quieting social relations in their commands. The programs and policies that Davison and his subordinate commanders introduced in West Germany between 1971 and 1975, particularly the reforms of the military justice system and the drug abuse policies, later served as models for implementation in the entire army.

The discontent among black soldiers in 1968 in Germany surprised their officers. The U.S. armed forces had officially become an integrated institution in 1948 with Truman's executive order.[21] The last unit in Germany was integrated in November 1954 before *Brown vs. Board of Education*. Twenty years later officers in USAREUR faced black soldiers displaying black power symbols and calling for black unity.

Members of the Black Panther Party were agitating among soldiers in 1971. Riots involving battles between black and white soldiers were frequent. Events that had rocked society, such as the race riots in major U.S. cities starting with the Watts Riots in 1965 as well as the formation of the Black Panther Party in 1966, seemed to have caught up with the army. Black soldiers in Germany claimed rampant discrimination in the military justice system, in promotions, in housing, and in off-duty facilities. They believed that the army was suppressing and ignoring their cultural heritage.

Part 1 of this study deals with racial conflicts in USAREUR. The history of racial discrimination of black GIs in Germany before the 1960s is briefly explored in chapter 1. Chapter 2 then analyzes the situation as it presented itself to observers between 1968 and 1971. Gen. James H. Polk's attempted solutions as radicalization among black troops reached its highest mark form the focus of chapter 3. The final analysis in chapter 4 shows how the new commander in chief, Michael S. Davison, helped calm the situation between 1971 and 1975 by initiating a more aggressive public relations campaign and opening up more channels of communication.

The emphasis of this analysis will be on African American soldiers and their relations and conflicts with white soldiers and superiors. This topic received the most attention from contemporary media and other observers. The problems of other ethnic minorities, such as soldiers of Mexican or Puerto Rican descent, received far less coverage in the early 1970s.[22] Only toward the end of the decade did other minorities and women receive similar attention.[23]

Black soldiers were not alone in their dissatisfaction with social conditions in the army. Many white enlisted men also felt the need to express their disagreement with army policy and the war it was involved in. One way for a soldier to dissent was to go AWOL, to desert from the army. Despite the fact that they were in a foreign country and most were unable to speak the local language, many GIs deserted their units in Germany and went underground, often making their way to France or Sweden. In Paris, an organization formed that would play an essential role in voicing GI protests: Resistance Inside the Army. RITA was founded in 1967 and relocated to Heidelberg in 1969. As an organization, it brought together dissatisfied soldiers and outside organizers. RITA provided soldiers with another way to voice their grievances. RITA published or supported the publication of pamphlets, newsletters, and underground newspapers through which GIs could anonymously voice their opinions about their superiors and the army as an institution. Contributors to the underground newspapers not only criticized U.S. involvement in Vietnam but also questioned army regulations that they believed unnecessarily inhibited their freedom.

GIs also used the military courts to express their dissatisfaction and to fight injustice. In 1972, the Lawyers Military Defense Committee sent two lawyers, Howard J. De Nike and Robert Rivkin, to set up an office in Heidelberg.[24] The lawyers offered their services to GIs who preferred the counsel of outside civilian lawyers in their courts-martial cases. The Lawyers Military Defense Committee specialized in impact cases involving civil liberties. The lawyers associated themselves with RITA, and they fostered dissent within the army through the publicity of the trials they got involved in.

Part 2 explores opposition and resistance inside USAREUR in areas not related to race relations. The issues that aroused opposition in many GIs, such as the Vietnam War, hair and clothing regulations, and other limits on their personal freedom will be mapped out. The study will also attempt to measure the scope and the influence of the resistance movement. The army leadership's response to this form of dissent, which differed somewhat from its approach to race-related problems and drug abuse, will also be analyzed.

If the outbreak of racial and social discontent appeared surprising, the increase in drug use and addiction among servicemen in Germany seemed even more sudden. American society had grappled with the problem of drug abuse since at least the beginning of the twentieth century, but the issue rose to unprecedented prominence in the 1960s. The counterculture whose members experimented freely with drugs and rejected traditional mores questioned the consensus that illegal drugs posed an unmitigated evil. Rampant drug abuse among soldiers in Vietnam contributed to the rising prominence of the issue in government policies.[25] Congressional commissions and U.S. reporters found the problem to be equally disturbing in Germany where young GIs were isolated in their desolate barracks with little money to spend and bored because the army had insufficient funds and materials to have them exercise regularly. Drugs were easily accessible in Germany, which due to its central location in Europe had many entry points through which drugs could be smuggled. Moreover, commanders complained about the German government's lack of experience and commitment in combating the drug traffic in Germany. Army leaders found that in order to maintain an effective army, they had to navigate between suppression of the drug abuse and traffic and the rehabilitation of the soldier.

After providing a brief historical overview of drug abuse as a social and political issue in the United States, part 3 analyzes the appearance of drug abuse as a social problem in USAREUR. It will explore the links between drug abuse in Vietnam and the emergence of the problem in West Germany. The term "drug abuse," which could be interpreted as a misnomer, is used because that was the term generally used in 1960s and 1970s to refer to problems relating to drug consumption and addiction. The Nixon administration displayed an increasing preoccupation with the issue of drug abuse that culminated in the "War on Drugs." The rising prominence of the issue in the U.S. government coincided with the growing concern over rampant drug abuse among troops in Germany. The attitudes and approaches of military commanders were often similar to those of government officials, despite some marked differences, particularly after 1972. Commanders tried to find a sensible approach between penalizing the drug user and rehabilitating him. This work will also show that the strategies used to alleviate the drug abuse situation after 1971 were strikingly similar to those employed to harmonize race relations.

The social unrest within USAREUR did not go unnoticed by West Germans. Just like their American counterparts, German journalists reported on the unrest and tensions in barracks around Germany. The Vietnam War stirred passions within German society almost as much as in the United States. For student protesters, U.S. military sites and their personnel became targets of their activism. They offered an opportunity to directly confront the U.S. war machine. Civilian activists tried to enlist young GIs for their cause. Many protest activities within the army could not have been carried out without the material and moral support of German and expatriate U.S. civilians. For German communities around U.S. bases, increases in unrest and crime were a natural concern, since they tended to spill over into the communities. On the governmental level, the possibility that the U.S. Army's readiness had suffered was a major concern. West Germany was at the frontline of the Cold War. Many Germans viewed a weakening of the U.S. military presence as an existential threat. The final chapter explores West Germans' responses to the social crisis.

As he was replacing James H. Polk as commander in chief in West Germany in September 1971, Michael Davison gave an interview to Wilson and Johnson that appeared along with the first article of the "Army in Anguish" series. In the interview, Davison voiced his concern over the situation in his new command. He believed the army faced the toughest period in its history. He argued that as the conflict in Vietnam was winding down, if there were to be "an army of the future," that future was "going to be determined right here in the United States Army, Europe." The social crisis among U.S. troops in West Germany had now taken center stage.[26]

RACE DISCRIMINATION
AND BLACK POWER IN
THE U.S. ARMY, EUROPE

The issues of racial discrimination and race relations in the U.S. Army are as old as the army itself. African Americans have served the United States as soldiers since the Revolutionary War. During the entire period from 1776 to the present, their role in the armed forces has been a source of struggle and debate. The debates normally reflected those occurring in civilian society. From the Revolution to the Civil War, the question was most often whether African Americans could serve at all. By the turn of the twentieth century, the debate shifted to the question of separation or integration of black troops. Since Harry Truman's executive order of 1948, issues of equal treatment and opportunity have caused the most conflict. Black soldiers have been part of the U.S. forces in Germany since the end of World War II. While many of their experiences reflected that of other black GIs at home, their experience also differed markedly. The history of black GIs in postwar West Germany reveals that the struggles of African American soldiers during the Vietnam War were not new. While Truman's order ended segregation as an official policy, its implementation in Germany took six years. USAREUR integrated the last units in 1954.[1]

The end of segregation did not mean an end to discrimination or unequal treatment. Civil rights activists inside and outside the army had to combat predominantly white commanders' prejudice and complacency regarding racial discrimination on numerous occasions during the 1940s and 1950s. However, as an institution that had abandoned segregation as its official policy in 1948, the army did not face the same scrutiny as institutions in the southern states during the 1950s and 1960s. Only when the focus of black activists shifted to structural discrimination in communities and institutions outside the South did the army become a major stage for racial struggles as well.

1

Black GIs in Postwar Germany

During the immediate postwar period, black GIs stationed in Germany and elsewhere in Europe became an issue for the army as well as African American civil rights activists. As U.S. armed forces entered Germany in 1945, concern arose whether the population, which had been exposed to and had participated in a racist ideology, would accept supervision by "racially inferior" Negro troops. Germans really were apprehensive at first about the black troops among them. Many people in the southwestern region of Germany remembered the French occupation forces in the Rhineland after World War I, which included between 14,000 and 25,000 colonial troops from Morocco and Senegal. In a propaganda effort, German politicians and journalists depicted these troops as "wild beasts" let loose upon the German people to humiliate them. The event became known in Germany as the *schwarze Schmach* (black humiliation) and evoked images of black savages raping German women. Colonial troops were no more vicious or barbaric than their white counterparts in the French army, but the image of the *schwarze Schmach* remained vivid in the minds of many Germans. During the last months of World War II, the National Socialists intensified their racial scare propaganda about African American soldiers.

Despite these early anxieties among Germans, their experiences would turn out quite differently. As a matter of fact, many Germans agreed that the black soldiers "distinguished themselves through their generosity and friendliness toward the Germans."[2] Many Germans preferred the black GIs to their white counterparts, because the former were more generous with their food rations and "approached the defeated Germans with less arrogance."[3] In their defeat and humiliation, the Germans may have also felt a sense of solidarity with the black GIs because white Americans treated the latter as second-class citizens.

As the army settled into its new role as an occupation force in the American sector of Germany, commanders not only maintained the system of segregation that was still the norm in the army but made an unsuccessful effort to rid themselves of black soldiers in their command. Ironically these efforts were taking place at a time when the number of black soldiers in the army in Europe was rising. The army did not demobilize black GIs as fast as white soldiers, because it gave preference to combat veterans. Prejudice and segregation had kept the number of black combat soldiers low. African Americans were also more likely to reenlist or to newly enlist in the army.[4] While the number of black troops in Germany never exceeded the percentage for the entire army, overseas commanders insisted that they had more black troops than they could absorb. They reported some 19,000 black soldiers in excess of billets in black units and some 2,000 men above the theater's current allotment of black troops.[5]

Despite the fact that the segregated black units were overcrowded, commanders in the European theater refused to assign black soldiers to other units or occupations. The black combat units that had existed during the war were now mostly deactivated, and their members were absorbed into quartermaster or general service. No black soldiers served at the headquarters of European Theater Operation (ETO) in Frankfurt, and the commander of ETO, Gen. Joseph T. McNarney, did not employ a single black officer on his staff. African Americans held no positions in the military government. They had not been integrated into the military police units either and were therefore suspiciously absent at the Nuremberg trials.[6] The army's maintenance of segregation and the resulting discrimination continued to negatively impact morale and discipline among black GIs in Germany.

The unfavorable comparison between U.S. barracks in 1970 and the victorious troops occupying Germany in the wake of World War II carried some irony considering that in 1946 the army in Germany suffered from an increase in crimes committed by its soldiers accompanied by an increase in venereal diseases. The rise in venereal disease cases was seen as an indicator of bad morale and lack of discipline. The relaxation of discipline and the heightened level of lawlessness were not unusual for a victorious army. The need to reorganize and redeploy large numbers of troops as well as take over the administration of the occupied territory caused much confusion within the army in 1945 and 1946. The breakdown of German society and its economy provided GIs with ample opportunity for looting and illegal marketeering. Moreover, the poverty of the population made sex an easily available commodity. The rate for soldiers afflicted with venereal disease jumped from 75 cases per 1,000 before VE day (May 8) to 251 per 1,000 at the end of 1945. The rate remained this high for the next two years.[7] While high levels of criminal and sexual activity were apparent across the army, the statistics from the early occupation period contained a racial twist. Black soldiers were represented in these statistics in disproportionate numbers. Historian Morris MacGregor presents a statistic according to which the disease rate among black soldiers was 806 cases per 1,000 black soldiers as compared with 203 cases per 1,000 white soldiers. Court-martial rates were also significantly higher for black soldiers, 3.48 per 1,000 compared with 1.14.[8]

These numbers point to a high level of frustration among black soldiers at the time. They are also indicators that despite the army's official dedication to a policy of "separate but equal," black soldiers widely experienced discrimination. Black officers were scarce. White officers and the military police were often hostile and prejudiced toward African Americans, and black units were often housed in poor camp locations. Many of the black soldiers had been sent over to Europe without basic training, came from poor educational backgrounds, and served under young and inexperienced noncommissioned officers.[9] The high crime and disease rates among black GIs drew the attention of the Senate's Special Investigations Committee and the attention of noted criminologist Leonard Keeler. In response to a study by Keeler, who recommended excluding African Americans from Europe, DOD aide Marcus Ray, who advised the department on racial matters, argued that the statistics were a result of the high concentration of blacks in a few places separate from white units. Ray believed that if the army afforded black soldiers at least the same opportunities for advancement and acquisition of special skills as their white counterparts, the situation in Germany would improve.[10] Ray had toured the German bases himself in December 1946. While he did not call for an immediate end to the system of segregation, he did favor integrating black specialists. He strongly criticized the exclusion of African Americans from combat units and certain occupations because of assumed prejudices on the part of the German population.[11]

Attitudes about race among commanders in Germany bore similarities to the attitudes of commanders in the 1960s. Most of them maintained that African Americans made inferior soldiers. However, like later commanders, they believed that the poor performance and state of indiscipline among black soldiers was not the result of prejudice or discrimination but of social upbringing or conditioning of African Americans in their communities in the United States. The army, these officers believed, was not the place to initiate social reform. Officers stationed in Germany also argued that the presence of black soldiers in Germany needed to be limited in order not to offend the perceived racial sensibilities of the Germans. Even though Germans were seen as the vanquished enemy, their presumed sensibility to race was used as a rationale not to change potentially discriminatory practices.[12] An example for this practice was the military police. African Americans were kept out of the constabulary because this would put them in a position where they supervised and wielded police control over German nationals.[13]

Sensitivity to African Americans in positions of authority reflected the preconceptions of white U.S. officers rather than the feelings of the

German population. Marcus Ray condemned officers for taking into account racial sensibilities that were the result of a wrong and defeated ideology. Like the Negro Newspaper Publishers Association (NNPA), he had found that Germans had not reacted in the expected hostile fashion to the presence of black troops. He "found no carry-over of Nazi racial ideologies."[14]

Black GIs often experienced their service time in Germany and Europe in general as liberating. This was due to the unexpected friendliness of the German people as well as the fact that blacks could enter any bar or store. Moreover, while black soldiers associating with German women did cause resentment, they could still do so without facing arrest or the kind of physical violence they would have encountered in many parts of the United States.

The depictions from black reporters of the NNPA, however, should not be taken as an indication that the German population did not exhibit any prejudice or hostility. When these reporters favorably depicted the racial atmosphere among Germans, they did so to indict the situation that awaited black GIs at home. By showing that black soldiers received better treatment from former Nazi Germans than from their own countrymen, the black journalists shed a most unfavorable light on their own society. African Americans in Germany continued to experience segregation and discrimination within the army, but they also faced limits to the Germans' tolerance particularly in regard to interracial relationships between black GIs and German women.

Brawls between black soldiers and German men over women were common during the early occupation period. Willoughby and MacGregor argue that records of the period indicate that Germans interpreted such clashes over women as a German-American problem rather than an issue of race.[15] The NNPA alleged that it was U.S. officers and military policemen who often racialized these clashes. They discouraged associations between black GIs and white women by often employing strong-arm methods "at the mere sight of a Negro soldier and a white girl."[16]

While white Americans may have imported many of their racial attitudes, indications are that German men and women objected to relationships between black men and German women due to their own prejudices. Germans would publicly insult women associating with black soldiers. These women were often prostitutes squatting in camps outside the towns. German officials harassed and arrested such women.[17]

In 1947 the deputy theater commander, Lt. Gen. Clarence R. Huebner, and Marcus Ray, who left his DOD position to become a lieutenant colonel in Europe, started a program to improve the status of black troops. Recognizing that most black enlisted men sent from the United States were poorly educated and badly trained, Huebner and Ray established a three-month training program. The soldiers were drilled in both military and academic subjects. A training center was established at Kitzingen Air Base. The education of soldiers was continued on duty, as a soldier was required to undergo academic instruction until he passed the general education development (GED) test. Black soldiers who had undergone training at Kitzingen scored an average of twenty points higher on army classification tests.

While it is hard to demonstrate a direct connection between the training program and the improvement in the morale and discipline of African American troops, a dramatic improvement had taken place by 1950. The venereal disease rate and the serious incident rate dropped closer to the average rates among white troops. The training program demonstrated that educated black soldiers performed their duties just as well as their white counterparts. It also demonstrated that segregation normally meant discrimination. But it would take the army a few more years to accept this fact.

In 1948 Truman began to take a stronger interest in civil rights issues. With the presidential candidacy of Thomas Dewey and Henry Wallace and the defection of Southern Democrats from the party, the urban black minority vote became important to Truman's quest for reelection.[18] Civil rights leaders pressured the Truman administration hard to integrate the armed forces, and they threatened to start a campaign of civil disobedience, a threat not easily overlooked by the administration considering that at this point 10 percent of the military population was black.[19] Since Truman could not pass any kind of civil rights legislation through Congress, he had to rely on the instrument of executive order. Executive Order 9981 officially desegregated the armed forces, declaring "equality of treatment and opportunity for all persons."[20] A presidential committee was organized that would review the manpower policies of the services and the implementation of the order.[21] Despite the somewhat vague language (for example, the word "integration" was omitted), the order was a turning point in the civil rights struggle and the history of the armed forces. It was widely interpreted as an order to make integration a federal policy.

However, the new dedication of the commander in chief to racial integration did not translate to an immediate acceptance of this policy by senior officers, who tended to believe that integration of the army was neither necessary nor feasible. They maintained that the army could not serve as a vehicle for social experimentation, that black soldiers, because of social and educational disadvantages, could not compete with their white counterparts, and that therefore racial segregation was the fairest and most efficient system that the army could offer at that time.[22]

The most important factor in ending segregation in the army was the Korean War. As in previous wars, the increased demands in manpower forced change in racial policies. During the initial phases of the war, the black units were up to 60 percent overstrength because of the high reenlistment rate of black soldiers and because the army insisted on assigning newly enlisted black soldiers to existing black units. At the same time the predominantly white combat units in Korea were unable to replace their losses at a sufficient level to maintain their battle strength. Without any sanction from the Department of Defense, commanders in Korea started to assign incoming black soldiers with combat specialties into white units to make up for their battle losses. By May 1951, more than 9 percent of the black soldiers in Korea served in unofficially integrated units. Another 9 percent were in integrated units that were predominantly black. On May 14, 1951, Far East commander Gen. Matthew B. Ridgeway formally requested that all the units in his command be integrated. Surprisingly, Ridgeway's proposal met with little resistance and was officially approved on July 1, 1951. The integration of the Eighth Army went smoothly and caused none of the problems senior officers had always predicted.[23]

The successful example of Korea convinced the army chief of staff, J. Lawton Collins, that integration was not only workable but also the most efficient way of organizing the army. On December 29, 1951, Collins ordered all major commands, continental and overseas, to prepare integration programs. After some initial resistance from senior officials in those commands, especially in Europe, Collins ordered the worldwide integration a year later in December 1952.[24] The last segregated army unit was eliminated in the first half of 1954. For the remainder of the decade and well into the next, the army became the most integrated institution in the United States. Despite the fears and predictions of most senior army officials, integration went smoothly and without any major disturbances. Subsequently the army's success in the area of race relations became a source of pride to its officers and enlisted men.[25] For the first time in its history, the army was ahead of developments in general society with respect to desegregation and integration.

The last black unit in Germany, the Ninety-Fourth Engineer Battalion, was deactivated in November 1954. Initially European commanders had been reluctant to follow the example of their colleagues in the Far East. When briefed about the successes of integration in Korea in November 1951, commanders voiced their skepticism. They believed integration was impractical for Europe. Once again officers pointed to the racial homogeneity of the host country. They argued that blacks serving with whites would cause social problems. The army chief of staff largely ignored the concerns of the European commanders and ordered the European command headed by Gen. Thomas T. Handy to submit a plan for racial integration on December 14, 1951.

On January 24, 1952, Collins accepted Handy's proposal to integrate combat units over a period of six months at the end of which all units would be 10 percent black. The army's insistence on a de facto quota of 10 percent strength per unit would slow the process down. Since overall black strength in Europe exceeded 10 percent in 1952 and 1953, it took European command until 1954 to properly balance and integrate its units. Despite the anxieties of many officers, integration of the army in Europe proceeded smoothly. Combat readiness increased. The army was now less vulnerable to Communist propaganda, and the civilian population took little notice.[26]

Throughout the 1950s, black GIs sought out service in Germany. According to military investigations conducted in the early 1950s, black GIs encountered no discrimination when frequenting German restaurants, bars, and shops. The investigations also found that Germans generally were friendly. While army assertions of a discrimination-free environment were overly optimistic, a tour in Germany offered black soldiers an "unprecedented level of prosperity, social mobility, and freedom."[27] They could date German women without fear of facing the type of violence they would have encountered in parts of the United States if they had dated white women. Black families living in German villages often developed friendships with their landlords. However, as Maria Höhn puts it, "the fact that many black soldiers experienced their time in Germany as a moment of liberation probably says more about the level of discrimination that blacks faced in the United States than about German racial tolerance during this period."

Despite the end of officially sanctioned racial segregation in the army and despite the relative freedom and acceptance that black GIs experienced in German communities, it is important to note that discrimination and off-base segregation remained widespread during the 1950s. On-duty integration in USAREUR progressed rapidly after 1952. But off-duty relations between black and white soldiers were still problematic. While any form of discrimination on base had been prohibited, white GIs had found ingenious ways of keeping black soldiers out of their clubs, such as playing only country western music. White soldiers were even more successful in maintaining a system of segregation in the surrounding German communities. Officially German law prohibited segregation, a fact army leaders liked to point out when facing criticism about racial problems in Europe. But white soldiers could use economic pressure to persuade German bar and club owners to exclude black GIs. In response, black soldiers established their own exclusive places. This was a process that allowed army leaders to claim that patterns of off-duty segregation were voluntary and therefore out of their hands.[28]

Commanders in Germany often not only accepted these forms of segregation but even condoned them. The military police in many places reinforced racial boundaries in the communities surrounding a base by warning soldiers to stay within their racial sphere. While all soldiers were admonished in this way, the predominantly white MP force was much heavier handed when black soldiers transgressed boundaries than when their white comrades did so.[29]

Physical violence between the races was common. Soldiers were unable to act out their negative feelings about integration when they were on duty. Frustrations in this regard would flare up when soldiers were off-duty socializing in the German communities. Army commanders played down such conflicts, claiming that most brawls resulted from fights over girls and were not racially motivated. Most violent incidents occurred when members of one race overstepped racial boundaries and transgressed into the perceived territory of the other. The civil rights struggle in the United States also added to the racial tensions. German authorities and the U.S. military police were put on alert when a civil rights confrontation took place back in the United States. On the other side, African American soldiers inspired by events at home became increasingly unwilling to accept the segregated system that white GIs had imposed on the local communities. Black GIs in Baumholder, for example, staged a sit-in at a local bar whose owner had put up a sign prohibiting "colored soldiers" from entering.

Throughout the 1950s and well into the 1960s, commanders and the Department of Defense maintained that they were powerless to interfere with local customs, which they held responsible for patterns of off-base segregation. This attitude was similar to that of their predecessors during occupation who tried to limit the influx of black troops in order not to offend German racial sensibilities. Patterns of segregation in communities around bases in the United States often predated the existence of the military installations, especially in the South. But it is unlikely that German customs or racial attitudes were primarily responsible for the segregation of German bars and restaurants around military bases. As a matter of fact, many Germans were amazed at the racial intolerance displayed by the Americans. Liberal Germans even developed a sense of superiority, believing that Germany had overcome its racist past by putting a prohibition against racial discrimination in the German Basic Law.[30] However, any sense of superiority on part of Germans in regard to racial matters was ill-founded. While much of the discrimination taking place may have been inspired by white soldiers, this does not mean that they often did not fit in well with German preconceptions and prejudices. That Germans retained their own prejudices and stereotypes about African Americans, or other people of African origin, becomes evident in the terminology they adopted. Germans distinguished between "American soldiers" and "Negro soldiers" (Amerikaner Soldaten and Negersoldaten) as well as "Negro children" (*Negerkinder*) as opposed to "American children" (*Amerikanerkinder*) for offspring of white GIs and German women.[31]

The end of segregation was not synonymous with an end to all forms of discrimination for black soldiers, independent of where they lived. The 1950s brought the organizational integration of the army, as the sociologists Charles C. Moskos and John S. Butler termed it. Any formal discrimination in recruitment, training, retention, and on-base living arrangements had ended.[32] But at bases in the southern states, integration did not extend outside the confines of the base. Recruitment of black officers remained low, and black enlisted men were promoted at a slower pace. Although officially the army had abandoned any formal quota on black recruitment and enlistment, an informal quota continued to exist disguised as an "acceptable" percentage of African Americans in individual units. According to MacGregor, these flaws created little friction in the 1950s, which people retrospectively saw as a quiet and harmonic period with regard to race relations in the army.[33] Maria Höhn's research indicates that conflicts ran closer to the surface than army leaders were ready to admit.[34] The far more open racism of the segregated South made problems in the officially integrated armed forces seem relatively benign. As the gaze in the United States shifted to other forms of racism and discrimination at the end of the next decade, the problem of discrimination and these unresolved issues would come back to haunt the army as well, especially in Germany.

President Kennedy's appointment of Robert McNamara as secretary of defense brought many changes to the administration of the armed forces. As the government became more concerned about civil rights issues, especially in the South, so did the DOD. But this change of attitude was gradual. McNamara was at first reluctant to act vigorously with regard to off-base discrimination. In a letter to Sen. J. William Fulbright, he claimed that military personnel and resources were not instruments of social change. Only as the decade progressed and the government as a whole became more proactive with regard to race relations did the policies introduced by the DOD become more forceful.[35] The Pentagon under McNamara made discrimination in the armed forces an issue, but since race relations remained comparatively tranquil, commanders rarely approached problems of discrimination on and off base aggressively. Moreover, as attention turned to Vietnam, these issues took a backseat to the war effort.

The response of DOD officials and base commanders initially was to maintain that the military could not control social customs outside the army bases. McNamara and his staff directed most of their early equal opportunity measures in 1961 and 1962 at ending patterns of discrimination on base. Until 1963 those initiatives that the DOD did introduce to address the problem of off-post discrimination remained limited in scope and timid in their language, trying to encourage voluntary desegregation. However, on March 8, 1963, McNamara issued a memorandum stating that all military leases for off-base family housing would contain a nondiscrimination clause in accordance with Kennedy's executive order no. 11063.[36] He followed up with DOD directive

5120.36 of July 26, 1963, which represented an important shift in the DOD social policies: it ordered military commanders to work hard to achieve equal opportunity in *and* outside military bases.

The change in policy came as a response to a highly critical committee report. In June 1962, Kennedy had appointed the Advisory Committee on Equal Opportunity in the Armed Forces under its chairman, Gerhard A. Gesell, a Washington attorney. He charged the Gesell Committee not only with investigating current policies and procedures regarding equal opportunity within the armed forces but also with suggesting measures "to improve equality of opportunity for members of the armed forces and their dependents in the civilian community, particularly with respect to housing, education, transportation, recreational facilities, community events, programs, and activities."[37] The committee held hearings involving installation commanders and DOD representatives and visited installations in the United States and overseas. Its findings shed light on the question of why race relations in the armed forces had regressed so much by the late 1960s and offered suggestions on attracting more black enlisted men and officers, improving promotion procedures, and removing vestiges of on-base discrimination. The recommendations with regard to off-base discrimination revealed how much the DOD had ignored this issue.[38]

DOD directive 5120.36 created the position of a deputy assistant secretary of defense responsible for civil rights and charged commanders with ensuring that their men and their dependents were treated equally *outside* as well as inside of their military bases.[39] The initial version of the directive did not provide commanders with the administrative tools to enforce nondiscrimination in the communities surrounding their bases. The directive expressly prohibited commanders from sanctioning civilian facilities that discriminated against black customers without the prior consent of the DOD.[40] The administration still faced pressure from Southern Democratic senators who rejected any interference by the federal government with segregation policies in southern military communities.[41] Throughout the decade the DOD continued to issue statements and directives encouraging military leaders to work to eliminate discrimination but mainly asked its base commanders to persuade the communities to change voluntarily.

Until the end of the decade, the focus on combating discrimination in off-base communities remained in the continental United States, especially the South. As tepid as its efforts were in the United States, the DOD remained even more reluctant to force any change in overseas communities. The Gesell Committee had also studied patterns of discrimination in overseas military communities. In its report the committee recommended that commanders undertake "vigorous efforts . . . to eliminate patterns of segregation and discrimination affecting troops off base," particularly in regard to "places of amusement which cater to our servicemen, and to housing."[42]

The Gesell Committee was specifically concerned that discrimination reflected the "attitudes of some of our own military personnel and is not generally practiced by nationals of the host country involved." The committee had found that discrimination existed only in host communities directly surrounding U.S. military bases inspired by a minority of white soldiers. This was the case in bars as well as in housing. The situation in Germany was among the most serious. This assertion contradicted the traditional wisdom of military services according to which, as guests in the country, commanders should do little to interfere in off-base affairs and traditions of the hosts. Overseas base commanders, with some exceptions, had "paid insufficient attention" to the problems black soldiers faced in the off-base economy and had "allowed discriminatory conditions to become more severe and more rigid, and the resulting disorders to become more widely publicized."[43]

While the authors of the report believed that the problem of off-base discrimination in Germany was more complex and more acute than in the United States, the forms of on-base discrimination were similar to what they had found at home. One of the main problems was that the army had not set up channels of communication through which black enlisted men could report instances of discrimination. This meant that many individual cases of discrimination went unnoticed by superiors who for the most part showed a lackluster attitude toward racial problems. Although the lack of communication was a widespread problem, this inadequacy had "an adverse effect on morale in overseas areas because the men affected" were far from home and had "neither family nor friends nearby to consult or call for help."[44]

Initially USAREUR officials responded negatively to the results of the Gesell Committee investigation. They demonstrated little willingness to work toward change. Speaking at a press conference in Bonn one day after the committee's results had become public, an army spokesman charged that the committee assessment was outdated because the members had based it on an investigation conducted in 1962. USAREUR, the spokesman argued, had made progress since then and there was "no discrimination whatsoever on army bases and very little in the German communities surrounding the bases." He also rejected the committee's assertion that commanders were paying insufficient attention to discrimination: "All command levels in the United States Army Europe, from the commanding general to every squad leader, are engaged in a program to eliminate racial discrimination from the army both on post and off." The spokesman did not deny that many restaurants and bars around army posts in Germany did "in fact serve exclusively Negro or white clientele." But he believed that this was a result of preference by the customers rather than any form of coercion.[45]

After the Gesell Committee's report, interest in the issue of overseas discrimination faded until the end of the decade. The growing conflict in Vietnam took precedent over any social problems the army might be having in Germany or at home. But the eruption of racial problems in USAREUR in 1969 and 1970 shows that the situation had not improved since 1964. Over the first two decades of the U.S. military presence in Germany, commanders' responses to complaints about racial discrimination and initiatives to identify underlying problems met with similar responses. One was denial that problems black enlisted men faced were in any way due to their superiors' prejudices or that the army as an institution was prejudiced. If they had to acknowledge at least the existence of discrimination outside the bases, they emphasized their inability to influence or the impropriety of affecting civilian social norms. The official response to the Gesell Committee showed the self-satisfaction among officers in Germany regarding the treatment of black soldiers. They felt confident in the army's institutional color blindness and their own lack of prejudice. Not unlike many white Americans in the northern states, these officers equated the absence of legal segregation with social and cultural equality.

This pattern of willful ignorance and neglect regarding racial discrimination would be disrupted when a new generation of black soldiers found the language and methods to call attention to the persistent forms of discrimination they faced on and off duty in the late 1960s. The increasingly vocal and visible ways in which black GIs in West Germany expressed and protested their inequality reflected the shifting discourse on race away from African Americans' legal status toward more insipid forms of institutional, cultural, and social discrimination. They found allies among civilian activists in Germany who closely followed race-related protests and movements in the United States. They shared many soldiers' interest in concepts of black power and saw African Americans as domestic victims of U.S. imperialism providing them with a chance to actively participate in the black freedom struggle.

2

Growing Racial Tensions

On September 13, 1971, the *Washington Post* featured a second article in its series "Army in Anguish," titled "GI Crime, Violence Climb Overseas: Race, Drugs, and Idleness Mix Together in Explosive Combination." It revealed an alarming number of violent incidents between black and white GIs all over Germany. Robberies and conflicts between competing white and black drug rings were supposedly common. The mix of racial tensions and illegal drugs aggravated by the poor housing conditions and the foreign, sometimes even hostile environment in Germany made the situation explosive. African American soldiers were especially frustrated because they faced the additional burden of discrimination. When commenting on these difficulties, officials often asserted that the army merely mirrored American society. Just as black power had increasingly superseded civil rights in the late 1960s, sentiments among many black soldiers had also hardened.

Despite these general trends, the authors of many of the newspaper and magazine articles maintained that the situation in Germany was especially bad. They claimed, often without further explanation, that the social climate in Germany was particularly hostile toward black soldiers. On November 18 and 19, 1971, the *Times* reported on an inquiry of the Black Congressional Caucus into the problem of race relations in the army. It summarized and quoted the testimony of a black sergeant who had served in Germany who claimed that readiness for violence among blacks and whites had increased.[1] After a decade of relative tranquility from the early 1950s to the early 1960s, the issue of racial discrimination had resurfaced within the armed forces with a vengeance. But how had the racial atmosphere turned explosive in an institution that from the 1950s onwards had been considered one of the most integrated? Why had Germany become such a hotbed of resistance among black GIs?

The first question is not hard to answer. Even though many observers seemed surprised at the level of frustration emerging among African American GIs in Germany, none of the grievances were new. Inferior housing and off-post discrimination had already been a major source of complaint. This was not so much the result of a new set of problems or any increase in discrimination. Instead the black servicemen emboldened by concepts such as black power and black pride became more willing to speak out or take action to address the existing systemic problems.[2] Patterns of off-base discrimination remained most pronounced in the still segregated South of the United States. Here discrimination extended beyond housing to the use of public accommodations such as restaurants, theaters, and saloons. Somewhat less blatant patterns of discrimination persisted in the continental United States and on and around bases overseas.

In Vietnam black soldiers were among the most outspoken and effective critics of the war.[3] This was partially due to the fact that they had a somewhat different view about the domestic protest movements from their white peers. While many soldiers viewed the wider antiwar movement as largely elitist and self-righteous, black GIs did identify with black activists in the United States. They shared their white counterparts' doubts about the justifications for the war and the viability of their mission. But their experiences as African Americans in the armed forces also gave them a unique perspective on the war. While they confronted racial discrimination within the institution they were serving in, they were fighting a war that had highly racialized aspects. Particularly during the early years of the conflict African Americans were overrepresented in the combat units. This meant that the casualty rate among black soldiers was initially higher than for white soldiers. As the war progressed, the overrepresentation in the combat units diminished. However, the perception that African Americans were dying in disproportionate numbers would remain throughout the war and play an important role in the civil rights movement at home and in the armed forces.[4]

According to historian Herman Graham, there had always been noticeable antiwar sentiments among black GIs, but they had little impact at first. As was the case for many Americans, soldiers and civilians, the Tet Offensive was a major watershed. Prior to Tet most black GIs had either backed the war enthusiastically or had been willing to put aside their doubts, assuming they were serving the best interests of the nation. As in previous wars, these soldiers expected that their service would earn them respect and equal treatment upon their return.[5] As would be the case in Germany, their actual treatment in the army would disabuse many black GIs of the notion that their service led to equal treatment. The slower pace of promotions, inequities in the administration of military justice, and the greater likelihood of receiving unpleasant assignments made black soldiers in Vietnam become increasingly receptive to black nationalism and antiwar ideas. The rhetoric and images of black power and the struggle of black protesters against racism did resonate with the young black soldiers and provided them with the language to critique the military establishment and voice their opposition to the war.[6] The anti-imperialist and antiracist critique of the Vietnam War voiced by black activists caused some black GIs to reflect on their own role in Vietnam.[7] Their own status vis-à-vis the Vietnamese became more complex because in the context of their own struggle the Vietnamese were their fellow oppressed, allies in the Third World struggle against white colonial exploitation.[8] Black GIs in Germany, some of whom had served in Vietnam, would draw the same parallels often supported by local antiwar activists.[9]

In 1969 the army chief of staff, Gen. William Westmoreland, ordered the army staff to assess the racial situation in the army and to identify the problems underlying the growing racial tensions. Army command was concerned that racial tensions would "negate past accomplishments" in regard to race relations. Racial disharmony could threaten the army's "ability to accomplish its Mission."[10] The assessment and the growing number of racial incidents in Germany, documented in the press, would show that the concerns of the army leadership were not unfounded. On October 27, 1969, the Office of Deputy Chief of Staff (Personnel) of the Department of the Army held a briefing for the commander in chief of USAREUR and Seventh Army general James H. Polk analyzing racial tensions in the army.

The officer in charge of the briefing was Lt. Col. James White. In the briefing, he presented among other things the findings of a Defense Department fact-finding team that had investigated nineteen military installations in the continental United States and six major overseas commands. White mainly focused on the situation in Germany but also provided more general impressions. His briefing showed how black soldiers reflected recent shifts within the black liberation movement. The first conclusion he presented was that the army indeed had a race problem. At this time the issue of race was receiving much attention in the United States. Because of television and the press, soldiers were well aware of what was going on with regard to race in general society, or as White put it, they were "not naïve on the subject of race." They were aware of the subject even before they entered the army, and this awareness was not "tuned out" when they put on their uniforms. Therefore, officers could not assume that by becoming soldiers their subordinates had left their racial differences behind. "A Negro in uniform" did not "cease being a Negro," nor were white soldiers "instantly cleansed of years of experience and attitudes." Ignorance among commanders as to these differences was dangerous, because "the cries of the Negro soldier" had "never been so loud."[11]

To clarify what commanders were potentially facing, White argued that the attitudes of black soldiers had changed over the years. He made several references to the importance that soldiers placed on "racial pride." He acknowledged that these soldiers had legitimate grievances that went unheard by their commanders. However, he also warned that this new generation of soldiers' response to those grievances differed from previous generations. Whereas a black soldier's typical response to his continuing perception of discrimination used to be "hard work and endurance," a young black soldier now would likely exhibit "more personal and racial pride; more bitterness at real or imagined injustice; and often a chip on the shoulder." Previous generations had responded within the framework of traditional and therefore legitimate American liberal values of "hard work and endurance." This new generation acted entitled and would be susceptible to militant messages if commanders did not act.

White also argued that confronted with often blatant racism on one side and "black militants who preach violence and black separatism" on the other, the typical black soldier was "longing for military leadership throughout his chain of command to recognize and communicate with him." White was convinced that most black soldiers were not militants or radicals. They resented having their "newly found racial pride confused and interpreted as evidence" that they were militants or racists. Despite the frustration of many black soldiers, White felt certain that the activities and success of the Black Panther Party remained limited.

White used the threat of militancy as a means to spur white officers into action to confront the very real problems of their black subordinates. While he conceded that racial pride in and of itself did not denote militancy, he did draw connections between the changed attitudes of young soldiers and militancy. These fears of a black militancy reflected in White's comments generally corresponded with white responses to tropes of black power or pride that the national media tended to portray as "violent, angry, controversial and antiwhite."[12] The predominantly white officers struggled to concede any legitimacy to displays of black power or black pride among their troops.

The negative media depictions of the movement not only reflected the hostile attitudes of white officers and most white Americans at the time. They also had a lasting impact on the historiography of the black liberation struggle. Early histories of the civil rights movement portrayed black power as a disruption. According to this narrative, the new focus on black nationalism and militancy brought an end to the "golden era" of nonviolent protest.[13] However, more recent histories of the black power movement have noted its crucial contributions in advancing the black liberation struggle.[14]

By 1969 "black power" had become a well-known, if controversial, concept in American society. Richard Wright and W. E. B. Du Bois had already used the term. But the Student Nonviolent Coordinating Committee (SNCC) and Stokely Carmichael popularized it. By 1966 the leadership of SNCC believed that the traditional civil rights movement had reached the limits of what it could achieve.[15] Dominated by white liberals and middle-class African Americans, the civil rights movement had focused on the integration of the individual rather than the empowerment of African Americans as a community. This type of integration, according to Carmichael, had done little to improve the lives of the black Americans living in the ghettos of American urban centers. Working as part of one united black community for the liberation of the whole community, not just individuals, could liberate these individuals. Only a united black body in which African Americans held all leadership positions could achieve power. African Americans, Carmichael believed, had to cease trying to become part of the white power system and culture and instead assert their pride in their own culture and strength.[16]

The emphasis of the black power movement on ending racism imbedded in culture and society made it more applicable to the situation of the soldiers than the traditional civil rights movement. Unlike society in general, the army had ended legal segregation long before the passage of the Civil Rights Act in 1964. But like their civilian counterparts in the United States, black soldiers in Germany faced the more intrinsic forms of discrimination and developed a need to demonstrate their unity and their pride in their own distinct culture. By 1970 a growing communication gap separated minority group personnel and their white company grade officers and noncommissioned officers. The complaints of the black soldiers ranged from the use of racial epitaphs when being addressed by superiors, discrimination in promotions and assignments of duty, to receiving harsher and more frequent punishment for offences.

In 1969 and 1970, black soldiers in Germany and elsewhere became increasingly vocal about their grievances and more assertive about their racial heritage. Many black soldiers greeted each other with black power salutes. Soldiers started to wear Afro hairstyles. They demanded a change in regulations making the Afro an acceptable hairstyle. Once the army had modified its regulations, they directed their efforts toward combating any prejudice officers might have toward black soldiers wearing such haircuts. They made certain that army posts in Germany trained personnel to cut black hair according to their needs. In Friedberg, for example, five black enlisted men shaved their heads, which was not a popular hairstyle in 1970, to protest the prejudice and daily harassment soldiers faced when they wore Afros, despite the change in regulations.[17] Another commonly voiced complaint was the lack of black magazines and literature from on-post newsstands and bookstores, as well as a lack of opportunities for soldiers to be educated on black culture and history.[18]

Overall, black soldiers had become less inclined to tolerate discrimination in the army as reflections of attitudes in the general society that the army was powerless to change. Many of the soldiers stationed in Germany had been to Vietnam. Black soldiers were aware that black casualties had been high in the initial stages of the war, and unlike their predecessors, they were more likely to know about the service of their ancestors in every major conflict. These soldiers expressed dissatisfaction with the progress made regarding discrimination and believed that drastic steps were necessary fast. Pvt. Eugene Franklin, chairman of the Black United Soldier in Karlsruhe, demanded in a *New York Times* interview that "America live up to the Constitution since we have put our lives on the line every day to possibly die for it."[19]

The findings of Colonel White had little immediate impact on USAREUR. During the fall of 1969 and all through 1970, race relations at bases all over Germany began to heat up. In October 1969 simmering racial tensions flared in Neureut Caserne, Karlsruhe. According to the *Overseas Weekly*, a group of about twenty black GIs had formed an informal organization dedicated to protesting unequal treatment by the military. Complaints made by the group had been concerned with issues such as the unavailability of barbers able to create black hairstyles and the lack of black publications in the dayroom. The post commander reacted by shipping out three members of the group and ordering the others to request permission for any future meetings they might plan to hold. When members met informally at the enlisted men's club on October 25, they got into a brawl with military police who arrested two black GIs. During the ensuing trial, members of the group charged that the MPs had roughed up the arrested soldiers and that the conviction of one of the two arrested GIs was mainly based on prejudice.[20] A similar incident occurred in Erlangen on December 23 when a fight between black and white soldiers broke out at the local enlisted men's club. One black specialist 4 was arrested and convicted. The *Overseas Weekly* described the convicted soldier as a militant who had previously claimed an interest in the Koran and had worn a Black Panther style outfit on the night of the fight.[21]

In March 1970 a series of racial incidents occurred in Baumholder. During the first weekend of March, about 120 black soldiers met at the post gym to discuss their problems in the military. In the subsequent weeks, racial tensions flared up. Black soldiers responded to the arrests of fellow enlisted men with angry protests leading to brawls between black and white soldiers. On March 28 tensions reached a high point. Reports suggested that one hundred black GIs had roamed the post tossing rocks and breaking windows. Black soldiers in Baumholder questioned by the *Overseas Weekly* claimed that "they had problems with racial prejudice within the ranks that extended up the chain of command. And nobody was listening to their complaints."[22]

The Mannheim Stockade was a frequent source of racial tensions in 1970. The first riot occurred on March 14 instigated by black militants according to the *Overseas Weekly*.[23] Race relations were not the only source of tension in the prison. Once the riot had started, white prisoners had joined in. In its coverage of the incident, the *Overseas Weekly* cited the "lousy mess hall chow," mistreatment by the guards, as well as racial prejudice as the underlying causes for the riot. As the year progressed, race took on an ever-greater importance as the source of disturbances in Mannheim. In April, black prisoners claimed that their breakfast juice had been poisoned.[24] The *Rhein-Neckar-Zeitung* reported the claim to be false.[25] But tensions in Mannheim persisted. Black prison guards accused their white colleagues of discriminatory behavior and reported several incidents of white guards beating up black inmates.[26] Brawls between black and white inmates and mess hall workers broke out in August and October.[27]

One of the most violent race-related incidents occurred in Hohenfels. On May 21, 1970, a grenade was lobbed into the officers' and NCOs' mess hall injuring ten people. This outbreak erupted in a racially heated atmosphere. Reports of black power meetings on the base had preceded the attack. On May 20 Brig. Gen. Marshall Garth, the commanding general of the First Infantry Division stationed at the base in Hohenfels, had met with senior officers to discuss the racial troubles there. On the same day, black enlisted men had organized a march during which they demanded a meeting with Garth. Garth only granted the meeting after the attack had taken place.[28] One of the spokesmen during that and previous meetings, Sgt. James Hobson, was arrested on May 22, and less than a month later he was declared the prime suspect for the attack.[29]

The accused had been a social success story for the army until his arrest. Growing up as an orphan in Chicago, he had been a gang leader at the age of seventeen with convictions on forty-three minor charges before a judge placed him in the army. Hobson rose to noncommissioned officer rank, earned a Bronze Star in Vietnam, and received Chicago's Medal of Merit. After coming to Hohenfels, Hobson became a spokesman for black activists. During the trial, the army prosecutors attempted to portray him as a militant. Prosecution witnesses testified that during the meeting with Garth he had accused Garth of bearing responsibility for the attack. Hobson's company commander testified that he had overheard a conversation between Hobson and other black soldiers during which he had predicted a night of fire and violence. In a letter to General Polk, Hobson pleaded his innocence. He claimed that he had become a spokesman to restrain the more militant "hotheads" among his fellow soldiers.[30]

Ultimately, the jury acquitted Hobson on most of the charges. His defense counsel presented evidence that two key witnesses had been promised amnesty if they implicated Hobson.[31] However, Hobson was convicted of disobeying a direct order to attend a field exercise following the incident.[32] Gen. Wilton B. Persons, who studied the file of the case when he became judge advocate in the spring of 1971, stated that the investigation was very confused, with finger pointing from all sides. Black soldiers "felt they were being tagged with this crime," while some white soldiers felt the black soldiers "were being mollycoddled."[33]

But violent outbreaks were not limited to the black servicemen. Reports of cross burnings and the existence of Ku Klux Klan cells in USAREUR suggest that white servicemen responded with great hostility to black soldiers' activism and displays of racial pride. In 1970 the media reported two cross burnings.[34] The *New York Times* reported that a group of white sergeants had beaten SP4 Edward Kaneta, a white soldier, because he had associated with black soldiers at a Fulda post. Kaneta charged that a Klan unit with forty-seven members existed at the base. An army investigation found no evidence for that claim.[35] One article in the *Overseas Weekly* that described a cross burning incident in Hanau offered no proof that there really were KKK members among the soldiers, but white soldiers did voice their complaints about the behavior of their black comrades. These complaints ranged from rather banal issues, such as black soldiers not waiting their turn in the food lines at the mess hall, to accusations of black groups roaming the streets and occasionally attacking white soldiers. White soldiers questioned by the *Overseas Weekly* expressed their dislike for black soldiers exchanging black power salutes. They further claimed that commanders were afraid of punishing black soldiers. This complaint presented a mirror image of how black servicemen believed commanders administered Article 15 punishments.[36]

Many of the protests by black GIs reported in the newspapers appeared to be spontaneous. But they also made efforts to establish more organized and formal means of protest. In May 1970, black soldiers in Karlsruhe organized the Black Defense Group. Frustrated by "the prejudiced racial atmosphere," members expressed grievances through legal and legitimate channels. The first event organized by the group was a Black Mother's Day celebration. Its purpose was, according to an *Overseas Weekly* article, "to honor black and Puerto Rican mothers and let guys in this area know that the brothers have finally gotten it together."[37] The grievances expressed at the meeting were similar to those that surfaced at most other bases in Germany: the segregation of German bars, discrimination in the administration of military justice, and commanders unwilling or unable to change the circumstances. Similar groups formed at other bases, such as the Black Action Group in Stuttgart, the Black United Soldier in Heidelberg, or the Black United Soldier from Karlsruhe.[38] Pvt. Eugene Franklin, chairman of the Karlsruhe group, demanded in a *New York Times* interview that "America live up to the Constitution since we have put our lives on the line every day to possibly die for it."[39] These groups organized a more public event on July 4, 1970, when a crowd of 700 to 1,000 people, mainly black GIs, gathered at the auditorium (Neue Aula) of the University of Heidelberg.[40] The soldiers wanted an enlisted men's review board that would rule on pretrial confinement of black soldiers. They demanded the appointment of "a civilian inspector general, the end of discrimination in assignments and duties, and the employment of more blacks in overseas civilian jobs." However, the grievances voiced went beyond discrimination in the army. The soldiers demanded the "immediate withdrawal of all troops from Indochina."[41]

These activities and the general state of unrest did not go unnoticed by the U.S. government, which in August 1970 started another analysis of race relations on bases overseas. White's report of 1969 had pointed out the issues that frustrated black enlisted men when serving in USAREUR and the army in general. Black soldiers could not express their racial pride freely; they felt discriminated against regarding promotions and job assignments; and they felt that they were punished more harshly and more often for infractions against the Uniform Code of Military Justice.[42] The CINCUSAREUR, James Polk, credited White with calling the problem of racial tensions to his attention. However, he showed little initiative in dealing with it. Before his subordinate commanders, he emphasized the need to prohibit any kind of protest activity on base. Polk called upon commanders to prevent meetings of soldiers with grievances by "pinning down organizers in advance," asking about their grievances, and offering to help if the grievances were determined to be real. He emphasized that commanders should have an open-door policy so that complaints could reach them. Polk was mainly concerned about maintaining discipline and having any complaint follow the regular chain of command.[43]

The prevailing attitude among Polk and his subordinate commanders exemplified White's characterization. They maintained that it was possible to disregard soldiers' skin color and treat them all as soldiers. Gen. C. E. Hutchinson emphasized the official color blindness of the army in a memorandum for V Corps:

> It is fortunate that we, in the Army, have had so much good experience in the realities of racial equality, born of the tradition that if a man acts like a Soldier he will be treated like a Soldier, without respect to the lightness or darkness of his skin. This tradition is a living thing. Thus it was no surprise to me to hear a unit commander, in his unit, reply that he knew only how many Soldiers there were.[44]

According to Hutchinson, the chain of command could best preserve racial equality. Polk himself emphasized maintaining the chain of command in dealing with race relations in a letter to a civilian who had asked for a position as a counselor on race relations. Polk refused the request because the army had no such civil service positions and because race relations were a problem that the army had to solve on its own "from within the chain of command."[45]

Polk and Hutchinson were more concerned about maintaining discipline than solving racial grievances. They admonished officers to eliminate the causes of even the smallest degradation in discipline. They mentioned unfair treatment as a possible cause of such degradation, but they advocated a color blind approach in which "every man's transgression" was to be weighted by precisely the same standards." If officers could maintain an atmosphere of impartiality, but also concern for the soldier, "then the nationwide problems related to civil rights" would not affect USAREUR.[46] Polk emphasized dealing with any disruption immediately and on an individual basis, not necessarily identifying underlying causes for disruptive behavior. He continued to see black soldiers protesting mainly as a threat to discipline and morale.[47]

To be fair, both Polk and his successor, Michael S. Davison, were performing a difficult balancing act. The Vietnam War proved that the army was not sufficiently prepared to meet contingencies outside of Europe, while maintaining its readiness in West Germany. After 1965, U.S. Army, Europe, quickly became the replacement depot for Vietnam.[48] Experienced officers, noncommissioned officers, and equipment were transferred to Southeast Asia often without replacement. The drain affected support units more than combat units. John Robert Bauer, a radio repair specialist, recalled in his oral history interview that he worked a service post alone that had previously been manned by four specialists in Würzburg in 1970.[49] In addition, pressure from Senator Mike Mansfield to reduce troops in Germany led to the implementation of the dual basing policy whereby units assigned to Europe were now based in the United States, while their weapons and equipment remained in Europe. The units returned to Germany for the annual monthlong REFORGER exercises, but otherwise they were unavailable.[50] Manpower in USAREUR had dropped from 272,000 at the height of the Berlin Crisis in 1961 to 170,000 by the end of the 1970s.[51] Despite these shortfalls, which contributed to the social unrest and decline in morale, Polk and Davison had to maintain USAREUR as a credible deterrent against the Warsaw Pact. Maintaining morale and social harmony was only one of many challenges they faced. Their response differed markedly, with Polk generally reluctant to acknowledge any systematic problem regarding race relations and morale.

Unsurprisingly, Polk was unable to control the situation. Racial incidents kept occurring throughout 1970. Only one year after White's briefing of Polk, President Nixon decided to send a new inquiry team to Europe to assess the racial situation. This team came into being with a sense of urgency because reports of "civil unrest and turmoil among military personnel in the European theater" had reached the Department of Defense.[52]

During a press conference, a White House official cited reports of racial conflicts between individual members of the army as well as reports about Ku Klux Klan and Black Panther activity as reasons for sending a new team of investigators to Europe.[53] The tour of European bases took place between September 12 and October 7, 1970. The team included Assistant Secretary of Defense (Manpower and Reserve Affairs) Frank W. Render II, his aide, L. Howard Bennett, the president's special consultant on minority affairs, Leonard Garment, and Robert J. Brown, a special assistant.[54] The aim of the tour was to make "an assessment of the effectiveness of present policies and programs of the Department of Defense and the Military Departments related to equal opportunity and race relations." The team wanted to verify the existence of organized conflicts between groups like the Klan and the Panthers. The scope of the investigation reached beyond on-base race relations to what was going on in the communities.[55]

The report submitted by Render and his team conjured a more alarming image of the racial situation in USAREUR than White's. It found "a higher level of frustration and anger among blacks than was anticipated." The members of the team had not expected "such acute frustration and such volatile anger" among the African American soldiers. They were also surprised to find that young white soldiers were feeling increasingly frustrated as well, if with somewhat lower intensity. The high degree of frustration became apparent when soldiers came to the team's meetings, only to disrupt them. These soldiers used "verbally inflammatory language rank with profanity and obscenities." At the barracks in Mannheim and Karlsruhe, Render and his team found what they termed "small cores of alienated blacks who could not be reached." These soldiers used revolutionary language that left little room for compromise. They referred to Vietnam as a white man's war, claiming that they needed to return to the United States "where they could fight to liberate and free their black sisters and brothers from the dirty, stinking, teeming ghettos and from all forms of racial bigotry and oppression." Liberation could only be achieved through violent confrontation, since this was the only approach "whitey" would understand." They accused Render and his team "of coming over to brainwash them."[56]

An article in the *Overseas Weekly* supports the description of disruptive behavior by some GIs. During a meeting at the Minuteman Theater in Karlsruhe, attendees accused Render and his team of being Criminal Investigation Division (CID) informers. The *Overseas Weekly* quotes some black soldiers as saying that the whole inquiry was just another "honky CID plot to expose us and quiet the movement" and that "Render was just another brown-skinned honkie."[57] The language used by the soldiers reflects the pervasive influence of black power and the revolutionary rhetoric of organizations like the Black Panther Party.

Render noted, somewhat condescendingly, that in more private talks many of the radical soldiers could be convinced "of the folly of their view," but there always remained some individuals who were "beyond the influence of reason and discussion." The *New York Times* reported that some black activists refused to meet with the investigators because they believed the Seventh Army was monitoring these meetings and that they wanted to whitewash racial problems in Germany.[58] Like White, Render used the threat of radical militants as a means to stress the urgency of the problem of race relations in USAREUR. Render had put the description of such radical positions at the beginning of the report. Subsequent parts of the report paid little attention to claims of radicalism. Instead, the report emphasized that complaints and grievances came from average black GIs.

Overall Render identified five major problem areas: discrimination in promotions, assertions of racial pride, the military justice system, discrimination in the German community, and the failure of leadership.

The question of representation within the army hierarchy formed one of the major factors contributing to dissatisfaction among black soldiers. While African Americans' general representation in the army was proportional to that in society, their representation in the officer corps and among the senior enlisted ranks was not. The White briefing couched the concern over misrepresentation of black and white personnel in the different ranks in carefully optimistic terms. It pointed out that the number of senior noncommissioned officers and field grade officers had steadily increased since 1964. However, by 1968 the number of black enlisted men making sergeant had decreased and the army continued to have problems procuring and retaining black junior officers. Already black majors outnumbered lieutenants, and lieutenant colonels outnumbered second lieutenants.[59] The Render report dealt only briefly with the issue of promotions and argued that the perception of discrimination in this area was more significant than the question whether this was actually true. But the report did state that "statistics indicate that there are some obvious discrepancies in numbers and percentages of blacks and their distribution at various levels even when comparing individuals with similar records and equal time in service."[60]

Discrimination in promotions was not a problem that was specific to USAREUR. Sociological studies conducted in the 1970s indicate that black soldiers received promotions at a slower rate than their white counterparts and were underrepresented in the officers' corps.[61] Studies conducted in 1972 put the ratio of black and white officers at 1 to 25.[62] Another study published in 1976 indicated that blacks perceived inequalities in promotions because it took them more time to move upward than their white counterparts.[63] In this study published in the *American Sociological Review*, John Sibley Butler found that it took black soldiers nineteen months in the service to make E4, while it took white soldiers fifteen months. To make grades E5 to E6 it took black soldiers sixty-eight months but white soldiers only fifty-nine.

Black soldiers were also less likely to make it into specialized technical occupations, such as medic, electronics maintenance engineers, or data processors.[64] Army leaders argued that this was mainly the result of the educational disadvantages of African Americans in general society and not the result of overt racism in the army.[65]

Butler's study disproved this assertion. Butler compared the time it took for black and white soldiers to make their grade with their scores in mental aptitude tests and their educational level. He discovered that "smart" black soldiers moved through the system the slowest. Black soldiers at the same educational level as their white counterparts still moved through the system at a slower pace. To put it differently, black soldiers "who were matched up with whites on key universalistic criteria still suffered discrimination on the basis of race."[66] Butler concluded that the data he had collected suggested that black soldiers' educational and economical disadvantages offered an insufficient explanation for inequality in promotions. Many army leaders erred when they assumed that institutional racism operated "without the racist actions of real-life individuals."

The Render report also suggested that the underrepresentation of African Americans in leadership positions led to a perception among black soldiers that they had nobody to turn to. The army assigned too many of the black officers to desk jobs. Moreover, "there was tokenism in the appointment of black flag and general officers." Apart from blacks in leadership positions, soldiers also complained about the lack of visible minorities in the support activities, such as base services, the post exchange, or the dependent schools.[67]

An NAACP investigation into racial discrimination in the army and the air force in West Germany conducted in January 1971 came up with similar results. Equally qualified black soldiers rose through the ranks at a slower pace than whites. Black enlisted men could not advance at the same rate as their white counterparts because of their uneven distribution among the different occupations. Younger black soldiers piled up in less skilled occupations competing for slots already filled by African Americans, a phenomenon referred to as "logjam."[68]

The NAACP committee sent to Germany also noted a lack of black officers in command positions. Black officers also felt discriminated against regarding their advancement. They were often slow to advance and more likely to be given dead-end assignments. Few black officers received command positions or were put into tracks that would allow them to acquire the experience and training that would qualify them for such positions.[69] The NAACP argued that one important way to overcome race problems in West Germany was to put more black officers in command positions where white junior officers would be accountable to them.

As mentioned previously, expressing their racial pride and solidarity through outward symbols had become an issue. During a visit to German army bases, sociologist Alvin J. Schexnider observed that explicit symbols had been "specifically designed to promote feelings of group solidarity" among the black enlisted men. Schexnider described black soldiers "dapping in the mess hall in a protracted and intense manner both before and after chow."[70] While such demonstrations sometimes were somewhat "cosmetic," Schexnider did believe that the symbols employed by black soldiers were "serious and genuine," serving as expressions of racial unity and solidarity.[71] Schexnider's essay in the *Journal of Black Studies* enumerated symbols of black solidarity used among soldiers. The most important were the dap, Afro haircuts, the black fist, and wristbands.[72] Schexnider concluded from interviews he conducted with black soldiers that the Vietnam experience was the source of this enhanced race consciousness. Returnees from Vietnam had introduced these symbols to those soldiers who had never been in Southeast Asia.[73] In 1970 and 1971, veterans formed an important part of the activist groups in Germany. Such veterans were disappointed that despite the fact that they had fought for their country, they still felt discriminated against, even in the army.[74]

Assertions of black pride caused resentment on the part of white enlisted men and officers, who often took them for expressions of black militancy or black racism.[75] In a letter to General Collins, General Westmoreland sent a picture from the newspaper depicting two black soldiers in Germany giving the black power salute to an officer. The picture contained a scribbled note reading: "This is terrible. What kind of Army are you running these days?"[76] Like Westmoreland, many senior officers and noncommissioned officers had little tolerance for open displays of racial pride even when they were less demonstrative than in this example.

One issue that took on major importance in debates over racial discrimination in the army was Afro haircuts. Black soldiers frequently complained that they had to wear their hair according to the same guidelines as their white counterparts, despite physical and cultural differences. Furthermore, barbers working for the army did not have the training to cut black hair, and special hair care products for African Americans were often not available at local commissaries and post exchanges in Germany.[77] What might have sounded like a mundane problem to many white Americans was of great cultural significance to black soldiers who took pride in their cultural heritage and wanted to be able to outwardly express this pride.

Commanders in Germany reacted differently to black soldiers' demands to wear their hair in Afro styles. In Augsburg the commanding general and the community commander saw the issue as an opportunity to demonstrate their openness to black demands for equal treatment. Augsburg community leader Brig. Gen. George H. Young Jr. ordered installation shops to get "Afro products."[78] The commanding general, Maj. Gen. Woodrow W. Vaughn, declared that Afro haircuts were permissible as long as they were neatly trimmed and did not hinder the black soldier from wearing his cap, helmet, or gas mask. He asserted that Afro haircuts were "a source of great pride and identity to the Negro."[79]

Not all officers and noncommissioned officers were as understanding as Vaughan and Young. The same issue of the *Overseas Weekly* that reported on Vaughan's policies also ran an article on a black GI in Frankfurt on trial for wearing an Afro.[80] Moreover, permission to wear Afros according to regulations did not automatically mean acceptance of the hairstyle by officers and NCOs. White officers and soldiers asked about their opinion on Afros stated that they believed black soldiers wearing them did face prejudice from their white comrades and superiors: "Blacks wearing Afros do get discriminated against. Their hair sticks out, so some hardcore Army people would probably accuse them of being militants."[81] During its investigation, the NAACP found much the same complaint among black soldiers. Displays of black pride such as "Afro hair styles, handshakes, and 'power salutes'—led to confrontations with white superior officers."[82]

The Hobson trial demonstrated the problems that individual black soldiers faced. Claims of being harassed for speaking out on issues of discrimination and expressing their black pride were widespread. Soldiers also complained that white leaders labeled any black soldier resisting the status quo as a militant: "These whites they think that every time colored guys get together, well, he's a Panther. He's a militant."[83] White officers and noncommissioned officers were insecure when dealing with questions of black activism and militancy. Not all black soldiers expressing their opinions faced courts-martial, but complaints of harassment were widespread. The *Overseas Weekly* reported on a conflict between a black private and the major in charge of his transportation company in Finthen. The private had drawn black power pictures and hung them on the wall. The major considered the pictures to be in bad taste. While the officer did not order Edward E. Gates to remove them, he insisted that Gates at least have them framed. When black troops started to hold what they described as impromptu meetings underneath the pictures, the major accused them of holding black power meetings. The conflict heated up when Edwards was implicated in a beating of two white soldiers.[84]

The *Overseas Weekly* article strongly insinuates that the fault in this conflict lay mainly with the major. Despite the slant, the article also shows that the major tried to appear open-minded when he did not insist on removing the pictures. He also tried to deescalate the situation by offering Edwards an Article 15 punishment for the beating of the white soldiers. Edwards and the other black soldiers implicated insisted on a court-martial. Black soldiers asking for a trial when they felt their superiors had unnecessarily disciplined them was not an unusual occurrence. A trial offered a more public forum to voice their grievances and to demonstrate the injustice of the current system. A particularly notorious case was the trial of the so-called Darmstadt 53, discussed in the next chapter.

Overall the tensions between black soldiers and their white superiors led to a disproportionate number of disciplinary actions taken. This was one of the aspects of military race relations that received the most attention from the DOD and outside organizations such as the NAACP. Both the White briefing and the Render report mentioned the administration of military justice as a major source of discrimination.

In his briefing White focused not so much on the court-martial procedure as a source of discrimination as on punishments under Article 15 of the Uniform Code of Military Justice. Article 15 allowed commanders to offer soldiers the possibility of punishment without a court-martial for minor offences. If a soldier accepted punishment under Article 15, the commander decided on the form, which could range from pay reductions to reductions in rank or brief prison terms. Acceptance of an Article 15 by the soldier did not require an admission of guilt. Despite the complaints, White believed that "commanders were not administering punishments in a racially discriminatory manner." At the same time the team had discovered that "a larger percentage of Negroes than Caucasians were reduced for their first offense." He noted a "clear disparity in the number of Negro soldiers administered nonjudicial punishment in contrast to his Caucasian counterpart. Approximately one of every eight soldiers in U.S. Army Europe" was black. However, the black soldiers received "slightly more than one of every four nonjudicial punishments imposed in that command."[85]

Two years later, statistics in the Render report drew a similar picture. According to the report, "an overwhelming number of blacks" were being "processed through the system of military justice." This included the use of Article 15 proceedings as well as special and general courts-martial.[86] Moreover, black enlisted men complained that they were punished more often and more severely than their white counterparts. According to the report, "there was also the implication of excessive pre-trial confinement for minorities." Furthermore, minority soldiers received insufficient counsel about their rights and the procedures under the Uniform Code of Military Justice.[87]

In an interview to AFN a little more than a month before the Render visit, the commander in chief of USAREUR had denied any discrimination in the administration of military justice. According to Polk, his command reviewed the legal system in USAREUR and had not found any evidence of widespread discrimination in the courts and boards. He acknowledged some rare occasions of discrimination, but argued those were few and far between and dealt with immediately. Polk went on to describe the changes made in the military justice system to ensure more qualified legal representation for defendants in military courts. Since 1967 the army had been providing a fully trained legal officer not only for the prosecution but for the defendant as well. Defendants had the right to hire a civilian lawyer. Polk stressed that the average sentence in the Mannheim Stockade had gone down from five to three months. The general was confident in the fairness of military justice in his command: "I believe that we do administer justice, administer it well and with impartiality." Polk acknowledged that a disproportionately high number of inmates at the Mannheim Stockade were African American, but he denied that this indicated discrimination in the justice system. He insisted that those prisoners were there for a reason, having "committed various offenses punishable under our legal system."[88] Polk's comments demonstrated that he misunderstood or misrepresented the issues that upset black soldiers under his command. His underlying assumption was that black soldiers got into trouble more often because they came from underprivileged backgrounds with less education and fewer resources. Thereby he placed the responsibility on American society for the racial imbalance in regard to punishments meted out. The findings of the Render team and findings of subsequent investigations contradicted Polk's assertion of the basic fairness of the military justice system. Polk was unable to dispel concern over the treatment of black soldiers by the military courts and boards.

The NAACP's team of investigators in West Germany focused on investigating the administration of military justice.[89] The final report showed that black soldiers were overrepresented in the penitentiaries in Germany. Blacks were more likely to receive formal and informal punishments.

The rate for punishments under Article 15 was double the white rate for offenses such as disrespect, disobedience, insubordination, "provoking gestures," and assault. In Berlin black GIs composed 15 percent of the command, but they received two-thirds of the punishments according to an estimate. Company commanders often induced by NCOs most often imposed the punishments.[90] The numbers provided by the NAACP were not the result of a survey. The team compiled them through interviews with officials and black soldiers at bases in West Germany. They show that the soldiers' perception of racial discrimination in the military justice system differed markedly from the perception of their commander in chief. Numbers compiled by a DOD task force seem to bear out the GIs' perception. The task force found that out of 4,082 instances of nonjudicial punishments it had included in its study, black GIs had received 25.5 percent. This number exceeded their proportionate number at the installations participating in the study (15.8 percent) or their proportionate number in the armed forces (13.1 percent). The task force conducted its investigation in 1972. Considering that by that time the army had already started to raise awareness among its officers about remaining problems of racial discrimination, it is not unreasonable to assume that the numbers were close to the NAACP's claim of two-thirds in 1970.[91]

Black soldiers believed they were punished for offenses that their white counterparts got away with. They pointed to long hair specifically as an infraction that only black soldiers received punishment for. Open displays of racial pride were likely to lead to confrontations with white superiors. Black soldiers reported to the NAACP that they were "goaded into technical violations by unsympathetic white officers."[92] One indication that the high number of confrontations between black soldiers and white officers was not just a result of young inexperienced soldiers still learning the boundaries of military life was that an unusually large number of higher ranking enlistees were also punished under Article 15. The NAACP claimed that there had been a significant increase in the number of E5s receiving nonjudicial punishments. These soldiers testified that "many disciplinary actions developed from an incident of racial discrimination."

Pretrial confinement appeared particularly discriminatory. Pretrial confinement was intended as a measure to ensure the presence of a defendant at the trial, to confine anyone whose alleged crimes were too severe to let him run free, or to confine someone who could potentially endanger life or property. The NAACP found that commanders misused their right to put their subordinates in pretrial confinement as a tool to enforce discipline. Black soldiers experienced this abuse of power in disproportionate numbers. Half of the black soldiers detained in prisons were in pretrial confinement. Black soldiers constituted half of the overall number of soldiers in pretrial confinement, according to the NAACP. The report of the NAACP showed that both black and white soldiers suffered from the abuse of pretrial confinement.[93] The guidelines protecting these soldiers from misuse were toothless and not properly enforced by commanding officers. The officers were often remiss in their duties to their subordinates. They were required to pay monthly visits to their men in pretrial confinement and to make sure that the men received their pay, letters, and fresh clothes.

The numbers given by the task force in 1972 were not quite as alarming, but they too indicated that more than 21 percent of the enlisted servicemen in pretrial confinement were black. They also had the longest average length of confinement of any racial or ethnic group identified (34.5 days). That was almost five days longer than the average for white enlisted men. This remained true regardless of whether or not the individual soldier had a prior military justice record. The task force also found that "proportionately more minority group personnel" were "placed in pretrial confinement (39.8% of all blacks and 35.2% of all Spanish Surnamed) for alleged commission of offenses which tend to directly confront or challenge military authority or are equivalent to civilian felony offenses (as compared to 15.4% of the whites)." Black soldiers in pretrial confinement were also more likely to actually go to trial and less likely to get a discharge in lieu of a trial.[94]

The number of African Americans serving regular prison sentences was also disproportionately high. A survey conducted in January 1971 showed that up to 50 percent of the prisoners were black. The NAACP team thought it significant "that blacks were more likely than whites to be confined for offenses that involved a challenge to authority, usually a superior white officer. More than 3 out of 5 soldiers convicted for the offenses of willful disobedience were black."[95] The NAACP argued that soldiers detained in pretrial confinement were likely to return to the stockade for a more serious offense, because the time in prison had a hardening effect on the detainee. The task force reported that of the 1,471 servicemen tried in courts-martial, 34.3 percent were black. The task force also found that 47 percent of a random sample of 207 servicemen imprisoned at the U.S. Disciplinary Barracks, Fort Leavenworth, Kansas, were black. These prisoners had received longer sentences to confinement at hard labor and had "a larger percentage of sentences including total forfeitures and dishonorable discharges." Black soldiers were also slightly more likely to have received a prior Article 15, summary court-martial, or special court-martial.[96]

Officers ignored, bypassed, or did not enforce reforms already in place to reduce Article 15 cases and stop the misuse of pretrial confinement. For example, acting on a suggestion from army judge Capt. Curtis Smothers, Polk ordered that Article 15 cases against the lower four enlisted grades (E1–E4) had to be published. He believed this would make proceedings more transparent and demonstrate that officers did not single out black soldiers for punishment. Most officers ignored the order. Polk's measure was telling regarding his attitude toward the racial tensions in his command. Polk did not believe that the system itself or the people administering it were flawed. Instead, African American perceptions of unfairness had to be changed. This fit in well with his assertion in the AFN interview that those black soldiers imprisoned were there because they had "gotten into trouble."

The problems of black GIs with the military justice system were exasperated by the distrust many of them felt toward the legal counsel available to them. Polk had asserted in his interview that since 1967 all defendants had the right to a fully trained legal officer or could hire a civilian lawyer. From the perspective of a black enlisted man, this did little to alleviate his problems. Except for two black judges, the Judge Advocate General (JAG) personnel serving in Germany was all white. Moreover, there were no black civilian lawyers available to the soldiers. Many black GIs believed that military lawyers were prejudiced and biased not only because they were white but also because they were part of the military hierarchy. Turning to a civilian lawyer was not a good alternative, because legal fees were high and civilian lawyers often paid insufficient attention to their clients. The NAACP team concluded that "so far the military has not found a way to provide objective and appropriate legal aid to its black soldiers."[97] Upon their return to the United States, the NAACP team called on the government to help defray the cost of sending black civilian lawyers to Germany.[98]

When he became the judge advocate of USAREUR in the spring of 1971, Brig. Gen. Wilton B. Persons conducted an internal investigation to evaluate discrimination against black soldiers. Many of his findings matched those of the NAACP. In a disposition to the chief of staff, Persons reported that black soldiers in the European command did receive "a disproportionate number of courts-martial in relation to their population." He also found that black soldiers were sentenced to confinement at hard labor more frequently than white soldiers and for longer periods of time. Moreover, a higher percentage of African Americans ended up in pretrial confinement, and the acquittal rate for black soldiers was lower.[99]

The conclusions that Persons drew were similar at first glance to General Polk's findings two years earlier. Like Polk, Persons made the point that the soldiers ended up in confinement for a reason. Almost half of confined blacks had committed an assault or robbery. He noted that black and white convicts came from similar social backgrounds that would make it more likely for them to get into trouble. Persons believed that "the basic military justice system is a sound one conceived in terms of fundamental fairness and designed to ensure justice and equality for all."

Unlike Polk, Persons did believe that discrimination was possible and did happen. Persons argued that discrimination was not inherent to the system but caused by individuals. Many judges, juries, and attorneys believed "that blacks usually lie on the witness stand, that they stick together, and that the racial makeup of witnesses is a factor in determining credibility." Individuals acting out their bias were responsible for instances of racial discrimination, not the system of military justice itself.[100] Persons argued that since the prejudices permeating American society also found their way into the army, the people needed to change. Even a "perfect system operated by prejudiced people" could not "eliminate racial discrimination." While Persons admitted that prejudices of the judges, attorneys, and juries could lead to discrimination, he believed that the crucial factor was the decisions made before a case went to court. More often than not, junior commanders (lieutenants and captains) and their NCOs had to decide how to deal with infractions committed by members of their units. They made the decision whether a soldier went to court-martial, received an Article 15, or received a warning. These were the decisions where racial bias had the most impact. These findings were similar to those of the NAACP, which had argued that tensions between black soldiers and their white superiors constituted the root cause of many punishable incidents. Black soldiers saw the unfair administration of Article 15s as a greater source of discrimination than their treatment in the military courts.[101] The Task Force on the Administration of Military Justice in the Armed Forces left no doubt in its report that by 1972 the question was no longer whether discrimination in the military justice system existed but how far it reached and where it originated.[102] This investigation, unlike the NAACP's, was not limited to Europe or the army. Its report showed clearly the disparities in the treatment of black and white military personnel.[103]

One of the greatest problems and one that also affected the German community was the polarization of enlisted men during their spare time activities. In on-post clubs as well as in off-post restaurants, bars, and clubs, soldiers tended to polarize according to race.[104] The Render report argued that coercion played a role. Coerced polarization came about "when blacks put down other blacks who associated with whites and whites reject other whites who associate with blacks." Of course African American soldiers would also keep to themselves voluntarily as a manifestation of the "covered wagon complex," where for self-protection both psychologically and physically black GIs had formed informal groups and tended to socialize among themselves. Render believed that "after a long history of experience of being intentionally rejected by whites purely on the basis of race," it was "understandable why this type of antisocial behavior" took place. Social polarization among black soldiers caused another discriminatory practice. White soldiers and officers often viewed groups of three or four blacks as a threat "prone to disruption or riotous activity." Officers and noncoms would disperse them without provocation, whereas groups of white soldiers were "considered to be merely carrying on social conversation."

Black servicemen complained that even though officially they had access to base clubs, they felt that these were still alien and hostile places. A black Vietnam veteran in Germany told the NAACP that the music played at his NCO club had a white bias. "Soul music was played only during weekdays, while prime off-duty weekend time was reserved for Country and Western." Black soldiers bringing German women to the enlisted men's club posed an even greater problem. This provoked drunken white soldiers to fight. The situation at off-base bars and clubs was even worse. Black GIs found that discrimination at local bars and inns was often even more overt and complete than in the United States. According to the NAACP, white-only and membership-only bars abounded around bases in Germany, while black soldiers found themselves segregated into one or two bars considered for blacks only. The NAACP found that blacks at one installation had declared their bar off-limits to white soldiers.[105]

The tendency to seek out members of one's own race also affected the German community. The army had exported American racism into the local population. In many cases white military personnel imposed "economic sanctions and threats on local businessmen," threatening that white personnel would cease to frequent businesses that provided services to African Americans. Given that most soldiers were white, German business owners acquiesced out of economic necessity.[106]

Sociologist Charles Moskos analyzed patterns of off-duty separation between black and white soldiers and saw them as most pronounced in Germany and Japan. He argued that the social difficulties of soldiers in USAREUR were due to their declining economic status. Unlike their predecessors fifteen to twenty years ago, soldiers were no longer affluent by local standards. The status drop of the American soldier vis-à-vis the German working man had particularly affected the black serviceman. This was most apparent in their access to women in Germany. According to Moskos, "the good old days" had ended for the black soldier as he found "his previous access to other than prostitutes severely reduced. Moreover, he now had to compete with foreign laborers for the same girls."[107] Maj. Gen. Frederic Davison, commander of the Eighth Division in 1971, remembered that in Mainz the entire community had been hostile to black troops. Only after the intervention of the president of the Bundestag, Anne Marie Renger, was he able to have a talk with the city's mayor on this subject.[108]

But even at this time of heightened racial tensions in the army in Germany, black GIs' experience of their host nation was not entirely negative. Overseas duty in Germany, Moskos argued, still gave black enlisted men an opportunity to witness a society "where overt racial discrimination is less practiced than it is in their home country." Sixty-four percent of the black soldiers Moskos had interviewed believed "that there was more racial equality in Germany, 30 percent saw little difference between the two countries, and only 6 percent believed blacks were treated better in the United States." Moskos discovered that black servicemen were five times more likely to learn conversational German than their white counterparts.

Despite these more positive findings, Moskos believed the racial situation in USAREUR to be critical. Regardless of its origins off-base, segregation became a source of frustration among black troops. Discriminatory behavior by Germans extended beyond the bars or personal relations to housing. According to the Render report, racial and price discrimination in off-post housing had "reached overwhelming proportions." Servicemen felt that the army condoned this type of behavior because it took no action to eliminate discrimination by German landlords.[109] The NAACP stressed that "experience with discrimination and housing and public accommodations" had prompted many black soldiers "to regard West Germany as an unfriendly country."[110]

As seen previously, the Department of Defense under McNamara had been reluctant to grant base commanders the authority to impose sanctions on businesses and landlords without prior consultation. Only as the racial tensions in the army mounted in the late 1960s did the DOD provide its commanders in the United States with the necessary administrative tools to enforce equal opportunity directives outside the military bases. The secretary of the army issued a regulation in December 1969 giving military commanders the authority to impose off-limit sanctions against civilian facilities that discriminated against black soldiers.[111] However, AR 600-18 was limited to bases within the United States. The regulation expressly excluded commanders in Germany and other overseas military bases from using sanctions against civilian establishments. The assistant secretary of defense, Roger T. Kelley, reinforced this point in DOD directive 1100.15 issued in December 1970.[112]

When the NAACP investigated racial discrimination in housing in USAREUR, army spokesmen claimed that they received few complaints from black servicemen. However, the NAACP reported that contrary to those claims, housing discrimination was a major grievance point among black soldiers at every base visited. Black soldiers expressed their frustration with German landlords and housing agents who practiced discrimination often with support from white personnel. They were equally frustrated with their commanders who "had ignored the issue and until recently failed to actively intervene to protect the rights of black servicemen."

Housing on German bases was limited. Therefore, the army discouraged its junior personnel from bringing their families along to Germany. Only enlisted personnel at E5 or higher qualified for U.S. government housing. Younger servicemen had to find housing "on the economy" (the German housing market) if they insisted on bringing their family along. The task of finding housing in a foreign environment was taxing enough for a young soldier. Black soldiers often found that after making an appointment with a German landlord to see a vacant apartment, these landlords would claim that they had already rented out the place as soon as they came face to face with the enlisted man. When black soldiers did manage to obtain housing, it was often located far away from their base in sometimes hostile environments. The wife of a soldier reported taunts such as "Look at the Swasi" or "Look at the N——."[113]

Dissatisfaction about the housing situation in Germany among some black soldiers ran so high that on December 25, 1970, a group of officers and enlisted men applied for a court of inquiry against the commander in chief of USAREUR. The seven petitioners alleged "widespread discrimination against your Petitioners in access to economy housing and that such discrimination is due solely to Petitioners' race."[114] The petitioners claimed that Polk had been aware of this type of discrimination since 1968. He had received information on this subject through official and unofficial channels but had not fulfilled his obligation to act, for example, by imposing sanctions on German landlords. But the allegations of the petitioners went even further. They believed that family-housing officials aided and abetted such discriminatory practices of German landlords. The petitioners asked for a court of inquiry because they did not have the means to conduct a full investigation into the matter.[115] One of the petitioners, Maj. Washington C. Hill, a doctor, also wrote a letter to the *New York Times* describing his difficulties obtaining housing in Germany.[116]

The DOD denied the petitioners' request, at least in regard to Polk. In a letter to Major Hill, the deputy assistant secretary of the army, John G. Kester, expressed confidence in Polk's handling of racial matters.

He reminded the petitioners that army regulations had forbidden "the referral of private rental quarters that were not available without regard to race, color, creed, or national origin of prospective tenants." He also assured them that in 1970 "because of increased allegations of racial discrimination," Polk had indeed started to impose off-limits and restrictive sanctions against businesses and landlords who practiced racial discrimination. Kester did not question that racial discrimination among German landlords was taking place, but he expected the actions taken by Polk to have a material effect in the future. While Kester was unwilling to criticize Polk, he did promise to look into the allegations of aiding and abetting by housing officials.[117]

While the NAACP did not charge that family housing officials were aiding and abetting, it did claim that officials were doing little to improve the situation. The report cites the case of one German landlord who refused housing to a black soldier. After the soldier appealed to his equal opportunity officer, the landlord gave in but raised the rent by 100 Deutschmarks. The equal opportunity officer advised the soldier to take the apartment. Black soldiers in the Heidelberg area "produced affidavits from Army Housing investigators attesting to the fact that 85 percent of the landlords listed with Family Housing offices" discriminated on the basis of race. The soldiers believed that housing officials were aware of this but did nothing about it.[118]

The NAACP did mention that in December 1970 Polk had been ordered to place businesses discriminating against service members off-limits. However, the NAACP team also noted that placing a business or an apartment complex off-limits involved a lengthy bureaucratic process in which a complaint had to be forwarded up the chain of command and an off-limits order had to be approved by CINCUSAREUR. Even worse, many commanders proved reluctant to report complaints about racial discrimination to their superiors out of fear that such a report would be interpreted as a failure on the commander's part. Soldiers felt that only if they themselves could pursue a complaint without being branded a militant or a troublemaker could appropriate results be brought about.[119]

Overall, the three fact-finding missions to USAREUR in 1969 and 1970 revealed how pervasive discrimination and racism were in the officially integrated institution. They also revealed how black soldiers had embraced black power concepts and rhetoric to demand equal treatment and an end to discrimination on and off duty. Faced with a strong institutional resistance to change, the more radical rhetoric and the threat of militancy were important factors in triggering government scrutiny and an acknowledgment that there might be a problem. Polk's response to revelations about systematic discrimination was slow and reluctant, but even he could not deny that some changes had to be made.

3

Failed Leadership Responses and Black Power

The Render report stated that there was no "problem or situation at the present time in the Armed Forces" that required "more resourcefulness of a commander and his leadership capabilities" than the problem of race relations. The failure of leadership constituted "the most overriding single factor" for the critical state of race relations. Despite the plethora of documents and statements issuing from the DOD that provided commanders at all levels with the necessary authority to monitor and provide for equal opportunity and treatment, many commanders had failed to do so. Consequently, incidents with racial overtones had "proliferated over the last several months in the European Theater, mostly in Germany." Racial incidents were not spontaneous or chance conflagrations. They resulted from "a history of long unresolved differences, misunderstandings, improper and inadequate communication."[1]

Conflagrations only appeared sudden because of deficiencies in the transmission of information up and down the chain of command. "Middle managers (junior NCOs and junior officers) seemed not to communicate adequately." Officers were often afraid to admit their inability to understand and address the racial tensions in their units and so failed to report the problems.[2] The report stressed that officers had little reason to feel ashamed, since very few of them had ever received adequate training in this field of military management.

The failures of leadership went further than just communication. Many commanders failed to make distinctions between militants and activists who were "very concerned about the system" and wanted to do what they could "through some activity of their own in conjunction with already identified leaders."[3] Instead military leaders often saw anyone who resisted the status quo as militant. They saw advocacy of "black consciousness, black civil liberties, even the expectation of equal treatment" as expressions of militancy.[4] The Render report argued that black soldiers expressing grievances in regard to racial discrimination were not generally militants. Even among soldiers labeled militants, distinctions had to be made between those who wanted to work within the system and those who wanted to destroy it. Commanders needed to become more sensitive to these differences in order to be able to utilize the activists in advancing the goal of more harmonious race relations.

The Render team itself experienced the undistinguishing attitude among commanders by quoting a communication between two commanders about the approaching visit of the team: "Mr. Render is a top grade militant. If he were not in the Army he would be a leader in the Black Panthers."[5] In the *Overseas Weekly*, white soldiers referred to Render's team as "a bunch of Commies inside the Government comin' 'round to agitate and stir up trouble."[6] While these quotes represented the more extreme end of the spectrum of attitudes among the USAREUR leadership, the report stated nonetheless that "most commands did exhibit to varying degrees an apprehensive, less than positive attitude relative to the business" that the team had come to carry out. Commanders were reluctant to discuss human or race relations problems openly, fearing the team would carry these problems into their command.[7]

These kinds of sentiments toward DOD officials who were investigating civil rights issues in the military extended beyond enlisted men and junior officers. In a letter exchange between General Polk and John J. Flynt Jr., a member of the House of Representatives, Flynt expressed his concern that the secretary of the army might unwittingly encourage action by black militant groups. Flynt believed that when the secretary reported such incidents to the secretary of defense, he did so in "a light most favorable to such militant groups."[8] Polk himself was less than enthusiastic about the visit of the Render team to his command and the report that the team had prepared. In a letter to Westmoreland, Polk did not criticize Render directly, but he did comment that public statements from DOD officials on the problem of race relations exacerbated the tensions: "These overtones create doubt that the command is sincere regarding equal opportunity matters."[9]

Like many of his subordinate commanders, General Polk was unwilling to admit that some of the problems in regard to race came from within USAREUR. Instead he argued that these problems came from the outside. The interview he gave to the American Forces Network (AFN) before the visit by the assistant secretary of defense indicates that for a long time Polk had underestimated the explosiveness of the racial situation in his command. Polk claimed that he had only learned of the dissatisfaction on the part of the African American troops through the briefing given by Lt. Col. James White the year before. In the interview Polk admitted that USAREUR had a race relations problem, but stressed that it originated from the United States. According to Polk, there was "very little discrimination in Europe."[10]

Polk also believed that the media bore some responsibility for the racial tensions in his units. In letter exchanges with Gen. David A. Burchinal, the deputy commander in chief of the U.S. European Command, and Westmoreland, he complained about the coverage by both overseas newspapers, the *Stars & Stripes* and the *Overseas Weekly*. In a letter to Westmoreland, Polk attached an article from the *Overseas Weekly* that he found particularly inflammatory.[11] The article from July 19, 1970, described the activities of the "USAREUR Defense Committee."[12] What particularly incensed the general was that the article publicized "not only the dissatisfaction of certain black soldiers" but also "the fact that certain blacks are prepared to use force and have weapons to gain their ends." Aside from the measures Polk intended to take in order to suppress the defense committee, the general was also contemplating suppressing "a particular issue of the *Weekly* in the event a similar article is published." Polk regretted that he could not talk to the publisher because he was not in Europe and would not return until September. However, the *New York Times* reported in August 1970 that the editor of the *Overseas Weekly*, Curtis Daniell, had been forced to resign after General Polk had communicated his displeasure over the *Overseas Weekly*'s coverage of USAREUR's racial problems to the paper's majority owner, Joseph B. Kroesen.[13]

In his letter to General Burchinal, Polk criticized some of the editorial choices made by the *Stars & Stripes* in the days before July 4.[14] The paper had run two articles on June 30 and July 1 describing black soldiers' discontent in Vietnam. Polk believed that the timing of these articles had been poor because they ran just prior to the widely publicized demonstrations by black soldiers in Heidelberg. He also stated that articles such as these tended to create dissatisfaction if published without some counterbalance. Polk was especially disappointed because he believed that the editorial policies of *Stars & Stripes* were "generally wholesome."

The reaction of Polk's two superiors differed. Westmoreland claimed to be equally concerned about the press coverage of the racial tensions in USAREUR. But he cautioned Polk that prohibiting distribution of the *Overseas Weekly* would be difficult at best and would require evidence that the publication presented a danger to the discipline, loyalty, and morale of the troops. Westmoreland was also convinced that suppressing a particular issue of the *Overseas Weekly* would probably have the reverse effect of increasing circulation. He warned Polk that he required the approval of EUCOM as well as the Defense Department in order to suppress circulation. Moreover, Westmoreland admonished Polk to check into the validity of the claims made in the article of the *Overseas Weekly* and to work more closely with the equal rights branch of the Defense Department in order to get the racial situation in Germany under control.[15]

General Burchinal's answer to Polk's complaints was more favorable. Burchinal believed that there had never been a time when the press had been more critical of the military than at present. While the military could do little about coverage in the United States, Burchinal did believe that the commanders in Europe could do more to make sure that the soldiers there got "more recognition for their sacrifices, their professionalism, and for their accomplishments." Burchinal reported that he discussed the coverage of race relations and drug problems in the military with editors of *Stars & Stripes*. His report sheds some light on the independence of the newspaper in Europe. According to Burchinal, the editors regretted the timing of the articles. They had known about the July 4 demonstration and had instructed their reporters to stay away. However, they had been unaware of the racial aspects of the demonstrations. Burchinal concluded that tightening up control would be healthy and "help reduce mistakes in taste and judgment to a minimum."[16]

To Polk and Burchinal, the racial unrest apparent in West Germany occurred as a result of outside agitation rather than structural or institutional problems. In his letter to Westmoreland, Polk complained that up to this point individual complaints garnered too much attention. He criticized Render for wanting to mandate "the entire issue of interpersonal relationships." According to Polk, suggestions of this nature "advanced by high ranking Department of Defense officials who should know better, contribute more to the problem than to its solution."[17] Polk was reacting to public statements made by Render, who had faulted field commanders for not wanting to "face up to dealing forthrightly with problems." When field commanders neglected the problem, their subordinate officers and NCOs tended to ignore or cover up smoldering racial difficulties. Young officers were afraid to admit to having racial problems in their units because that could have made them look incompetent. The *New York Times* published Render's criticism.[18] The tensions between the assistant secretary and the general would later lead to speculations in the press that it was Polk's inability to calm the racial situation that led to his early retirement in March 1971.[19]

Despite his complaints about Render's suggestions, Polk did introduce measures to improve race relations in his command. USAREUR published a Commanders' Notebook on Equal Opportunity and Human

Relations. With the aid of the notebook, commanders at all levels started to implement equal opportunity programs. By January 5 they had established more than one hundred human relations councils. Increasingly, unit commanders appointed equal opportunity officers in their units. Inspection teams were created specifically to investigate "unit records and procedures to determine if discriminatory practices" existed.[20] Race relations instruction increased from two to four hours at NCO academies. Education centers started to offer black studies courses and sensitivity training. Housing regulations were changed. Commanders in Germany were now able to use restrictive sanctions against landlords who discriminated. This meant they could declare a house that did not rent to black soldiers off-limits to all soldiers in the command, so that no soldier could live there anymore. Polk also made public appeals through U.S. and German media "to landlords and rental agents to end discrimination by making their establishments available to all U.S. soldiers." Performance reports now contained comments on the sensitivity of individuals rated "to human relations and especially as to performance in analyzing and solving the problems of race relations."[21] A new regulation guaranteed a lawyer to enlisted personnel confronted with a punishment under Article 15.[22]

The NAACP acknowledged in its report, which was issued five months after the Render visit, that "various policy changes" had been initiated recently at the higher levels of the command "to deal with many of the inequities of which the enlisted men complained." The problem was that the inquiry team had found much greater awareness of race-related problems at the higher levels of command than among the junior officers. Noncommissioned and junior grade officers were unaware of the new programs and policies. Because of that, "the newly announced programs and policy changes were not, in a meaningful way, being implemented at a level that had an impact on the lives of most black servicemen." For the moment problems in Germany remained "real, critical, and complex." The grievances articulated by black soldiers were pervasive and intense. The NAACP also believed that at this point "the overwhelming number" of black servicemen were prepared to fight for change within the system as long as they could be convinced that those possessing power to bring about meaningful change also had the will to do so. But the report also warned that "an uncomfortable number" of younger servicemen were disenchanted, alienated, and had lost faith "in the capacity and the will of the Armed Forces to deal honestly with their problems." These younger servicemen were intent on pressing change outside of the system, a trend that the NAACP deemed to be potentially catastrophic for both the soldiers engaged in such actions and for the military.[23]

In *The Taming of the Troops* Lawrence Radine outlined the different strategies the army employed to maintain social control and make potential dissidents ineffective. Writing in 1977, Radine believed that the army's emphasis was shifting from the more traditional professional paternalist techniques to co-optive rational techniques. The paternalist approach to dissidence included "the clarification of regulations and dissemination of propaganda on soldierly character."[24] Polk's insistence that black soldiers just needed to be shown that they were being treated fairly by publicizing army regulations on equal opportunity can be interpreted as an example that fits Lawrence's definition of a paternalist approach. While Polk demonstrated concern about unrest among his soldiers, he was unable to convince black soldiers that he was taking the underlying grievances seriously. He was reluctant to have the racial problems discussed outside of the "family," and so he allowed only limited communication on the subject.

According to Radine, co-optive techniques centered on the careful management of hostile attitudes. A co-optive leader had to draw out antagonistic sentiments into the open "in a setting that allows him to 'cool them out,' rather than allow them to coalesce in a counter organization." In order to achieve this, an officer could give the impression that he would redress voiced grievances "or otherwise correct the problem." He could also deal with the soldier as a therapist, "helping him surmount his maladaptive behavior and feelings." Moreover, open discussions and classes, as well as informal question-and-answer sessions were also techniques to dissolve the development of counter consciousness.[25] While some of Polk's measures indicate that he was moving in the direction of a more co-optive leadership style, he was unable to convincingly communicate this change. It also seems doubtful that he ever completely believed in a more open style of leadership. Consequently, Polk was unable to break the momentum of dissidence in USAREUR in late 1970.

The policies Polk had introduced to alleviate racial problems by early 1971 had done little to calm the racial tensions in the command. In fact, protests became more organized and more radical. Members of the Black Panther Party started to take an interest in the racial situation in USAREUR. In April 1971, 450 black enlisted men once again met in a meeting hall at the University of Heidelberg. As during the meeting on July 4 of the previous year, the rhetoric employed at the demonstration went beyond GIs' grievances. Declaring the war in Vietnam racist, speakers came out against capitalism and imperialism, which they identified as the major source of their oppression.[26] The connections made between domestic racism and U.S. imperialism echoed ideas popularized by Eldridge Cleaver, the Panthers' former minister of information and current leader of the disavowed International Section of the Black Panther Party.[27]

On July 4, 1971, black activists called a meeting at the University of Heidelberg. The featured speaker was Kathleen Cleaver, Eldridge's wife and communications secretary of the International Section. Cleaver called upon black GIs to stop fighting for their white oppressors. Even though African Americans had fought in every major conflict the United States had been involved in in the name of freedom, they still lived in slavery, Cleaver claimed. Independence Day, she believed, was not a cause for celebration for America's black population.[28] The rhetoric at both meetings had become more radical than at the meeting of the previous year. Cleaver referred to the army as the "Green Machine" and to white oppressors as "pigs."

Besides the more general grievances against white discrimination and oppression, both meetings in Heidelberg voiced a more specific grievance. The soldiers demonstrated for the release of two members of the Black Panther Party who had allegedly been involved in a shooting at the Ramstein Air Base.[29] The case of the so-called Ramstein Two became an important rallying point for political activists in West Germany, both American and German. William Burrell and Lawrence Jackson were former GIs who had chosen to remain in Germany after their release from the army. They had been touring American bases in southwestern Germany to distribute posters announcing an upcoming rally with Kathleen Cleaver.[30] When the Burrell and Jackson along with one or two unidentified persons tried to enter the Ramstein Air Base on November 19, 1970, they refused to show their identification to the guard. After the guard asked them to step out of the car, a firefight ensued. The German police took the two into custody that same day.[31] Their trial before a German court took place in June 1971. Black Panther activists in Germany saw the trial as an example of white oppression and covered it in their underground newspaper, *Voice of the Lumpen*.

Voice of the Lumpen made its appearance in early 1971. "Lumpen" was an obvious reference to the term "Lumpenproletariat."[32] Many of its articles dealt with incidents at various barracks in Germany. *Voice* also contained articles informing the soldiers about larger issues that the Black Panther Party was involved in, such as the trials against Black Panther founder Bobby Seale and Ericka Huggins or the trial against Angela Davis.[33] As was often the case with such underground publications, the editors of the paper remained anonymous. From the information given in the second issue, it is reasonable to conclude that they were not GIs themselves:

> We the editors of the "Voice of the Lumpen," are the Black Panther Task Squad in Germany, which means we are representatives of the BPP. We are here to inform and educate our Brothers in particular, and GIs in general, about the Black Panther Party and developments; to counter-act any pig press lies about the Black Panther Party; to expose the harrassments [*sic*] of the Military pig system against GIs.[34]

Incidents reported in the paper often involved members of the party trying to distribute literature among soldiers.

The Black Panther Party originated in Oakland, California. Huey P. Newton and Bobby Seale founded the party on October 15, 1966. Frustrated with more traditional civil rights organizations, they were looking for an organization with a new agenda. Newton and Seale were not so much concerned with political integration as with the material and social discrimination that African Americans faced in the ghettos of the inner cities. The Black Panthers did identify themselves with the concept of black power in that they sought the political and social empowerment of urban African Americans. However, they differed from the more nationalist interpretations of black power in that they endorsed the Marxist principle of the universal brotherhood of the exploited.[35]

The Black Panthers consciously rejected the label of a movement, preferring instead to organize as a centralized revolutionary party. Marx, Lenin, Frantz Fanon, Mao, Che Guevara, Robert Williams, and Malcolm X were important influences. They interpreted the struggle of African Americans as a class struggle and identified themselves with anti-imperialist movements in former colonies in Africa and Asia.[36] Its socialist outlook also allowed the party to forge alliances with white political activists, and it informed its more internationalist outlook. Until 1971 Eldridge Cleaver was the party's most influential leader in emphasizing international solidarity with Third World revolutions.[37] The ideology of the party was not entirely coherent, as its various leaders emphasized different aspects of their ten-point program. Especially in the last years of the decade, rifts developed between sections of the party in the East and its headquarters in Oakland as well as with the International Section.[38]

Several months after his involvement in a 1968 shoot-out with Oakland police, Cleaver went into exile first in Cuba and then in Algeria. In 1970 he founded the International Section with an embassy building in Algiers.[39] From 1969 to 1971 Cleaver maintained high-level connections with the National Liberation Front, North Vietnam, and North Korea. The Vietnamese played a key role in Algeria's decision to recognize Cleaver and the International Section. Given these connections Cleaver became even more invested in the revolutionary and Marxist identity of the party.[40] This increasingly put him at odds with the leadership at home who had become more committed to community engagement, emphasizing programs such as the Free Breakfast for Children. By early 1971 the Central Committee of the BPP saw immediate insurrection as counterproductive and instead advocated a social democratic approach to build support and membership through community-oriented programs. After a televised disagreement between Newton and Cleaver in February 1971, the *Black Panther* announced the defection of the International Section on March 20, 1971.[41] So the International Section, which exerted the most influence on activities on German military bases and on the *Voice of the Lumpen,* had severed ties to the party back in the United States.

Despite the disavowal, the *Voice* covered broader issues, such as the imprisonment of BPP members in the United States. It also made an effort to voice the grievances of black soldiers in Germany. The Ramstein Two were political prisoners trapped by the same oppressive machinery as Black Panther members in the United States. The West German court was a lackey to American "capitalist and fascist" interests. Other articles also focused on the persecution that black activists and regular GIs experienced in West Germany. On May 11, 1971, for example, German police arrested another civilian activist of the BPP in Augsburg while he was handing out newspapers to GIs. The police arrested him for selling without a license. However, for the trial, authorities charged him with possession of subversive material that called for acts of insubordination and could therefore potentially undermine army readiness. The article denounced the Bavarian court by informing readers that Bavaria was the birthplace of the National Socialist Party and proclaiming it to be a stronghold of neofascism. The authors referred to all political opponents as pigs, the United States as Amerikkka.[42]

Several articles dealt with racial disturbances at various bases in Germany, as for example a night riot in Kirch-Göns on May 20, 1971, the setting on fire of a command jeep in Schwetzingen, or the setting on fire of the private vehicle of a lieutenant at McNair Kaserne in Höchst.[43]

The main focus of the *Voice of the Lumpen* was not to inform GIs about inequities in the army or racial disturbances at bases in West Germany but to agitate them into action. Whether they dealt with the struggle of black activists in the United States, West Germany, or other parts of the world, almost all articles ended with the famous Panther slogans "Free all political prisoners" or "All power to the people." Race riots and destruction of military vehicles and buildings were revolutionary acts long overdue. The paper featured a section called "GIs Speak Out," which featured anonymous letters supposedly written by soldiers. The letters contained admonitions to fellow GIs to take an uncompromising attitude regarding racial discrimination and the army authorities referred to as "pigs." In one of the letters a pig was defined as a "low nature beast that has no regard for law, justice or the rights of people; A creature that bites the hand that feeds it. And the pig uses lies to divide and conquer the people as his chief means of suppressing the people and keeping the people of Amerikkka in a constant state of turmoil."[44] One letter proclaimed that revolution was the only solution, since compromise with the "pigs" was not possible.[45]

Western Germany was the equally capitalist and fascist lackey of the United States. In one of the articles describing the case of the Ramstein Two, the anonymous author explained that the two accused had originally settled in Germany after their service because it had offered "a glimpse of something different than what existed in America." However, this difference was vanishing quickly as German society was changing "into an exact replica of the decadent racist American system." The "almighty dollar" had corrupted the German government, traditions, and Germany's youth.[46] Another article described German bars in Frankfurt and the practice of bars segregating along racial lines. According to the articles, German bar owners were even more "blatant" and "disgusting" in their approach to the two races than their American counterparts. Germans, the author believed, disliked American GIs in general but welcomed the dollars they spent. For black soldiers, the situation was especially cruel: "First you have suffered exploitation, racism, and police brutality constantly back in

Babylon, and now you are confronted with the same racist situation here in Germany."[47]

The writers featured in the *Voice* recounted many of the same injustices as the NAACP report of January 1971: discrimination in the justice system, promotions, and duty assignments.[48] They also claimed that black GIs were dying in disproportionate numbers in Vietnam. However, unlike the NAACP, they denied any progress in army race relations. In one article, the writer denounced the creation of race relations committees and Afro-American study groups as smoke-screens designed "to make Black GIs believe that the problems lie not within the military structure, but with a few individuals." This writer denounced peaceful coexistence and nonviolent actions as just another method to cover up acts of white racism. The author also called the NAACP report on military justice a farce. To make this claim, the author misrepresented the conclusions made by the NAACP team as more accommodationist than they were.[49] The author had earlier asserted that the U.S. military faced universal rebellion. He portrayed black soldiers in West Germany as part of an international struggle for national liberation: "Adhering to the teachings of Brother Malcolm X and the revolutionary principles put forth by the Black Panther Party, Black GIs have become actively involved in destroying the machinery that enslaves the world." Black GIs in Germany were demanding "exemption from military service, freedom for all political prisoners and prisoners of war, and freedom and self-determination for all the communities around the world."[50]

The author's claim of universal rebellion in the U.S. military was somewhat hyperbolic. The fact that 200 to 450 GIs participated in demonstrations that proclaimed comparatively radical aims indicates that the ideas and slogans of the BPP resonated with some black soldiers. But the fact that attendance at the rallies had dropped by about 50 percent compared with a similar rally on July 4, 1970, indicates that the revolutionary emphasis of the International Section resonated with fewer GIs than the *Voice* wanted its readers to believe.[51]

Many articles in the *Voice* itself contain clues that the response of

African American GIs to the appeals made by the paper was disappointing. The second issue of *Voice* featured a report by the Mannheim Liberation League, which had been founded during "the latter part of 1970" out of a need for a "vanguard element to guide and politically educate the masses of the people to the truth of this fascist decadent system." The term "vanguard" already indicates that the league was not a mass movement, but the report went on to note that from its beginnings the organization had suffered from often having to operate with insufficient funds and from a "lack of TRUE revolutionary brothers and sisters."[52] In the article "Black Bars in Germany," the author, not a GI himself, complained about the apathy of soldiers in the Frankfurt area when confronted with the segregation of clubs and bars there:

> It is amazing that while the individual Brother, when questioned concerning his rights and place in today's society, usually responds with beautiful, Black, ultra-militant rhetoric, but when faced with a situation that demands action, he assumes the complacency of a well fed domesticated animal. . . . It appears young Blacks in the Frankfurt community are still afflicted with the now centuries-old attitude of many American "Negroes." That is, "Be Satisfied With What You've Got."[53]

The rhetoric used at the two demonstrations in Heidelberg in April and July 1971 indicate that some of the black activists within the army had radicalized and seemed no longer interested in reforms from within. But the drop in attendance and the complaints about apathy found in the *Voice* lead to the conclusion that most black GIs did not support revolutionary action. This was also the conclusion of the Render team and the NAACP.[54]

Race relations in USAREUR remained tense throughout the first half of 1971 but had passed the high-water mark. Nonetheless, public perception of the matter was that of a situation out of control, as demonstrated by the *Washington Post* series in the fall of that year. The revolutionary rhetoric at the demonstrations in April and July and other activities surrounding the case of the Ramstein Two lent credence to the admonitions by Render and the NAACP that more decisive action was needed.

In January 1971, the DOD recalled Gen. James Polk three months ahead of time, effectively ending his tenure in March. Rumors persisted that his early retirement was due to his loss of control of the racial situation in Germany. A memorandum for correspondents from April 9, 1971, stated that Polk had discussed his retirement with the secretary of the army in 1969 but that the secretary had refused then. Then in September 1970 Polk "submitted a request for voluntary retirement citing personal family reasons."[55] At a convention of the National Urban League later that year, Frank Render rekindled the rumors. He claimed before the press that as part of a more vigorous campaign to end discrimination in the military, a number of high-ranking officers had been relieved of duty or disciplined because of their failure to obey the new civil rights regulations. He went on to claim that at least one general officer had been retired early "due to his inability to understand the military's new civil rights philosophy."[56]

Render never named the general, but members of the press concluded that he was referring to Polk. At two Defense Department morning briefings on July 28 and 29, a spokesman refused to deny or confirm it was Polk. While the official seemed less than supportive of the statements made by Render, he would not refute them. When pressed to at least outright deny that Polk had been retired because of the racial situation, the official would only say that the army stood by the memorandum of April 9. This seems to indicate that the difficulties regarding race relations were at least partially responsible for Polk's early retirement.[57] Polk himself rebuffed such contentions by claiming he had already intended to retire in 1969.[58]

Whether it ultimately caused his retirement or not, Polk's response to the racial grievances proved inadequate. Despite the multiple investigations that unveiled long-standing structural problems within USAREUR regarding racial discrimination, Polk maintained that this was an outside problem carried in by the media and civilian activists. He continued to insist on the inherent color blindness of the army and its officers. To him the major problem in communication lay with black soldiers not realizing how fairly they were being treated rather than with officers not listening to their minority personnel's real concerns.

The increasingly radical language used by black activists and the visibility of the Black Panther Party contradicted Polk's assurance that the situation was under control and required little institutional adjustment. Moderate observers, such as the Render committee and the NAACP, used that same visibility of black power activism to demand a more proactive and self-critical approach from the army in Germany. In Polk's successor they found a leader far more willing to consider USAREUR's institutional failings and to address race-related problems in his command more openly.

4

The New Race Relations Policies

The year 1971 was crucial regarding race relations in the U.S. Army, Europe (USAREUR). At first it seemed activism among African American GIs was becoming more radical. But the shrinking number of black GIs attending rallies and the tapering off of incidents in the following years indicated that protests had peaked in 1971. During the year, a change of command took place. Gen. Michael S. Davison replaced Gen. James H. Polk. Major General Persons became the new judge advocate, and Davison brought the highest-ranking black officer, Maj. Gen. Frederic Davison, to Germany as commander of Eighth Division and the deputy chief of staff for personnel in Europe.[1] These three commanders brought a more communicative approach to the problem that reduced the pressure even though the underlying problems were not immediately solved.

General Davison replaced Polk in June 1971.[2] From the start his approach to the social problems in his new command differed markedly from his predecessor's. Davison followed a strategy of being very candid about the difficulties USAREUR and Seventh Army were going through. Only a few months into his new command, he gave an interview to Wilson and Johnson of the *Washington Post*. The interview appeared along with the first article of the "Army in Anguish" series. In the interview, Davison voiced his concern over drug abuse and race relations in Germany. He believed the army faced the toughest period of its history. There had been a breakdown in leadership and a breakdown in communications between officers and their subordinates. This was to Davison the cause of most of the problems, regardless of their nature. He always retained an upbeat tone. While this was the toughest period ever for the army, it was also a challenge that USAREUR could meet.[3]

In the interview Davison claimed that a year ago many areas in Europe had experienced serious racial problems and had been on the verge "of being completely riotous and out of control." However, at this point commanders had already turned the situation around completely, because "the commander got everybody appreciating their subordinates as individuals and listening to them. It opened up the channels of communication." Incidents later in the year and Davison's own dealings with his subordinates indicate that the views he expressed publicly in the interview were more optimistic than he really felt.

On September 22, 1971, Davison sent private letters to his immediate subordinates in which he described his views concerning leadership and race relations in his new command. In his letter to Lt. Gen. Fillmore K. Mearns, commander of VII Corps, Davison emphasized that the problem of racial relations within the command was "a matter of deep personal concern" to him. Davison would not tolerate a commander who was "insensitive to the requirement to establish conditions of racial harmony within his unit." Protests, demonstrations, or riotous assemblies were "prime facie evidence of a leadership failure" on the part of the commander in whose unit these kinds of occurrences took place. Any such event would "be cause to examine carefully the need to replace the commander of the unit."[4] He recommended that Mearns destroy the letter after reading it, but apparently kept a copy in his own files.

At a commanders conference on race relations in Garmisch around the same time, Davison had been equally firm on the importance of the issue. Even though his speech was less threatening toward his commanders than the letters, General Persons recalled that Davison had read his subordinates the riot act.[5] He again emphasized that the commander was the key to harmonious human relations. It was not enough that a commander tried to be fair in all his dealings with his subordinates; he also had to communicate this fairness to the black soldiers. He argued that "when the black soldier's perception of his commander is poor, it's usually due to lack of communication."[6]

This assertion seemed not so different from Polk's a year earlier that the black service member only needed to be shown how fairly he was being treated. When explaining Davison's viewpoint, Persons mentioned the importance of convincing the black soldiers that "the U.S. Army in Europe was not racist, not discriminating against him as a black, but as interested in him as in any white soldier." According to Persons, commanders had to make an effort "to clear up" the mistrust and real paranoia that many of the young black GIs had.[7]

But Davison's approach was different from Polk's, because to him communication meant awareness and sensitivity on the part of the commander on what was going on in his unit. If the perception of a commander was poor, he had most likely "failed to assert the necessary controls over those in his unit whose racial attitude produce friction" or he had failed to eliminate those that were unable to control their attitudes. Individuals who used their authority to vent their prejudice against black soldiers in their unit needed to be relieved.[8] White NCOs and the Officer Corps had to be educated in order to be able "to face squarely what the problem was, to understand what the perceptions of the blacks were, and to examine in their own hearts whether they really were behaving in a way that appeared to be biased or bigoted." The emphasis was on changing the outward behavior of soldiers rather than trying to change people's minds. Persons remembers Davison exclaiming: "I don't care how you feel about this, but bigoted behavior will not be tolerated."[9]

Davison's leadership qualities in regard to race relations came under scrutiny quickly in October 1971. One of the first major racial incidents that Davison had to handle when he assumed command of USAREUR was the case of the Darmstadt 53, sometimes referred to as the Darmstadt 29. The case became one of the most prominent incidents of racial tension, receiving coverage in the press on both sides of the Atlantic and drawing the attention of a congressional committee.[10] It also became a rallying point for dissidents inside and outside of USAREUR. The incident started with a mess hall brawl on July 18, 1971, between black and white soldiers at the Cambrai Fitch installation outside of Darmstadt occupied by the Ninety-Third Signal Battalion.[11] According to General Persons, the USAREUR judge advocate, the brawl had started because a group of white soldiers had sat down at tables usually occupied by a group of black soldiers. Moreover, the white soldiers were imitating the behavior of the African Americans, carrying swagger sticks and dapping.[12] The black soldiers in the mess hall felt provoked by their behavior, and a brawl ensued.

After the brawl had been broken up, authorities arrested one black soldier, Pvt. Lareon Dixon, and charged him with inciting violence. The next day a group of 49 black soldiers and 4 white soldiers demonstrated against the arrest and were in turn arrested after refusing to disperse. The commander in charge offered the demonstrators punishment under Article 15. Twenty-nine of the demonstrators refused and demanded a court-martial.[13] After an investigation, the army decided to let Dixon go. The only soldier arrested and charged in connection with the actual brawl was a white soldier, Specialist 4 Edwards, who had assaulted a black soldier with a steel rod.[14] By October 1971 the case of the twenty-nine soldiers who had failed to disperse remained unresolved. There had been several changes of counsel, which delayed the start of the trial (the defendants tried to obtain counsel from the NAACP and the ACLU).[15] A young black activist, Mary Richardson, who had been touring Germany to prepare a report on racism in Germany had taken up the cause of the Darmstadt 53 and founded a defense committee.[16] According to the judge advocate, Davison decided to dismiss the case on October 22, 1971, because it had been "blown out of all proportion." Moreover, he believed that the offenses of the defendants did not warrant a court-martial in the first place and that the case had been dragging on for too long.[17] In his testimony before Congress, Persons also mentioned that the battalion in Darmstadt had been in "a poor state of discipline" even before the incident. A previous commander had been dismissed, and the current commander had only been there for three weeks.[18]

Outside sources indicated that there might have been another reason why the CINCUSAREUR dismissed the case. The dismissal came one day before a group of lawyers (Bernard L. Segal, Melvin Wulf of the ACLU, Melvin Bolden of the NAACP, and Capt. Ralph Kirkman Mulford III, an Army defense counsel) arrived in Germany to take over the defense of the soldiers. At a press conference the lawyers stated that fear of their potential involvement had made Davison dismiss the case.[19] Persons denied the allegation and claimed that he and Davison had not even been aware that these lawyers were coming.[20] While Persons maintained that outside interest groups had not forced Davison's decision, he also carefully distanced himself from the decision. He pointed out that Davison had not consulted him when he made the decision and that legal considerations had not informed his decision. Persons implied thereby that Davison was mainly concerned with diffusing a potentially explosive situation and weakened his own assertion that outside pressures had had no influence.[21] According to Persons, Davison was concerned that the publicity would "go on and on" and "keep people stirred up."[22]

Dissident groups in Germany such as RITA (Resistance Inside the Army) played an important role in generating the publicity surrounding the case. The case inspired these American dissidents in Germany and the German SDS (German Socialist Student Organization) as well as other German dissident organizations to publish a number of leaflets protesting the trial. The leaflets described the incident as another example of the excesses of American racism and imperialism linking the incident with the war in Vietnam and called upon readers to join a demonstration against the trial and the war on October 4, 1971.[23] The case also drew the attention of CBS. The network reported on the case on August 31, 1971. The report contained two interviews with soldiers dissatisfied with their command. One of the soldiers blamed the incident on a lack of communication between the officers and the troops. The commander of the battalion would only listen to individuals voicing grievances, not groups of soldiers. Another soldier claimed that the army was "really getting over on the black man." Commanders were obsessed with maintaining control and preventing soldiers from organizing rather than addressing the actual problems.[24]

The dismissal of the case did not bring the matter to an immediate end, however. While those who had opposed the trial hailed the dropping of the case by Davison as a victory, they had little time to celebrate. Only three days after the dismissal, USAREUR transferred thirty-five of the GIs to other bases.[25] The transfer so soon after the dismissal was widely criticized by those active on behalf of the soldiers.[26]

Despite the transfer, the impression that Davison had buckled under the pressure from leftist organizations remained strong in the American press. One article in the *Los Angeles Times* was particularly critical of Davison's approach toward race relations. The reporter, Joe Alex Morris Jr., talked to white soldiers from the Ninety-Third Signal Battalion. Morris claimed that the dismissal of the charges had a demoralizing effect on them. White soldiers were frustrated with the failure of officers and NCOs to deal forcefully with the growing lack of discipline of black soldiers on the base. Officers and NCOs were intimidated because "an accusation of racial bias can soil an otherwise spotless record of dedication and devotion." Morris argued that Davison's strategy of better communication was failing because "rapping" with the black soldiers undermined the traditional hierarchy of the army, thereby paving the way "for black militancy and the solidarity which led 29 soldiers to demand courts-martial."[27] Morris did not take into account that Davison had barely assumed command when the actual incident occurred. He also appeared to be unaware that numerous racial incidents like that had taken place in the years before when the leadership had been far less open and had emphasized the importance of maintaining the chain of command in solving racial problems. The *Los Angeles Times* story followed the general mainstream media pattern of demonizing expressions of black power.[28]

The publicity surrounding the case of the Darmstadt 53 along with the *Washington Post* series of September led the House Armed Services

Committee to hold hearings on the matter of race relations, dissent, and drug abuse in USAREUR. Testifying before the committee, Persons defended Davison's actions in the case.[29] The hearings had no negative effects for Davison. Despite the initial outrage by dissenters in Germany and the hearings in December, his decision to dismiss the case had the desired effect of defusing an explosive situation. Davison's handling of the Darmstadt 53 case show his sensibility toward public perception of army policies. He used the case to demonstrate his devotion to racial fairness and harmony.[30] At the same time, the transfer of those involved showed the boundaries of his tolerance for expressions of dissent and his willingness to use suppressive methods to supplement his overall strategy.

Every year in November *Army* magazine published the so-called Green Book Report in which major commanders wrote reports on the status of their commands. The reports written by Davison presented a stark contrast to the previous ones written by General Polk. Even in his last report from October 1970 Polk tried to retain an image of success and readiness in USAREUR, when the reality seemed far more critical. Polk mentioned racial issues only briefly and never alluded to any problems, but instead insisted that all commanders in Europe strove "to instill understanding, promote racial harmony and provide for the needs of each soldier." The soldier, he believed, encountered "fairness and a favorable approach to promotions, housing, assignments and military justice."[31] Considering the reports of the Render Team and the NAACP, Polk's assessment appeared out of touch with the perceptions among his enlisted men.

In his first Green Book Report, Davison openly admitted that USA-REUR faced difficult times. He too provided an optimistic twist, saying he believed the army was also ready to meet them. He emphasized the need for better leadership and communication.[32] In hundreds of speeches he gave over the course of his assignment in Germany, Davison reiterated his message that improved communication and education would help overcome the crisis.[33] Overall Davison became much more involved in the management of people in USAREUR than his predecessor.[34] Like Polk, Davison had to maintain his command as a credible deterrent, while addressing the social crisis. His second in command, Arthur Collins, was in charge of training and took an important role in boosting readiness.

Commanders' conferences on race relations became a regular feature during Davison's tenure. Conferences took place every six months and included colonels and battalion commanders. Even before the DOD ordered it for the entire armed forces, Davison had started to require commanders to install equal opportunity officers in their units. In his opening remarks at the Equal Opportunity Conference in Berchtesgaden, Davison emphasized once again the responsibility of all commanders and community leaders "for eliminating negative situations that militate against racial harmony." However, eliminating the negative was not enough. Commanders were required to initiate "positive and imaginative programs to create racial harmony." To accomplish that goal, Davison directed all units down to brigade level and community leaders "to appoint a full-time equal opportunity staff officer with direct access to the commander." The equal opportunity officer could expedite investigations of grievances, supervise local programs, and make recommendations to optimize such programs.[35] The measure was unpopular among Davison's subordinate commanders because they felt that Davison was taking away responsibilities that were rightfully theirs, thereby interfering with the chain of command. The CINCUSAREUR responded that he would abandon these new channels of communication as soon as his commanders demonstrated that they were solving the racial problems by themselves.[36]

Davison emphasized the importance of "concerned leadership" in restoring discipline to USAREUR. He contrasted a traditional view of discipline through fear, punishment, and coercion, to his concept of discipline through positive actions. The majority of soldiers wanted to do the best job they could, Davison believed. By recognizing soldiers as a "warm, live human being[s]" instead of "faceless file[s]," people who possessed "hopes, aspirations and beliefs," but also "their own bag of problems," leaders could create an environment in the unit in which self-discipline and motivation thrived.[37] Davison was critical of the leadership provided by officers and NCOs at the company level so far. Too many company commanders were "bewildered and confused." They lacked a "real understanding of how to deal with their black soldiers."[38] Officers had no comprehensive background and training in contemporary social dynamics. Many company commanders had failed "to enforce a high standard of fair and equitable treatment for all soldiers." As a result, African American soldiers who might have felt heartened by policy pronouncements from the higher levels of command felt frustrated by the lack of progress at their level.[39]

Unlike officers during World War II and the immediate postwar era, Davison did not insist that the army was not the place to correct society's ills. Davison argued that while the army had not created the racial problems it was facing, it still needed to act decisively to solve them. Davison pointed out that the army corrected other deficiencies that soldiers brought with them from bad teeth to reading and writing deficiencies.[40] Like the proponents of integration in the early 1950s, Davison argued that military efficiency required army leaders to change racial attitudes. Davison became very involved in leadership and the management of people. Unlike his predecessor, who had not been involved in as much detail, Davison put out a number of policy letters called "CINC notes" on various subjects. The notes were posted publicly and were designed to get his subordinates to understand "his philosophy on how he thought things ought to be run."[41]

One important symbolic and practical gesture was Davison's appointment of Maj. Gen. Frederic Davison as commander of the Eighth Infantry Division. Davison thereby became the first black officer to command a division in Germany. Davison had started his career in the segregated army having received his commission in 1939. Despite the many institutional hurdles, Davison had risen to the rank of major general by 1971. His assignment to Germany received much publicity.[42] Frederic Davison gave several interviews in which he praised his commander's efforts in turning around the racial situation in USA-REUR. Davison, like his commander, emphasized the importance of open communication: "The USAREUR commander-in-chief feels very strongly and I feel equally as strong that this is where we've been goofing. You don't sweep those things under the rug. If there's something wrong, let's correct it. If it's right, let's keep doing it."[43]

On November 10, 1971, Davison invited Robert J. Brown, special assistant to President Nixon, Harold Sims, acting executive director of the National Urban League, and Nathaniel R. Jones, general counsel of the NAACP, to an equal opportunity conference in Berchtesgaden, Bavaria. The reason for inviting prominent black leaders to Germany was to demonstrate publicly the Seventh Army's dedication to the goal of equal opportunity and integration. At the conference, Jones and Sims raised the by now familiar problem areas of military justice, promotions, and failure to react vigorously to discrimination in the German community. But they also maintained that the army had the singular opportunity to create an integrated society that did not yet exist in the United States. Sims praised Michael Davison and his new chief of personnel for their commitment to racial equality and for their efforts to build up a force of full-time equal opportunity officers. Sims called upon black soldiers not to act as "exponents of a black nation, nor black spies." While African Americans were no longer Uncle Toms, neither were they separate from their nonblack countrymen.[44] The words represented a clear denouncement of black power and black nationalism, not entirely surprising given the organizations Sims and Jones represented.

Unlike Polk, who feared that black investigators such as Render distorted the image of racial fairness in his command, Davison actively encouraged prominent black leaders to come to Germany. Such visits created the impression that the leadership of USAREUR was aware of its problems and was actively engaged in solving them. Davison responded positively to a proposal by Brown that prominent African Americans should visit USAREUR over the course of the next twelve months. The purpose of the visits was mainly a matter of public relations. Davison recommended that the visits be "couched in terms of an invitation by the Army to black leaders to view our programs and assist in developing new ideas and approaches."[45] Aside from the publicity value of prominent entertainers such as Sammy Davis Jr. and Dionne Warwick visiting USAREUR, Davison also wanted leaders of black fraternal organizations and the National Bar Organization to attract more "talented young Blacks to enter the JAG Corps or serve elsewhere as officers to work within the Army towards our objective of equal opportunity and racial harmony."[46] However, the representatives and organizations chosen also demonstrated the limits of acceptable viewpoints on race. Racial grievances could only be stated in liberal integrationist terms represented by organizations like the NAACP or the National Urban League. Black nationalism and black power represented a form of militancy that officers needed to prevent from taking hold by implementing reasonable racial policies.

When questioned by the Special Subcommittee on Recruiting and Retention of Military Personnel on the measures taken by USAREUR command to improve race relations, USAREUR JAG Persons presented a fourteen-point list. Persons emphasized that to overcome the racial tensions, NCOs and officers needed "to convince the young black soldier that his leaders are concerned with his welfare and with treating him fairly." The JAG Corps had to "continually strive to convince their black soldier clients that they are receiving the same high quality of legal representation as the white soldier in trouble."[47] Among the points mentioned were items such as the publication of a commanders' notebook on equal opportunity, the issuance of positive guidance through command letters and upgraded command information programs, and the stocking of items in libraries, commissaries, and PXs favored by black soldiers. Davison installed equal opportunity staff officers at brigade level and established equal opportunity councils. Moreover, Davison encouraged the creation of more informal community human relations discussion groups.[48] Another point mentioned by Persons was the scheduling of the V Corps Race Relations Road Show. In 1972 senior personnel attended screenings of a "black power" film, because some commanders needed to "be jarred into awareness" about the more extreme viewpoints on the part of the black soldiers.[49] Davison also emphasized the observance of Brotherhood Week, admonishing commanders to become personally involved and to work harder against discrimination and toward equal opportunity and treatment.[50]

Housing became an important focus. Davison improved the housing referral system and the imposition of off-limits sanctions in discrimination cases. All persons who sought off-post housing were required to work through the Housing Referral Office. Such offices were set up all over Germany to assist soldiers in finding off-base housing. According to Davison, restrictive sanctions were now applied even "in the face of a critical shortage of rental units if racial discrimination by German landlords was evident."[51] Davison warned soldiers that individuals who sought "to gain a personal advantage by bypassing the system" set back USAREUR's efforts "to improve the rental housing picture for all affected personnel.[52] Improving USAREUR's own housing was another measure taken to improve race relations. Frederic Davison said in an oral history interview ten years later that the bad living conditions for enlisted men contributed to the racial tensions. Living conditions, he said, were abominable:

> In a barracks squad room that housed 8 to 10 men, for example, you might have a single ceiling fixture, electricity that might or might not be working, windows where the panes were missing in the wintertime, and space heaters that might or might not be working. Out of a whole row of showerheads, you might have one working. . . . There were shower stalls with no doors on them, urinals that were leaking, and face basins in which half the fixtures didn't work.

Both black and white soldiers were tense and frustrated over living conditions. For black soldiers, racial discrimination just added to this already considerable tension. Michael Davison was able to convince officials of the German government to contribute funds to improve living conditions in American barracks, a measure that was also important in regard to combating drug abuse.[53]

Persons testified before Congress that another part of Davison's strategy was the increased use of communications media in USAREUR to present problems, policies, and programs. Moreover, USAREUR command was conducting meetings with Federal Republic of Germany officials to enlist their help in improving relations between black soldiers and the German community. In some of his speeches Davison also stressed that highly placed officials in the German government had been very receptive to complaints of discrimination against black GIs. Both Chancellor Willy Brandt and Defense Minister Helmut Schmidt issued appeals for tolerance and equal opportunity. The army also asked members of the German Press Council "not to refer to the color of American soldiers in reporting incidents" unless it was pertinent to the story.[54] Davison stressed the importance of working "closely, frankly and candidly with the press" in a letter to the commander of VII Corps, Ken Mearns. Mearns had complained about the recent coverage of his unit in the *Stars & Stripes*, which he believed had shed a bad light on VII Corps' KONTAKT program and had reported a racial incident in Stuttgart. Davison defended the newspaper's right to publish negative incidents occurring in the army with its need to remain credible in the eyes of its readers: "If a bad incident occurs, we can expect that it will appear in print. If we could eliminate bad incidents, I'm sure we could eliminate adverse publicity."[55] Davison's attitude stood in stark contrast to his predecessor, who had tried to exert his influence on the newspaper to change coverage of racial incidents.

One of the most important measures implemented was the flying squad inspection teams. Davison's papers at the U.S. Military History Institute contain several brief reports of the USAREUR Equal Opportunity/Human Relations Team, which was an inspection team sent to various barracks and units throughout Germany. The inspections normally took place at the brigade level or at communities. The teams reported on a variety of issues. One frequently mentioned was whether the unit had a written Equal Opportunity/Human Relations program and whether soldiers of the unit understood its contents.[56] Similarly, the inspection teams tried to determine whether commanders followed enlisted promotion policies and whether their men were aware of these policies.[57] Were the channels of communication open between the commanders and their men?[58] Responses to these inquiries varied in the fall of 1972. The Third Brigade, Eighth Division received a commendation for its "effective use of the chain of command to conduct the brigade Equal Opportunity/Human Relations Program," but it also received a reprimand for the lack of a written EO/HR program.[59] The inspection teams also inquired whether the unit had a full-time equal opportunity staff officer. In the fall of 1972 the lack of such an officer was an often-reported deficiency.[60] Another issue was soldiers segregating themselves in the dining halls and excessive dapping.[61] Were there English-language programs for the Hispanic soldiers?[62]

Apart from conducting surprise inspections, the EO/HR staff officers also followed up on specific grievances. On May 25, 1972, E4 Paul Saunders, an African American soldier, wrote a letter to Davison claiming that he and other minority soldiers were being held back in their ranks by the leadership and unable to advance in the 545th Ordnance Company. He also claimed that an existing Enlisted Advisory and Race Relations Council had been discontinued. When the staff officer conducted interviews in the company, he found that the company did not "have a functional EO/HR Council" and that officers and NCOs were "not sensitive to the feelings and needs of minority group personnel." Communication and dialogue "to enhance racial harmony" in the unit were lacking, and soldiers in the unit did not know their EO/HR representative.[63] Davison not only informed Lt. Gen. Willard Pearson, whose corps the company was part of, but also sent a personal response to Saunders. In the note he explained that Saunders's superiors had not promoted him because he had not met the criteria for promotion to E5 yet. He acknowledged, however, the lack of an Enlisted Advisory Council.[64]

In a similar case SP4 Robert Lercy Coger, a member of the Ninth Maintenance Battalion, charged that discrimination was widespread in the First Infantry Division. The investigation team found that rumors and feelings of discontent among minority soldiers had increased as a result of "adverse personnel actions and inadequate communication by commanders concerned." Commanders at the company and battalion level were not actively participating in the EO/HR programs. The EO/HR personnel of the division "expressed feelings of disappointment and frustration in their programs because of a lack of concern and communication within the chain of command.[65] Davison revoked Coger's nonjudicial punishment and reassigned him to another unit. Davison also apologized for the occurrences in the unit, lamenting "that at times the attitudes and behavior of some of our people stem from inexperience and lack of concern about individuals of different skin color." These were issues that the Race Relations Education Program was designed to address and correct.[66] Showing concern and being responsive to the complaints of black soldiers was an important part of Davison's strategy in harmonizing race relations.[67]

In a speech Davison made at an Equal Opportunity/Human Relations conference in June 1972 he elaborated on the difference in perception between a white company commander and a black enlisted man. A company commander, Davison argued, would see the racial problems in organizational terms relating to the unit's effectiveness. To such a commander, racial problems were a cyclical phenomenon that depended on the presence of "militant troublemakers" in his company. The commander saw his objective as the avoidance of racial incidents. To Davison, avoidance of racial incidents was not enough. His goal was the creation of racial harmony. To achieve that, commanders had to understand that for most young black soldiers, the racial problem was "defined in a wholly different way." For a black soldier the problem was not cyclical "but continuous within every moment of their lives." Racial problems were not a matter of organizational efficiency to the black soldiers but "a conglomerate of grievances felt very personally."[68] The black soldier found himself in a difficult situation when he joined the army. After having lived in a "culturally comfortable environment," black communities in which most authority figures were black, black soldiers now faced an environment in which "the authority structure seems almost wholly white. He perceives it as a white man's organization run by white men for white men's purposes."[69] The foreign environment of Germany pushed the cultural shock even further. Commanders needed to understand the different experiences and motivations of their black soldiers. Once again Davison emphasized openness and receptiveness on the part of his officers. Minority soldiers had to be able to communicate their differences to their superior.

Commandwide equal opportunity conferences and the improvement of education programs also formed an important part of Davison's strategy. Parallel to the DRRI (Defense Race Relations Institute) created in Florida for the entire U.S. armed forces, Davison established the USAREUR race relations school in Munich.[70] The school provided a four-week course for part-time instructors and a one-week course for company commanders. The purpose of the first course was "to train qualified military personnel how to teach and resolve racial/ethnic problems by non-violent procedures" and increase the overall number of personnel with training by adding officers and noncommissioned officers who could be utilized on a part-time basis.[71] Participants received training in communication skills, racism and sexism, individual and group behavior, methods of instruction, and administration. Students went through an eighteen-hour core curriculum that they could use to educate soldiers in their units.[72]

The second course offered training for unit commanders. Such training would enable a commander "to maintain the highest degree of organizational and combat readiness by fostering harmonious relations among personnel under his/her control." The course was different from other courses offered in the army because it provided officers with training not as instructors but as commanders in their respective units. The terminal goals of the course were to teach "viable leadership techniques" that commanders could apply to the management of their units and to improve their communication skills. Moreover, they learned to "identify the commander's responsibilities inherent in the implementation of the U.S. Army Europe's Race Relations/Equal Opportunity Program" and to "apply race relations/equal opportunity management techniques."[73] Apart from emphasizing the education of soldiers on the subject of race relations, Davison also stressed the observance of such events as the annual National Brotherhood Week in

February. In a memo to his subordinate commanders, Davison admonished them not to treat the event with a passing nod or a perfunctory ceremony. Instead, he challenged "each member of the command to become personally involved . . . in seeking ways to further improve interpersonal relationships."[74]

While reports from the EO/HR inspection teams were frequent in 1972, the number of such reports declined a year later. By 1973 concern over drug abuse increasingly took precedence over race relations both in Davison's speeches and in his communications with his subordinates. The impression that race relations were quieting down by 1973 is also borne out by the report of two sociologists sent to Germany to assess the racial situation in USAREUR in 1976 and 1977.

The military justice system in Europe became another important area of reform for Davison and his judge advocate, General Persons. Polk had never been as involved in the details of the military justice system. When Persons came to Europe in early June 1971, he drew up an assessment of changes necessary. His analysis did not address racial discrimination specifically, but since African American soldiers were affected in disproportionate numbers, the issues Persons raised and the changes he recommended had an impact on race relations.

The most urgent problem Persons confronted was also the issue most indicative of the general disarray that had shocked Wilson and Johnson of the *Washington Post*.[75] According to Persons, "The USAREUR stockade was bursting at the seams."[76] With prisons overpopulated, commanders and NCOs were frustrated because they could not put soldiers who belonged there in the stockade. Aside from the overflowing stockade, Persons and his team identified deficiencies in the areas of training, manpower resources, the geographic distribution of legal services, delayed cases, administrative processing, facilities and equipment, and CID support.[77] Deficiencies in confinement, training of legal personnel, the delay of cases, and Article 15 punishments had the most impact on black soldiers.

Persons's report triggered a policy reassessment at various levels of USAREUR's military justice system. Davison asked commanders to conduct studies on what areas in the administration of military justice required improvement and then implement changes accordingly.[78] Among the measures Davison encouraged his subordinates to consider were the elimination of administrative bottlenecks, providing judge advocates with more assistants, increased legal training of officers and NCOs, and upgrading facilities such as courtrooms and offices.

One year later the JAG wrote another analysis of the military justice system. This time the focus was specifically on racial discrimination. The study came in response to the creation of the Defense Department Task Force on the Administration of Military Justice in the Armed Forces. Persons's conclusions matched those of previous investigations. Black soldiers received a disproportionate number of courts-martial. They were sentenced to confinement at hard labor more frequently than white counterparts and for longer periods of time. A higher percentage of them ended up in pretrial confinement, and a lower percentage of blacks received acquittals.[79]

However, despite these findings Persons would not concede that discrimination was the culprit. When comparing the backgrounds of those sentenced, Persons had found that both black and white soldiers had "spent roughly the same amount of time in the services." These soldiers were all about the same age and had "about the same amount of education and GT scores." The overwhelming majority in both racial groups came from large northern cities. They all had similar prior disciplinary records. Persons's argument was that the disproportionate number of black soldiers caught up in the military justice system was a result of the soldiers' upbringing, not their race. To Persons, "The subjective data gathered indicated that probably no racial discrimination existed in the administration of military justice, although black soldiers feel that it does exist." The basic military justice system, Persons concluded, was "a sound one conceived in terms of fundamental fairness and designed to ensure justice and equality for all."

Persons's assertion seemed at odds with the premises and conclusions of the task force that he wrote his assessment for. The task force's report stated clearly that discrimination in the military justice system was a reality. The task force's aim was to determine its extent and source and make recommendations to end it. Persons was not willing to go as far as the task force in his conclusions, but despite his belief that the justice system was fair and impartial, Persons was actually not claiming that no discrimination was taking place. However, he denied that the problem was systemic. Individuals largely caused the discrimination that did occur. Talks with judges, juries, and attorneys had shown that many believed "that blacks usually lie on the witness stand, that they stick together, and that the racial makeup of witnesses was a factor in determining credibility."[80]

These findings reinforced both Persons's and Davison's belief that individuals were causing the problem, not the system. According to Persons, both black and white soldiers often perceived the system as unfair regardless of objective fairness.[81] Consequently, changing perceptions and awareness became a major priority. Much like regular officers, military lawyers had to attend race relations seminars because many of them were "not sufficiently aware of the problem." Furthermore, most military lawyers did not realize how black soldiers perceived the military attorney's role in the administration of military justice.[82] Aside from heightening awareness, most of Persons's recommendations aimed at making the processes of the military justice system more transparent to the soldiers in general rather than specifically targeting discrimination.

Before Davison and Persons took up their respective commands, Polk and his JAG, Maj. Gen. George S. Prugh had implemented some reforms to improve the efficiency and the fairness of the system. Article 15s had to be posted on the unit bulletin board in order to "give every soldier the opportunity to see how he was treated in relation to his fellow minor offender." This would demonstrate the fairness of the system. Moreover, soldiers entering pretrial confinement were now appointed a defense counsel within seven days of their confinement. Thus far the law had only required that a counsel be appointed if and when the case went to trial.[83] Finally, they introduced a stockade visitation program. Military attorneys were required to "visit each of the

USAREUR stockades on an almost daily basis." The attorneys interviewed new prisoners to make sure that they were aware of their rights.

They assisted these prisoners in requesting defense counsel and gave them limited legal assistance. Persons expanded on these measures. Two of the most important measures he introduced were the magistrate program and the 45-day rule. The magistrate program was an expansion of the program requiring a JAG officer to be present at the stockades almost daily. The military magistrate was "required to review the circumstances of every prisoner in pretrial confinement, and to order his release" if he determined that further confinement was unnecessary.[84] The magistrate had to review a case within one or two days.[85] One of the effects of the new program was to lower the number of soldiers held in pretrial confinement by releasing those whose detention was unwarranted.[86] Persons found that officers had handled pretrial confinement "pretty sloppily" until he conducted his investigation. The magistrate program revealed that many commanders in USAREUR used pretrial confinement as a disciplinary tool. After magistrates discovered that many soldiers arriving at the stockade had never talked to a lawyer before they were brought there, Persons wanted to make it mandatory for soldiers to see an attorney first. This idea met with resistance from both commanders and legal officers. Persons found that officers were bringing up many administrative excuses against such a requirement. However, the underlying reason for their resistance was that "there was nothing wrong with putting someone in pre-trial whom you never intended to try, but rather to make an example or to keep him on ice."[87]

As a result of this discovery, magistrates now had the authority to order the release of prisoners who had not seen an attorney prior to their imprisonment, unless the command sent a lawyer there the same day. A few months later the task force cited the magistrate program initiated by Persons with the full support of Davison as an exemplary measure in alleviating "many of the problems associated with pretrial confinement in USAREUR" and found it useful in alleviating perceptions of discrimination as well.[88]

The other rule designed to alleviate the overflow in USAREUR stockades was the 45-day rule. Adopted in September 1971, the regulation required that charges referred to a summary or special court-martial had to be brought to trial within forty-five days from either the day charges were preferred or when restraint was imposed, whichever was earlier. Failure to meet the time frame led to a dismissal of charges.[89] As a result of this policy, the stockade population halved within a year.[90]

Persons had not implemented the magistrate program or the 45-day rule to explicitly end racial discrimination. They were important in improving race relations nonetheless. Regarding racial discrimination, Persons was most concerned over the human factor in the system. The most likely point where discrimination could occur was when an officer normally at the company level made the original determination as to how to discipline a soldier. Many commanders placed troublesome individuals in pretrial confinement, whether they actually intended to charge the soldiers or not. Due to racial biases, white commanders were apt to deem black soldiers more troublesome than white soldiers. The task force concluded that the disproportionate number of black servicemen in pretrial confinement had contributed to the belief among enlisted men that commanders were abusing their discretion and practicing racial discrimination.[91]

The magistrate program and the 45-day rule were important in counteracting the perception "that only blacks were thrown in there and kept and not told what was going on."[92] The new measures limited a commander's opportunity to impose confinement arbitrarily. They ensured that black soldiers received counseling within the first days of their imprisonment. They were made aware of the charges against them and could not be held in pretrial indefinitely.

In 1976 social scientists Marcia A. Gilbert and Peter G. Nordlie conducted a study on race relations/equal opportunity training in USAREUR on behalf of the U.S. Army Research Institute for the Behavioral and Social Sciences. The researchers went to Germany in October 1976 and May 1977 to conduct interviews and hand out questionnaires. The analysis of the current racial climate was not optimistic. The two sociologists saw no evidence "that the racial climate was improving" but instead claimed there was some evidence that it was worsening. The authors believed that after a less tense period during 1974, the responses to their questionnaire reflected a climate that was closer to what it had been in 1972 than 1974. White soldiers felt that the program had "overcorrected." Black soldiers, on the other hand, felt that the programs and policy changes had not met their expectations.[93] While the authors believed the racial climate was deteriorating, they conceded that this deterioration did not come with the violent confrontations of earlier years. This relative calm they believed obscured the severity of the problem.

The total amount of RR/EO training occurring in USAREUR was greater than anywhere else in the army, but while soldiers of both races agreed on the need for RR/EO training, the current training programs had a negative image. Black soldiers felt that the programs were mainly a public relations strategy, a token gesture aimed at vocal minorities. Many white soldiers believed that minority history and culture were overemphasized and that the RR/EO programs only benefited minorities. Overall the researchers were struck by "just how stable and resistant to change . . . the black-white differences in perception and attitude" were. The authors had two explanations for this lack of progress. First, personnel from the regular chain of command taught the classes. They often proved ill-prepared and unenthusiastic, giving soldiers the impression that the program was a low priority.[94]

When reading the findings of the two researchers closely, it appears that their interpretation was too pessimistic, but the findings of the researchers did show the limits of Davison's approach to changing the perception and the conduct, not the person. As General Persons said in his oral history interview: "The emphasis was always on changing of behavior, recognizing that you probably were whistling Dixie if you thought you could change the way people thought, particularly if they had grown up with a pretty deep-seated bias against people of the other race."[95] Nordlie and Gilbert were arguing that the army's efforts to improve race relations had fallen short because the attitudes among the soldiers on the issue had not changed significantly since 1972. But in drawing their conclusions on the progress of the last four years, the authors had overlooked how much structures had changed since before 1972. It is also significant to note that their own survey showed that physical confrontations between the races had decreased. Soldiers observed that fights rarely occurred. Fewer than 15 percent of soldiers of both races surveyed believed that such conflicts occurred often. When asked how often white personnel in their companies or work units got together in certain situations to harass or keep nonwhites out of facilities that were supposed to be open for all, only 4 percent of the white respondents and 18 percent of the black respondents answered that this occurred often. Sixty-seven percent of the black respondents said that this seldom happened.[96] A majority of the respondents of both races, 55 percent of the white soldiers, 46 percent of the black soldiers, believed that race relations in the army were fair, although 38 percent of black soldiers felt them to be poor. Most believed that actual physical confrontations occurred very infrequently. Less than 15 percent of either race reported that physical conflict occurred sometimes or often, and 90 percent of the white soldiers and 84 percent of the black soldiers reported that "whites" and "nonwhites" challenged each other to fights seldom or never. Thirty-four percent of the white soldiers and 39 percent of the black soldiers believed that race relations had been getting better in the past year. Fifty percent of the white and 47 percent of the black soldiers believed race relations had not changed.

The report by the two sociologists shows that many of the underlying problems that caused the racial tensions to flare between 1968 and 1972 had not disappeared by the time Davison retired in 1975. But while no similar survey for 1969 or 1970 exists, the numbers still indicate that racial tensions had calmed considerably during Davison's tenure as CINCUSAREUR. There were external circumstances contributing to the decline of the tensions. The fervor of the civil rights and the black power movement had died down by the mid-1970s. Radical organizations such as the Black Panther Party were losing their influence. The army itself had changed into an all-volunteer force. It no longer had reluctant draftees. However, in regard to race relations, that latter point was probably not important. Many of the soldiers involved in the protests earlier had been volunteers. The report of Gilbert and Nordlie shows that volunteers had many of the same concerns regarding race as the draftees.

If prejudices as well as discriminatory behavior still existed, had Davison failed in his goals? Not surprisingly, given the United States' long and tortured history of racism, Davison could not eliminate prejudice and discrimination in his command. However, he was able to improve race relations significantly by creating the DRRI and regulations that gave commanders increasing power to ensure equal treatment and opportunity. But the example of Davison's predecessor, Polk, shows that DOD policies to improve race relations were not effective unless commanders supported them enthusiastically. Davison's insistence that racial conflicts were mainly a leadership problem was essential in instilling a sense of responsibility and accountability in officers. By openly acknowledging the existence of a problem and talking candidly about it to his soldiers and the public, he was able to convey the image of a concerned commander. Through discussion groups, rap sessions, race relation counsels, and full-time equal opportunity officers, Davison opened channels of communication through which soldiers could vent their frustration. He put into place a network and a set of procedures that ensured frustrations could be channeled before they exploded.

Davison's strategy in restoring social peace in the army fits Radine's concept of co-optive rational control, which Radine sees as the army's preferred and most effective mechanism to counteract dissidence. Radine believed that co-optation was "a cynical approach to political commitment and values, which controls an underclass by accepting and including the opposition." The army would particularize GI gripes "to peripheral issues" that could be reformed.[97] While overall Radine's definition describes Davison's strategy well, his value judgment that this kind of a strategy was cynical is not necessarily accurate. Frederic Davison believed that his superior was genuinely concerned about the welfare of his troops: "Mike Davison was the most sensitive and the most people-oriented officer I ever met. It didn't mean at all that he was soft or that he was lax, but it meant that his first concern was always for his troops and their welfare."[98]

Critics of the army's methods could, of course, criticize the assessment as a statement from a member of the same power structure. The sources used in this study cannot prove or deny that Davison's motive for implementing changes in his command were cynical or idealistic, but it is clear that the racial situation in USAREUR was improved by Davison's measures and public relations efforts.

What is also clear is that the more militant rhetoric of black power and black nationalism remained unacceptable to Davison and his subordinate commanders. However, the presence of the Black Panther Party and use of black power terminology by black soldiers galvanized army leaders into adopting a more introspective approach designed to allow "more moderately" framed grievances to be heard.

POLITICAL PROTEST
AND ANTIWAR ACTIVISM

PART 2

E ven though the various reporters and commentators at the time cited dissent as one of the major aspects of the army's social crisis along with race relations and drug abuse, politically motivated protests not related to issues of racial discrimination elicited a very different public reaction from army leaders. The public response to soldiers engaged in antiwar activism remained far more subdued. At no point did antiwar protests evoke the sense of urgency that army leaders at least publicly displayed in regard to the other two problems. However, the lack of a public response did not mean that officers were unconcerned or failed to respond at all. Their response was simply less public and less accommodating than toward drug abuse or racial discontent.

As the Vietnam conflict progressed, a growing communication gap emerged between officers and career soldiers on one side and draftees on the other. Reports on the morale of soldiers in Vietnam were alarming. Morale problems were pervasive in the army in Vietnam, be it at the front or the rear. As soldiers increasingly harbored doubts about the justification for the war they were fighting in, they were less and less tolerant of officers willing to put them in harm's way to advance their careers or of officers in the rear insisting on their prerogatives and exercising their authority "as if the bases they ran were not in a war zone." Officers were invested in producing statistical results as measures of their success. They were afraid of failure or the perception of failure, leading them to a culture of overly optimistic reports and turning a blind eye to any deficiencies or negative developments within their units. After 1969, officers at the front had to be careful not to push their soldiers too hard for fear of becoming the victim of a "fragging," a euphemistic term for the attempted murder of officers or NCOs by their own men.[1]

The lack of connection and communication between officers and enlisted men was not a problem limited to Vietnam. The late 1960s saw an increasing number of antiwar activists trying to turn soldiers' discontent into active resistance at bases in the continental United States and Germany.[2] A growing number of college-educated draftees had come into the ranks by 1970. Many brought with them the political rhetoric, methods, and debates they had imbibed on American campuses. Some joined the army with the explicit goal of disrupting army routines and undermining its authority and structures of power from the inside. Organizing protest from within the army was difficult, since soldiers did not enjoy the full range of civil liberties, and they were limited in their ability to initiate reform in an organization that relied on hierarchy to function.

David Cortright went so far as to claim that restrictions on soldiers' civil liberties were "nearly absolute." Being politically active within "the draconian legal structure of the military" could be suicidal. Since there is no evidence of the army executing soldiers for organizing protest activities, Cortright's claims appear somewhat exaggerated. Nevertheless, soldiers were certainly discouraged from playing an active political role within the army and could face serious sanctions for organizing or participating in antiwar protests. The military's hierarchical organization and the transitory nature of military life made dissent among soldiers difficult. Continuity in the organization of political activities was difficult to maintain because of the frequent changes in the soldiers' assignments and transfers to other bases. In fact, military leaders frequently and intentionally used transfers as a strategy to isolate activists and limit their impact on fellow soldiers.[3]

5

Resistance and Dissent in the U.S. Army

Before the Tet Offensive in 1968, opposition to the war from within the military was limited. One of the first recorded instances was the case of Lt. Henry Howe. Howe was court-martialed and sentenced to two years of hard labor at Fort Leavenworth for taking part in a civilian peace demonstration in El Paso in November 1965 and carrying a placard reading "End Johnson's Fascist Aggression."[4] A famous incident from this earlier period was Dr. Howard Levy's refusal to train Green Beret medics at Fort Jackson, arguing that Special Forces units such as the Green Berets were responsible for war crimes in Vietnam. Levy was ultimately sentenced to three years at Leavenworth.[5]

Howe and Levy were active duty officers who objected to U.S. engagement in Vietnam. However, they had not entered the armed services as peace activists. Andy Stapp, who joined the army in 1966, represented a new kind of peace activist. Stapp had joined the antiwar movement while enrolled at Penn State in 1964. When draft resistance activities he helped organize met with little success, he decided to join the army in 1966 and organize resistance to the war from within instead of trying to dodge the draft. After completing basic training, he tried to turn fellow soldiers in his unit against the war by distributing antiwar literature and establishing discussion groups. The army was able to limit the success of Stapp's efforts by relocating any soldiers who participated in his activities and by assigning him to positions where he had little access to other soldiers. He was, at one point, assigned to the post office and placed on gardening and cleaning duty. Authorities later reassigned him to the mess hall to portion out food rations.[6]

Stapp's first chance to gain access to a larger public forum to advance his protest activities came in June 1967. He went before a summary court-martial at Fort Sill, Oklahoma, for refusing an order to hand over pamphlets and protest literature in his possession. The trial drew the attention of Youth Against War and Fascism (YAWF), an antiwar organization founded in New York in 1952. The YAWF send a delegation to Oklahoma to stage protest activities during the trial. A civilian lawyer from the National Emergency Civil Liberties Committee (NECLC) represented Stapp. The *New York Times* and CBS covered the proceedings. Stapp received a sentence of forty-five days of unconfined hard labor and forfeiture of twenty days' pay. He was also reduced to the rank of private E 1, the lowest rank possible. However, the trial served his aim of attracting more publicity to antiwar protests within the army.[7]

Stapp's intention in provoking a court-martial was to expose the limits on soldiers' free speech rights. When Stapp refused to open the footlocker containing his political pamphlets and literature, his commanding officer had the locker opened forcefully and the materials confiscated. Stapp and his lawyer argued that keeping such literature was part of his right to free speech and that the order to open the locker had been unlawful.[8] While Stapp could not avoid a guilty verdict, the trial allowed him to present his personal political convictions to a larger public. During the trial he referred to himself as "a socialist in a revolutionary society" and an advocate of "the destruction of capitalism and the establishment of a workers' state in the United States."[9]

Supporting soldiers facing court-martial was one of the most common strategies for promoting antiwar activism. The seven-member group of civilian antiwar activists supporting Stapp led by Maryann Weissman voiced their protest by chanting during the court proceedings.[10] Stapp had to go through another court-martial a month later for allegedly violating parts of his June sentence. The judge eventually dismissed the charges, but the trial drew press attention nonetheless because of actions taken by the base commander against civilian activists.[11] Once again Weissman stepped forward as the national coordinator of Youth Against War and Fascism, and her colleague Key Martin, chairman of the same organization, traveled to Fort Sill to demonstrate at Stapp's trial. When the post commander learned of their presence and intentions, he had the two activists evicted from their motel outside the post and barred from entering the army reservation.[12] When they demonstrated on base despite the ban, police arrested them, and a judge sentenced them to six months in jail and fined them $500.[13]

In subsequent years, protests in connection with military trials would become one of the most important vehicles for expressing antiwar sentiments. Stapp's trial established a pattern that would repeat itself often on army posts in the continental United States and in Germany. Activist soldiers whose views on the Vietnam War conflicted with those of their superiors would opt for a court-martial over lesser punishments because it provided a better platform for exposing what they saw as an encroachment on their civil liberties. Gaining publicity through trials was a popular tactic for activist soldiers who were otherwise isolated and could not organize sufficient numbers of dissidents to stage demonstrations or marches. Civilian supporters also tended to play an important role in fomenting dissent. They had the expertise on how to get press coverage, and they provided soldiers with legal counsel.

Another means of fostering antiwar sentiments within the ranks was the establishment of coffeehouses near bases. In his blistering analysis of what he referred to as "the collapse of the Armed Forces," Col. Robert D. Heinl estimated in 1971 that at least eleven, possibly as many as twenty-six, coffeehouses were plying "GIs with rock music, lukewarm coffee, antiwar literature, how-to-do-it tips on desertion, and similar disruptive counsels."[14] The coffeehouses indeed offered food and entertainment, and they offered soldiers an informal setting in which they could express and exchange their ideas about the war outside of the domain of military supervision. Activists established the first coffeehouses in late 1967 and early 1968. The Tet Offensive was a factor in galvanizing activities as more and more coffeehouses sprang up all over the country. Often communities that did not share activists' antiwar sentiments successfully blocked attempts to establish such coffeehouses. Local authorities would place administrative hurdles in their way, such as withholding licenses and enforcing health codes or noise ordinances.[15] The United States Servicemen's Fund (USSF) often helped with founding the coffeehouses. Fred Gardner and Donna Mickleson established the fund with the help of the Mobilization Committee to End the War in Vietnam. Although they originally initiated the fund to support coffeehouses, they would also use it for other projects later on. Administered in offices in Oakland and New York City, the fund not only provided financial aid to activists but also "assisted with films, entertainers, speakers, legal defense, and staff workers."[16]

Activists established one of the earliest coffeehouses, the UFO in Columbia, SC. The antiwar activists initiated the "Summer of Support" to demonstrate to servicemen that the antiwar movement was targeting not them but the policy makers. It was also a means to "make opposition to the war by draftees more articulate and to encourage servicemen to raise critical questions in the barracks." Three civilian activists functioned as managers of the UFO. These managers were not concerned with making a profit. They merely wanted to break even. The acronym UFO was chosen because of its close approximation to USO, the abbreviation used to designate the regular, officially condoned social clubs set up for servicemen near the army bases. It is also the abbreviation for "unidentified flying object," which in this case had "landed and remained."[17]

The UFO was located right in the center of Columbia where off-duty servicemen from nearby Fort Jackson were likely to hang out. The *New York Times* article described the interior as similar to what coffeehouses looked like in larger cities such as New York or Chicago: dim lights, red tablecloths, and psychedelic posters. Antiwar and anti-army publications laid out on the shelves. Folk singers, such as Phil Ochs or Barbara Dane, performed. The UFO did not serve alcohol, and its managers always maintained that they only encouraged soldiers to talk about their feelings toward the army and the war, not to defect. Openly calling for soldiers to desert would have provided the community and the army with a justification for closing down the establishment.[18] Nevertheless, such claims have to be taken with a grain of salt. Although the management probably did not directly advise anyone to defect, the coffeehouse did apparently offer counseling on subjects such as conscientious objection, desertion, emigration, medical discharge, legal rights, and legal aid.[19] Since authorities never legally charged the managers with encouraging desertion, they stayed within the legal boundaries, although that does not mean that the UFO, like other coffeehouses, did not face any harassment from the community or the army.

Dissenting soldiers meeting in the UFO organized GIs United against the War in Vietnam, normally abbreviated GIs United, claiming a membership of thirty-five soldiers in early 1969.[20] One of their first actions was to circulate a petition among fellow soldiers at Fort Jackson asking the army to authorize a meeting to "freely discuss the legal and moral questions related to the war in Vietnam and the civil rights of American citizens." One of the organizers was promptly court-martialed for passing around an unauthorized flyer.[21] The most famous incident involving the UFO and GIs United was the trial against the so-called Jackson 8, described elsewhere in this work. Members of GIs United filed a suit for an injunction against the commanding general and the secretary of the army to forbid harassment or interference of orderly meetings or the circulation of petitions and newspapers.[22]

On January 18, 1970, city and county police padlocked the UFO. They had arrested the three operators two days earlier and charged them with creating a public nuisance.[23] The American Civil Liberties Union took over their defense. The ACLU filed a class action suit in the federal district court in Columbia asking the court to declare the common law offense of "maintaining a public nuisance" unconstitutional. This effort failed.[24] The three defendants were found guilty and sentenced to six years in prison for a seldom charged common law misdemeanor.[25] While the coffeehouse remained closed for the remainder of that year, protest activity continued.[26]

One of the most important forms of protest the USSF supported in addition to the coffeehouses was the publication of GI newspapers. Underground newspapers were mimeographed sheets with information on antiwar activities and antiwar commentary on U.S. policy in Vietnam. A veteran turned peace activist in Chicago published the *Vietnam Vet,* one of the first underground newspapers to appear in the United States. Draft resistance groups all over the country distributed the newssheet to soldiers. The publishers had a mailing list of three thousand servicemen in Vietnam. One of the earliest papers initiated by active duty soldiers was *Strikeback* at Fort Bragg. Like many of the newssheets, the paper faltered after a few months. The transitory nature of military life made it difficult to keep an effort going as those soldiers who had started a paper transferred and often found no successors. Among the exceptions to this rule were *FTA* at Fort Knox and *Fatigue Press* at Fort Hood, which started in the summer of 1968 and continued for four years. Heinl claimed in 1971 that 144 papers existed worldwide.[27] The DOD put the number at 245 in 1972. Cortright lists 259 papers in the appendix of his book published first in 1975, although his estimates run as high as 300.[28]

The newspapers and coffeehouses at various bases in the United States provided an infrastructure for the organized events and various protest activities. At Fort Hood, for example, two hundred soldiers attended a "Love-In" and countercultural festival in Condor Park with rock music and antiwar speeches.[29] In San Francisco forty GIs marched at the head of a demonstration on April 27, and two hundred active duty soldiers participated in another demonstration on October 12, 1968.[30] In June of that same year, nine enlisted men from all four service branches who had gone AWOL took sanctuary in the Howard Presbyterian Church as an expression of their moral opposition to the war.[31]

Fort Hood, near Killeen, Texas, was one of the most active sites of antiwar organizing among soldiers. Fort Hood was an armored training center that experienced "extensive unrest" in the late 1960s. In mid-1968 Fred Gardner, a former reservist as well as a former writer and editor of the *Harvard Crimson,* established a coffeehouse, the Oleo

Strut, in Killeen with assistance from the Mobilization Committee to End the War in Vietnam and the "Summer of Support" project. Along with the Oleo Strut, activists launched an underground newspaper, the *Fatigue Press*, in Killeen. The first organized event was the already mentioned "Love In."[32]

A different act of dissent at Fort Hood during the summer of 1968 was at first carried out independently of the activities of the Oleo Strut/ *Fatigue Press*. On August 23, about sixty black soldiers from the First Armored Cavalry Division assembled to protest racism in the army and the use of troops against civilians.[33] The organizers anticipated that troops from Fort Hood might head to Chicago to maintain security during the Democratic National Convention.[34] The demonstration lasted all night. In the morning military police arrested forty-three of the protesters for failure to attend reveille.[35] The resulting trials received national press attention.[36] Most of the soldiers received comparably light sentences, probably due to the amount of public attention attracted by the trials and the fact that more than half of the arrested soldiers were Vietnam veterans, some highly decorated. Only twenty-six received any sentence at all. Thirteen were acquitted and four never went to trial.[37]

During the trial the army, the FBI, and local authorities harassed protest organizers. The army arrested PFC Bruce Peterson, first editor of *Fatigue Press*, for possession of a minute amount of marijuana and sentenced him to eight years of hard labor. Local authorities used the same tactic on one of the civilian organizers at the Oleo Strut before the Chicago convention. Police stopped him on his way to the airport and subsequently arrested him for possession of marijuana.[38] The sentence was overturned two years later.[39] Local authorities convicted Andy Stapp and two fellow ASU members of vagrancy.[40]

The Oleo Strut/*Fatigue Press* organization remained one of the most active in subsequent years. In 1971 it became the subject of a CBS documentary.[41] Two of the more successful protest actions of 1971 were typical examples of the kind of protest activities being carried on a number of military bases. In the summer of that year the activists formed "Ft. Hood United Front" to protest against the trial of two military prison inmates charged for their roles in a prison rebellion a few months earlier. The activists drew up petitions signed by nearly one thousand soldiers and organized a demonstration attended by twenty-five activists on September 12. Three days later, the charges against the two imprisoned soldiers were dropped.[42]

In another effort, the activists attempted to incorporate widespread everyday grievances into their agenda. In May 1971 they organized a boycott of a jewelry store in Killeen. The store was part of a chain that, according to the activists, used exploitive methods to get soldiers to make purchases.[43] The activists were particularly incensed about the fact that the store made use of the military command system to extract credit payments from soldiers. The activists demanded that the store stop soliciting and pressuring soldiers on the sidewalks, stop exploiting soldiers' homesickness, cease using the military as a collection agency, and take down the "Vietnam Honor Roll" of customers who had given their lives in Vietnam.[44] Soldiers at other bases with stores belonging to the same chain picked up the boycott.[45] Like many other organizations spearheading GI protest movements, the Oleo Strut/ *Fatigue Press* declined after 1971 with a small spike of renewed activity during the bombing campaign against North Vietnam in April 1972.

Army reactions to the coffeehouses around its bases were diffuse and sometimes contradictory. Because the coffeehouses were located in the neighboring civilian communities beyond base boundaries, army commanders had limited official means of dealing with them. Their most powerful weapon was off-limits sanctions, meaning they prohibited soldiers from patronizing a business. However, the army guidelines on dissent issued in September 1969 cautioned commanding officers against using the sanctions too readily. The guidelines asked commanders to refrain from preventing soldiers from exercising "their constitutional rights of freedom of speech at the coffeehouses, unless it can be shown, for example, that activities taking place in the coffeehouses include counseling soldiers to refuse to perform duty or to desert, or otherwise involve illegal acts with an adverse effect on soldier health, morale or welfare."[46] The guidelines were vague enough to allow varying interpretations, but ultimately a commander used his power to declare one of the better-known coffeehouses off-limits and to impose sanctions on violators only in one instance.

The Shelter Half was established in Tacoma, Washington, near Fort Lewis in early 1968. In January 1970 military authorities in Fort Lewis moved to have the house placed off-limits, contending that it was "a source of dissident counseling and literature and other activities inimical to good morale order and discipline within the armed services."[47] In the *Washington Post*, the commanding general stated that he could not condone the existence of any organization that counseled members of his command to refuse to perform their duty or to desert their military service. The owners of the coffeehouse denied that they advised their customers to desert. They claimed that they had tried to talk GIs out of deserting, because they believed that "the answer" was to stay and organize from within. They also argued that it was not their opposition to military order and discipline that was detrimental to morale but the army's inhumane treatment of enlisted men and the war itself.[48] The commander's efforts at Fort Lewis were ultimately unsuccessful, and the Shelter Half was able to stay open until late 1970.[49]

In several instances commanders did not have to take direct action against coffeehouses in order to hamper their activities. Instead, members of the civilian communities tried, sometimes successfully, to get rid of these sources of disturbance. In Muldraugh, Kentucky, citizens of the community felt obliged to step in, because the commanders at Fort Knox stuck to the army policy of toleration and refused to interfere.[50] The landlord tried to evict the managers of the coffeehouse after he realized that their business had political dimensions. The Muldraugh City Council established two new ordinances in order to withhold the business license from the coffeehouse. Officials withheld health permits as well. Police arrested some of the civilian organizers and charged them with creating a public nuisance much as their colleagues in South Carolina did.[51]

Local authorities in Washington DC also attempted to shut down a coffeehouse by withholding essential licenses and permits. They successfully delayed opening of the DMZ for several weeks because the managers at first could not comply with a number of health department and building regulations. However, these measures could not prevent the opening of the coffeehouse.[52] Similarly, community administrators prevented the owners of the Shelter Half from renewing their business license. A few extralegal efforts to shut down coffeehouses occurred as well. An unidentified assailant threw a firebomb into a coffeehouse near Fort Dix, New Jersey. Three people were injured, two of whom were GIs. One of the GIs had to be hospitalized. A coffeehouse in Fayetteville, North Carolina, was firebombed in May 1970.[53]

The ambivalent and contradictory stance toward protesters that marked the army's response in the United States would also become evident in Germany. Commanders often felt threatened by antiwar organizers. However, their options in preventing organizing efforts near their bases were limited. They also had to be careful not to violate their soldiers' constitutional rights. Their greatest allies, as would sometimes be the case in Germany, were local authorities who took a similarly dim view of antiwar organizers in their communities. Publicly the army leaders did very little in regard to protesters. However, in 1968 the army developed a surveillance plan. The army enlisted the help of several government agencies to collect intelligence on civil rights workers and antiwar activists.[54] These domestic spying activities caused a scandal when they came to light in early 1971.[55] Despite the public embarrassment, the army continued using counterintelligence measures against antiwar organizers in Germany.

Regardless of commanders' fears, antiwar organizing around U.S. bases never became a major part of the antiwar movement. While the morale and discipline among troops was not high, no mass movement emerged. While individual GIs or groups would sometimes voice their grievances or opposition to the war, no national organization run by GIs formed.

Much of the activism among soldiers depended on receiving help from civilian activists. Organizations such as the Student Mobilization Committee (SMC), the Young Socialist Alliance (YSA), and the Youth

Against War and Fascism (YAWF) were often essential in providing support to dissenting soldiers. Civilian activists assisted in the printing and distributing of leaflets and newspapers, helped run the coffeehouses, and staged demonstrations at courts-martial. Members of the Student Mobilization Committee, for example, cooperated with soldiers at Fort Lewis, Washington, in founding the GI-Civilian Alliance for Peace (GI-CAP) and its newspaper *Counterpoint*. One of the more successful events organized by the group was a peace rally in downtown Seattle on February 16, 1969, which included two hundred active duty service members and attracted a crowd of several thousand.[56] Members of the YAWF worked closely with founding members of ASU Andy Stapp, Paul Gaedtke, Dick Ilg, and Dick Wheaton. A delegation was present and active at the courts-martial of Stapp and Ilg.[57]

The Young Socialist Alliance was involved in a high-profile incident of soldiers' dissent, the case of the "Fort Jackson 8." In early 1969, soldiers concerned about racism in the army and the war in Vietnam, among them a member of the YSA, formed an organization that they named "GIs United Against the War in Vietnam." One of the more spectacular actions taken by the group was filing a lawsuit before the federal court demanding that the army comply with the freedom of speech provisions of the First Amendment. The title "Fort Jackson 8" refers to an incident during which members of GIs United addressed a crowd of approximately one hundred soldiers.[58] The event started spontaneously when a soldier decided to address the crowd that had gathered to watch a few fellow soldiers wrestle. Two officers and an NCO who witnessed the event testified that it was peaceful, even though the officer who tried to disperse the crowd described it as a riot. Authorities refrained from arresting anybody on the day of the "demonstration." On the following day, military police arrested eight soldiers and charged them with disrespecting an officer, participating in a public demonstration without approval, and breaching the peace. As the case drew more and more negative publicity, authorities dropped the charges against six of the defendants, and two received undesirable discharges. Officers who were not necessarily sympathetic toward dissenters testified that they believed the incident to have been harmless. This was a clear indication that the leadership at the base had overreacted.

The United States Servicemen's Fund, a civilian organization already mentioned above, funded numerous protest activities all over the United States. According to David Cortright, the USSF raised more than $150,000 in 1970. After being closed for four months in late 1970, the USSF reorganized in December 1970 and continued its activities until mid-1973. Another civilian support organization was the Pacific Counseling Service, which had offices near bases in California, Japan, the Philippines, and Hong Kong. One of the more influential support groups was the Chicago Area Military Project (CAMP) founded in early 1970. The organization published *Camp News*, a worldwide GI movement newsletter. Cortright claims that the organization "carried on extremely valuable coordination and political-education work and served as the most authoritative information source available on servicemen's dissent."[59]

Actress Jane Fonda and a former Green Beret, Sgt. Don Duncan, founded the GI Office in Washington. The office helped channel GI grievances to Congress and assisted with legal complaints. Fonda, one of the most famous figures associated with the antiwar movement, was also active in mobilization efforts of the GI movement.

Army veterans played an important role in GI organizing. A veteran started the first GI newspaper in Chicago. Carl Rogers, Jan Barry, and Steve Wilcox, early members of Vietnam Veterans Against War (VVAW), organized the Servicemen's Link to Peace movement.[60] LINK provided support to dissenting GIs from people who had experienced military life themselves and were consequently much more credible than any civilian peace activist with no military experience could be. Thus veterans were especially valuable in "bridging" a gap and establishing contacts. The members of LINK also believed that they were essential in making developments in the GI movement known to a wider public: "Suddenly we were discovering this enormous revolt going on within the military that nobody really had any other way of hearing was going on."[61]

Like other organizations involved with the GI movement, LINK worked to support GIs facing courts-martial, particularly the Presidio 27. This was a group of prisoners in the army stockade at the Presidio in San Francisco who protested when a guard killed a mentally disturbed young soldier. The soldiers were tried for "mutiny" and sentenced to fifteen years of hard labor. The case gained wide publicity and caused some embarrassment to the army. The judge advocate general intervened and reduced the sentence even before the appellate process had begun.[62]

Another attempt by Andy Stapp and other antiwar activists to organize and channel discontent among the soldiers was the creation of the American Servicemen's Union (ASU). Fourteen soldiers from different continental bases founded the ASU in 1967. Stapp continued his activities in the ASU even after his dismissal from the army in April 1968.[63] Originally the aim of the ASU was not to become a legally recognized union; instead, it defined itself as a resistance organization within the army. Membership was limited to the lowest five enlisted grades. Officers or career enlisted men, so-called lifers, could not join. However, the union did not make a distinction between draftees and volunteers.[64] The founders of the ASU believed that the concept of a union would reverberate with soldiers from predominantly working-class neighborhoods and poor rural areas.[65] Calling the organization a union also reflected the members' interpretation of their struggle as pitting working-class enlisted men against bourgeois officers.[66]

The ASU drafted ten demands. First, they asserted the right of a soldier to refuse any illegal or immoral order, particularly the order to fight in Vietnam.[67] By pointing specifically to the war in Vietnam, the ASU turned the demand into an expression of dissent. The general right to refuse illegal or immoral orders was not at odds with normal military practice, at least theoretically. However, the ASU argued that soldiers refusing to go to Vietnam could invoke this right, because the war was illegal due to the fact that Congress had never formally declared war on Vietnam.[68]

The ASU's second demand was for the right of the ranks to elect officers from their own midst to replace the officers imposed on them by the military hierarchy.[69] The military and particularly its officers were tools of the bourgeoisie who needed to be replaced, by force if necessary.[70] Third, they called for abandoning rituals reinforcing social hierarchy in the army, such as addressing officers as "sir" and saluting.

The fourth demand was for the elimination of racism in the army.[71] In interviews conducted in September 1970 and October 1971, Andy Stapp strongly identified the struggle of the ASU with the struggles of black GIs. He repeatedly referred to the military as a racist institution. Most of the examples of protest activity he cited in the interview were race related. He mentioned Ku Klux Klan activities in Fulda, Germany, the case of the Darmstadt 53, and the case of black soldiers in California who had allegedly killed two superior officers. Stapp conceded that frustrated black soldiers initiated most violent protests, but believed that white soldiers were joining in as well. Stapp interpreted racism in the army as an extension of U.S. imperialism. The United States was exploiting the working class both in Third World countries and at home. According to this interpretation, African Americans were members of the wider exploited masses.[72]

Demands five and six stated the ASU's opposition to using army forces for domestic law enforcement or peacekeeping efforts. The ASU demanded that the army not be used against antiwar demonstrators or striking workers. Demand seven targeted the military justice system.[73] The union criticized the process of selecting court-martial juries, made up of officers only, even in trials against enlisted men. The ASU demanded that the enlisted ranks should have control over who could sit on juries.[74] Demand eight was for the right to free assembly. Only demands nine and ten were truly concerned with traditional union issues. Demand nine called for the introduction of a minimum wage for the enlisted men, and demand ten entailed the right of union members to bargain collectively. Efforts to unionize the army would later also be made in Germany. Underground newspapers in Germany would publish the ASU's demands.

Another group that reached beyond a single military base was the

Movement for a Democratic Military (MDM), founded in the fall of 1969 at Camp Pendleton, Oceanside, California. Most of the founding members were black GIs who were associated with the Black Panther Party, but the MDM had some white members as well. The MDM particularly stressed Third World solidarity supporting self-determination for all people and working to end the war in Vietnam. The goal was "to end the exploitation of our brothers and sisters abroad, and the repression, both physical and economic, of those in our own land."[75] The demands of the MDM were similar to those of the ASU. Members demanded the right of collective bargaining and all constitutional and human rights. They wanted an end to all military censorship and intimidation. Individual soldiers should have "the right to refuse politically objectionable duty such as riot control, strike breaking, and imperialistic wars." The armed forces had to abolish mental and physical cruelty in military brigs, correctional custodies, and basic training. The organization further demanded the abolition of the court-martial system and nonjudicial punishment. Instead, soldiers were to be tried by a jury of their peers by rank. All cases were to be subject to civilian review.

Similar to the ASU, the demands also reflected some socialist ideas, particularly obvious in the call for the banishment of class structures in the military including the obligation to salute and "sir" officers and the call for the elimination of all special privileges allotted to officers. The armed forces needed to create enlisted rank review boards of officer conduct.

Like most GI organizations, MDM demanded an end to racism and combined this with a call to free all political prisoners, in particular Eldridge Cleaver, Huey Newton, Bobby Seale, and Erika Huggins, in return for captured American prisoners of war in Indochina. More unusual was a call to ban all glorification of war. The final demand was for an immediate withdrawal from Indochina. Soldiers should no longer be the puppets of U.S. imperial ambitions and the military industrial complex "tricked into fighting against the 'Peoples War.'" Instead members of MDM would fight "to force these genocidal rulers and the Brass to get out of Indochina Now."

According to Waterhouse and Wizard, who were active in the organization, MDM spread rapidly across bases in the western United States during the fall of 1969 with its reputation as a "heavy" revolutionary group quickly established. They believed the multiracial character made it "generally a successful and rewarding experience, as GIs of all races discovered their common oppression, talked openly with each other about racist attitudes and actions, and shared their ideas for change."[76] Despite these initial successes, the organization encountered difficulties by the summer of 1970. The chapters at different bases had problems communicating with each other. Because of its radical views, the organization had difficulties raising sufficient funds. Liberal sources became increasingly hesitant to contribute. Apparently internal racial conflicts also played a role in the mounting difficulties despite the MDM's claims to harmony. The MDM is one of the few cases where gender roles became an acknowledged contributing factor to the organization's problems. According to Wizard and Waterhouse, male chauvinist attitudes among the mostly male membership caused women to become "disillusioned with their role in the GI movement." Accordingly, the organization attracted few servicewomen.

Despite Wizard and Waterhouse's claim asserting the important role of the MDM, their own account indicates that its influence remained limited to the West Coast and was probably short-lived. They describe the impact of the organization in very vague terms claiming that MDM and "its list of demands served to raise the consciousness of GIs in many areas." The organization also "brought the GI movement as a potential revolutionary ally to the attention of other revolutionary groups."[77]

Ultimately the efforts of the ASU and the MDM to politicize and unionize enlisted men met with little success. While individual efforts at organizing at different bases in the United States did garner some media attention and contributed to the image of a troubled army, efforts at GI organizing never received the kind of attention that protests at university campuses and Washington received. The most lasting impact of antiwar activism in the army was probably to clarify soldiers' constitutional rights through a series of trials. However, GI activism in the United States was certainly an important precursor to what occurred in West Germany. GI organizing took on similar forms in Europe. Underground newspapers played a central role in offering GIs an alternative perspective of the war and U.S. society. Trials became important forums to stage protests. In many ways commanders treated the morale and discipline problems that protest activities in Germany unveiled with far more urgency than in the United States, since USA-REUR stood at the frontline of the Cold War.

6

The Situation in
USAREUR, 1968–1975

Resistance in USAREUR began with soldiers trying to escape the army and to avoid duty in Vietnam by going AWOL. Unlike their fellow soldiers in Vietnam, GIs in Germany had the viable option of leaving the army without permission. Not only were there countries in Europe that did not extradite deserters but a support network of civilian antiwar activists had formed to funnel them toward those countries. The so-called underground railway for American soldiers in Europe had its beginnings in Amsterdam and Paris in 1966. Some soldiers spending their weekend leave in Amsterdam decided not to return to their units in Germany and instead asked Dutch activists, "Provos," to help them go underground. The Provos normally smuggled these soldiers to Paris because they believed them to be safer there, since France had taken a fairly critical stance toward the war in Vietnam and had ceased its military involvement in NATO. In May 1967 the French government had granted a work permit to an American army deserter who had been arrested in the country, thereby legalizing his presence in France and creating a precedent and a safe haven for deserters. Over the years soldiers increasingly found help among German student activists and were able to move to France without the detour through Amsterdam. Sweden, which would become the most famous haven for deserters, did not start accepting GIs until later in 1967. Initially France remained more attractive for GIs because it was closer and shared a comparatively open border with Germany.[1]

Rising AWOL rates became an increasing problem for the army in Germany. A postproduction script for a radio program broadcast on August 17, 1967, describes the network that existed in Western Europe to provide assistance to deserting GIs. Reporter Peter Williams interviewed a number of deserters and activists, all providing pseudonyms only for the interview, on why and how they had left their units in Germany. While early leaflets on how to desert printed in London indicate some activity there, the main hub of underground activity was Paris.[2]

Some of the AWOL soldiers in France became politically active. While many had merely wanted to get away from the army and the possibility of ending up in Vietnam, others wanted to be active in the opposition to the war. They gave interviews to journalists in which they expressed their opposing views, and some started to organize a return to their units in Germany. In doing so they could carry their antiwar message and the information on how soldiers could successfully hide from the army. Naturally, not all the returning soldiers had an activist agenda. Most had probably never planned to leave permanently; others were often convinced by their families that a return would be preferable to a life in exile. Ultimately few of the soldiers who went AWOL actually became politically active.[3]

One of the soldiers who did was Richard Perrin, who claimed that he had turned against the war after overhearing two veterans in Fort Leonard Wood talking about how they had tortured a Vietnamese prisoner. When Perrin was assigned to Fort Sill, he met Andy Stapp and started collaborating with him. Like Stapp, Perrin was also court-martialed for his dissident activities. During the proceedings Perrin accepted a deal allowing him to avoid prison by transferring to Kitzingen, Germany. However, after arriving in Germany, Perrin decided to go AWOL and ended up in Paris. There he joined a protest group that at the time called itself AITA, Act Inside the Army, but was soon renamed RITA, Resistance Inside the Army, a designation that would stay in use throughout the 1970s. Along with three other soldiers and a sailor, Perrin founded the underground newspaper *RITA's ACT*, which was later abbreviated to *ACT*. *ACT* was a one-sheet newspaper that published only articles written by soldiers who were willing to have their name and RA number appear in the byline. *ACT* was the first GI newspaper to appear in Europe.[4]

After the student revolt in Paris in the summer of 1968, the GI activists began drifting apart. While AWOL soldiers continued to make their way to Paris, even fewer were politically motivated. Those who thought of themselves as activists went to Canada or Sweden. One activist GI, Terry Klug, turned himself in to stand trial as a deserter. He received a three-year prison sentence at Fort Dix, NJ, where he organized a chapter of the ASU and faced another trial for allegedly inciting a stockade revolt in October 1969. By 1969 the government policy in France had changed. Georges Pompidou replaced Charles de Gaulle, and France became less tolerant toward deserters.[5] Civilian activist Max Watts had to relocate to Germany where he continued the activities of RITA.[6] At this point resistance activities began mirroring events in the United States.

When researching RITA it is impossible not to come across the name Max Watts, and when reviewing the documents it is impossible to avoid the conclusion that Watts was the driving force behind the GI movement in Germany. This name is actually only an alias; Watts's real name was Thomas Schwaetzer. He was born in Vienna on June 13, 1928. According to an intelligence file from the JAG office of the Department of the Army, he went to the United States and became a naturalized citizen sometime in the 1940s, but he returned to Europe around 1950 to avoid the Korea draft. He took up residence in Paris, where he received a degree in geophysics.[7]

He became politically active in the leftist movement in Paris and was, at first, a member of the Paris American Committee to Stop-the-War (PACS). According to Watts, PACS was a middle-class and mostly middle-aged organization that supported draft resisters and dodgers in Paris. When the first deserters appeared in Paris, members of PACS were uncertain about how to deal with them.[8] Watts focused on supporting resisting GIs and became an active member of RITA in Paris.

According to an intelligence file, French authorities deported Watts to Corsica. Via Austria he ultimately ended up in Heidelberg in October 1969.[9] He conducted his organizational activities out of a bookstore in the historic center of Heidelberg close to the central buildings of the university.[10] Once in Heidelberg, Watts became deeply involved in organizing GI resistance. The *Politische Buchhandlung* was a hub of student protest activities in Heidelberg and became the official address of RITA.[11]

Watts was the editor of *Graffiti,* an underground newspaper written for American GIs. During this period, he assembled a collection of flyers and publications that he entitled "RITA Notes." When studying these texts, it is often hard to tell from whom they originated, since the texts generated by RITA were rarely signed. Authors either remained anonymous or used an obvious pseudonym, such as Rita F. Act. According to activist lawyer Howard DeNike, Rita F. Act was Watts's pseudonym. DeNike described Watts as "at the vortex of GI agitation in Germany, a good deal of it his own devising."[12] Watts's intense involvement and his efforts to conceal it in his writings make it difficult to tell in retrospect how many active duty soldiers were involved. Watts liked to pretend that GIs primarily ran RITA. To validate that claim, he made a distinction between "ritas," resisters inside the army, and "fritas," friends of resisters inside the army. But most sources indicate that the distinction was blurry at best.

Unrest and protest activities among GIs in Germany increased in 1969 and 1970. The number of racial incidents and antiwar protests rose. In May 1969 about fifty soldiers demonstrated across from the Daenner-Kaserne in Kaiserslautern, distributing antiwar leaflets to passing soldiers. Two soldiers subsequently started an underground newspaper, the *Ash.* Another demonstration occurred in September 1969 in Grafenwöhr. One hundred GIs gathered for meetings to voice their opposition to the war and the military justice system. The same number of GIs attended an antiwar meeting and film in Augsburg during the Moratorium demonstrations in October of that year.[13] The years 1969 and 1970 saw an increasing number of underground publications from the *Baumholder Gig Sheet*, to *Graffiti* in Heidelberg, *Speak Out* in Hanau, and *Venceremos* in Frankfurt.[14] In some cases individual soldiers initiated acts of defiance or protest. SP5 Randall Polack, a medic and Vietnam veteran, stationed himself in front of a mess hall in Schwäbisch-Gemünd on Easter Sunday with a sign asking his fellow soldiers to boycott Easter Sunday services as a form of protest against the war. Military police arrested Pollack after about thirty minutes, and he later accepted punishment according to Article 15 for violating army regulations against such demonstrations on base.[15]

However, despite this increase in antiwar protest, the race-related activities would always dominate the GI movement in Germany. RITA never became a mass movement within USAREUR. An article in the *Overseas Weekly* in which enlisted men were asked their opinion of protesters revealed that a number of soldiers were sympathetic toward some of their demands, particularly in regard to soldiers' free speech rights. However, few of the soldiers questioned seemed to be willing to become active themselves or saw themselves as part of a spreading movement. They were more concerned with "getting short."[16] While the specialist 4 quoted by the *Overseas Weekly* had little love for army life, he preferred waiting out his tour over actively resisting while in the army. Accordingly antiwar activism strongly depended on individuals and remained highly localized.

Early 1971 was the high point of the GI movement in Europe. This is particularly true if black resistance is interpreted as part of the wider GI movement and the most successful part at that. A large number of documents from congressional hearings through army reports and the already mentioned major newspapers cite 1971 as the most tumultuous year for USAREUR. According to an army report on "group dissent against authority," acts of insubordination had increased from once every two weeks in 1970 to twice a week by the summer of 1971.[17] Senator Stuart Symington (D-MO) and Representative Dab Daniel (D-VA) traveled to Germany and returned with the impression that discipline and morale were declining.[18]

Vietnam was, of course, the central issue for RITA activists. They wrote and distributed flyers among GIs and the German public condemning U.S. engagement in Vietnam. One of the RITA Notes from May 31, 1971, for example, tried to cast doubt on the official numbers given for casualties in Vietnam published by the *Stars & Stripes*. The note lists additional groups of casualties that the author believed were not part of the official counts. He alleged that the army did not count soldiers who died from wounds later, despite the army's claim to the contrary. The army supposedly left out accidental deaths such as heroin overdoses, friendly fire, fragging victims, and soldiers engaged in combat zones where the United States was not operating officially, such as Laos. To prove his point, the author cited two examples. He recounted stories about a Special Forces soldier whose tombstone in the United States read that he had died in Laos and about pilots who had smuggled opium out of the Laotian uplands. He followed up with a comparatively lengthy and somewhat unrelated account of the CIA's involvement in the Southeast Asia drug trade.[19] The flyer contained no information specific to USAREUR and made an argument indistinguishable from civilian protests in the United States or Germany.

Flyers also took the form of appeals for funds, asking GIs, for example, for contributions to provide medical aid to Hanoi. This particular flyer argued that it was time for Americans to demonstrate their opposition to the war. The note claimed that the majority of Americans felt disgraced by their government's failure to end the conflict in Vietnam.[20] The claim of representing a majority as well as an alternate America was a constant thread in RITA publications. In another flyer distributed in Stuttgart, activists protested against the German-American Friendship Week taking place May 2–10. The program of the festival included demonstrations of military equipment and barracks, concerts by the military bands, and paratrooper jumps. According to the activist authors of the flyer, such an event was not conducive to the friendship between the two peoples (*Völkerfreundschaft*), but merely served capitalists, politicians, and generals to "propagandize" about the war. The war and resulting war profiteering were being financed with

American tax dollars. The flyer contended further that the majority of these Americans did not support Nixon and the continuation of the war. The flyer also included an antiwar statement by a GI arguing that racism and capitalism were not a way of life he chose to protect. He would not "murder the Vietnamese people in order to defend the privileges and profits of the Military-Industrial-Complex." Instead he vowed that he would return home to "end racism, fascism, and imperialism." The flyer made race a central theme connecting the plight of the Vietnamese to American racism and imperialism, referring to the U.S. government as slave masters and the United States as Amerikkka, and calling for "power to all people. Power to all oppressed, Black, White, Red, Yellow."[21]

Court cases against enlisted men who came into conflict with the army hierarchy were often a vehicle for RITA activism. One such court case adopted as a cause by RITA was the trial against a Private O'Brien that took place near Heidelberg in August 1971. O'Brien, the RITA flyer maintained, had gone AWOL after his CO had threatened to kill him with a revolver. To RITA the trial demonstrated the farcical nature of U.S. military courts. The anonymous author of the flyer argued that the court had revealed its fascist nature when it had failed to take the CO's alleged threats into consideration. Even further "proof" was the judge's refusal to let the defense attorney question the defendant about conditions at the Mannheim stockade, a hot topic in that year. The judge, according to RITA, did not intend to put "the Mannheim stockade on trial." In RITA's view, the judge's refusal to hear about the brutality at Mannheim was a travesty of justice. The flyer stresses typical themes depicting the U.S. Army as a fascist organization that systematically violated soldiers' civil rights.[22] The vocabulary used put RITA far to the left of the political mainstream, a fact that at times made their organizing efforts among soldiers more difficult.

Activists intended the flyers not only for GIs but German civilians as well, trying to convince them of the existence of an alternative America. RITA members strived repeatedly to foster ties between German activists and GIs. A letter to RITA indicates that the group interacted with German activists and organizers, although it also reveals the difficulties of this work. The letter is a response from a German activist, a high school student from Niederstetten, thanking RITA for the materials received and reporting on the difficulties of organizing in a community with a population of 2,800. RITA activists might have mistakenly assumed an American presence in Niederstetten when they sent the materials. The student activist indicated that he saw little possibility for raising awareness about the United States' involvement in Vietnam and the suppression of African Americans given the lack of a base in town. Accordingly, the population did not realize "that the problems of U.S. are also its own." He promised to distribute the materials to GIs coming to the discotheques in the nearby town of Bad Mergentheim.[23]

Cooperation between German activists and GIs were more successful in larger cities with large student populations. On July 3, 1971, German students organized demonstrations in Heidelberg, Frankfurt, and Munich. The German National Union of Students (Verband Deutscher Studentenschaften) distributed flyers to GIs calling on soldiers to resist the war effort in Vietnam and promising that the People's Army of Vietnam would support any American soldier opposing U.S. policy.[24] The demonstration drew about 1,000 supporters in Heidelberg. Newspaper articles on the event did not indicate whether any GIs attended. On October 1, 1971, the Socialist Heidelberg Student Union (Sozialistischer Heidelberger Studentenbund) distributed a flyer urging the German public to support the Darmstadt 53. The flyer explained the situation and claimed that so far the German press had paid little attention to the incident out of solidarity with the U.S. government.[25] The flyer invited Germans to join a demonstration on October 4, 1971, in front of the barracks in Mannheim where the trial was to take place. The same information was also put out through a special edition of *was tun*, a socialist newsletter.[26]

In November 1969, Frankfurt student leader K. D. Wolff launched the Black Panther Solidarity Committee. One of its missions was to support black GIs in their protest activities. Wolff founded the publishing house *Verlag Roter Stern.*[27] The press became an important resource for activists. They were able to produce the pamphlets, flyers, and underground newspapers expressing soldiers' dissatisfaction with the current situation and calling upon fellow soldiers to join in the protest. German activists participated in the demonstrations in support of the Ramstein 2 or the Darmstadt 53.[28]

Despite such demonstrations of solidarity and flurries of German-American cooperation during high-profile events, cooperation between GIs and civilian activists was fraught with difficulties. One large barrier, of course, was language. Most GIs did not speak German, and their interactions with Germans were therefore often limited. In the cases where dissenting GIs were able to connect with German activists, the soldiers had either been in the country for a while or they had staged an action that drew outside attention and support from German activists. American civilians such as Max Watts and Karen Bixler played a crucial role in establishing contacts between dissenting GIs and German activists. However, regardless of this support, those few U.S. soldiers who tried to take political action encountered huge logistical obstacles in their organizing work, mainly due to the base structure in Germany with many small and midsized barracks spread out throughout southern and southwestern Germany.[29]

In many cases GIs and civilian activists, be they German or American, approached their activism with different motivations and goals. In one letter to an activist college professor about resistance in the armed forces, an anonymous member of RITA describes the problems arising from the limited education of regular soldiers. Most soldiers active in RITA were not inclined toward theoretical discussions. Few of the soldiers had high school diplomas. Accordingly, it was normally the civilian activists who wrote down and condensed the soldiers' grievances.[30] This description of the interaction between civilian activists and dissenting GIs showed the embarrassment felt by the civilian activist about suggesting that the difficulties arising in organizing and working with GIs might be due to differing levels of education. On the other hand, it also demonstrates why an assessment of GI involvement in

RITA activities is difficult, since the writer essentially admitted that it was often the civilian activists who wrote up and published the issues RITA was concerned with.

In the same letter the activist indicated that many civilian protesters and leftist organizations showed only very selective interest in GI resistance. Spectacular actions garnered some interest, but many civilian activists showed little interest otherwise. Groups and individuals involved in GI organizing were for the most part marginal to the wider protest movement. A further problem was the "fragmentation between (resisting) structurally alienated groups." GIs, found the factional fighting between different civilian leftist groups confusing and not relevant to their own concerns.[31]

Flyers and underground newspapers show that RITA activists repeatedly tried to bridge the gap between GIs and German protesters. One issue of the Berlin-based underground newspaper *Where It's At* described German Moratorium Day demonstrations in Berlin. The writers tried to reassure GIs that these demonstrators were hostile not toward them but toward those they believed to be in control in the United States and its armed forces. Acknowledging that "crowds of foreign demonstrators" did not "always look too friendly to the naked eye," the writers assured GIs that just like American protesters, the Germans were "AGAINST the military-industrial complex and the top brass only" but "FOR the American people and FOR the GI."[32]

A flyer from late 1972 invites GIs to attend RITA-Contact meetings to bring "Americans and Germans together." Naming the effort RITA-Contact was a reference to the official army program KONTAKT, which fostered meetings between GIs and young Germans.

Ultimately relations between GIs and peace activists remained difficult. Many of the peace activists were students who opposed the draft. They faced resisting soldiers who in many cases had joined the army voluntarily. On-base resistance was a concept the civilian activists outside of RITA had a hard time envisioning. Instead, such activists continued to encourage soldiers to desert. The daily struggles of GIs over issues such as hair length, mess hall food, or housing conditions meant little to them. On the other hand, GIs often showed little interest in concepts such as imperialism and communism and by no means always shared the same political goals. As one AWOL GI in France put it: "Communism sucks. I live inside a communist conspiracy, the United States Army, where you have no freedom, no private initiative; they issue you clothing, medical treatment, etc. That's communism, but no way, that's what we are against."[33] Ideologically minded civilian activists saw the United States and its military in the grips of fascist oppressors bent on an imperialist agenda. They encountered soldiers who, while possibly critical of what they experienced in the army, were not inclined to ascribe their criticism greater ideological significance.

As in the United States, underground newspapers formed an important part of antiwar and protest activity in Germany. One publication that received quite a bit of attention from local commanders was the *Witness.* The paper initially appeared as the *Green Weenie* in February 1970 in Schwäbisch-Gmünd.[34] The original title was an irreverent reference to the unit's green Pershing missiles. SP4 John Vater wrote and published the four-page newsletter. Vater remained anonymous until the army discovered his identity in April 1970.[35] The paper's main purpose was to vent the frustration that enlisted men felt about their unit.

The subjects of the articles were normally officers or NCOs. In its first edition, the *Witness* reported, for example, that of all the NCOs in the unit, only two had finished high school, or that another NCO had been turned in for drinking on duty hours. The paper ridiculed one captain for his bad breath. Other articles were more political. One article criticized a chaplain for not letting soldiers speak out about their frustrations over their unit's racial problems during a religious retreat for fear of sanctions from his superiors. The *Witness* also reported on the case of two black soldiers who had given the black power salute to the flag at the local theater while the national anthem played.[36] It exposed one officer's racial prejudices as well as his wife's arrogant behavior toward the wives of the enlisted men.[37] Another topic was the excessively abusive behavior of the military police in dealing with soldiers.[38] In one edition the paper started a protest week during which enlisted men were to salute everything they came across, from the cleaning lady to the fire hydrants. The rationale was that a salute was a sign of respect but that soldiers had to salute any officer regardless of how much respect they really felt toward him. The underground authors named the protest action "Salute a Dud Week."[39] The paper also reported on antiwar activities. Inspired by the *Witness*, one soldier, for example, started an Easter mess hall boycott to protest the war in Vietnam.[40] The topic choices of the paper make obvious that a GI actually wrote the *Witness*. It provided reports on incidents actually occurring on base giving voice to soldiers' frustrations and revealing the obvious gap between enlisted personnel and their superior officers and senior NCOs.

The paper's activities did not go unnoticed by commanders in Schwäbisch-Gemünd. Once they identified Vater as the editor, they charged him with "misappropriation of government property" for using six mimeograph stencils. Vater refused the Article 15 and opted for a court-martial. Authorities eventually dropped the charges, but Vater was continuously harassed by his command.[41] The *Witness* was a paper actually run by a GI activist, and like many similar efforts it was short-lived. Publishing an underground newspaper posed major obstacles to the few GIs who were inclined to do so. Soldiers could not legally produce or distribute such papers on base.[42] At first GIs had to fight for even the right to possess such materials. Another obstacle was the transitory nature of military life, which the army leadership knew how to exploit. Known activists or newspaper editors were simply transferred to other posts in Germany, to other countries, or back to the United States.[43] It comes as no surprise that civilians published the longest running underground newspapers in Germany, recruiting GIs as contributors.

One of these publications was *Forward* in West Berlin. *Forward* had its origins in two earlier publications, *Where It's At* and *Up Against the Wall*. *Where It's At* was originally published by American antiwar activists living in Berlin in 1967. These activists had been members of the U.S. Campaign Against the War in South Vietnam, but were dissatisfied with its progress, believing that the liberal members of the organization put too much faith in the beginning peace negotiations, another indication that RITA organizers were politically more radical than average peace activists. Looking for new allies in their campaign, the activists sought out soldiers stationed in West Berlin. The longest lasting editor was Dave Harris, who collected *Forward* and other GI movement publications at the Archiv für Soldatenrechte.[44] Through *Where It's At*, the activists tried to inform soldiers about the "progressive struggles" that were occurring all over the world and in all tiers of society, particularly in the military, such as the demonstrations in Chicago at the Democratic National Convention in 1968, and including the refusal of forty black soldiers in Fort Hood, Texas, to be deployed against rioters in the Chicago ghetto and the black power salute given by two athletes at the Olympic Games in Mexico City.[45]

As was the case with the attempts to get GIs to join in the other forms of dissent, civilians found it difficult to connect with soldiers. Only a few issues of the first edition found their way into soldiers' possession. Activists also had to confront their own class assumptions. Soldiers were often less interested in the larger political or ideological struggles taking place than in solving more mundane problems of army life. The difference between civilian and soldiers' concerns becomes obvious when comparing Vater's *Witness* to *Where It's At*. As shown above, Vater reported on on-base struggles between enlisted men and their superiors. The Berlin newspaper was more concerned with the wider antiwar struggle. Internal ideological struggles and the disintegration of the American Students for a Democratic Society additionally hampered civilian activists. However, by late 1969 the group had consolidated its membership and developed more effective strategies for reaching soldiers.[46]

The war in Vietnam remained at the heart of the publication. In fall 1969, for example, *Where It's At* published a special Moratorium Day issue. The first article cast doubt on the government's figures on troop withdrawals from Vietnam, citing among other things the fact that two hundred troops stationed in Berlin had received orders to leave for Vietnam. The other item on the front page was a letter from an imprisoned South Vietnamese student who applauded American students for their protest activities. The letter did not address GIs specifically. It was most likely a reprint from another publication.[47]

Another article commented on the chances of success for the upcoming M-Day on November 14–15, 1969. The editors argued that the M-Day of October 15 had not been effective because Nixon was "continuing the war" and had not provided a timetable for withdrawal in his speech of November 3. The editors expressed their skepticism toward the upcoming moratorium despite their general support for it, because the leading organizers had backed down from their original plan of starting a mass strike in solidarity "with the hundreds of thousands of GIs who don't want to be sent to Nam and with those there who want to come home immediately." Instead, organizers had settled for "parades, mourning sessions, and talks." People, the paper complained, were "supposed to talk about the war alone—as though it were merely a tragic mistake, a freak accident."[48] The editors believed that the establishment had taken over the event, and they called on readers to "do more than they had planned." The M-Day issue demonstrates the differences the editors had with the mainstream antiwar activists. It also shows their focus on a wider ideological struggle.

Where It's At, of course, also reported on past Moratorium Day activities that had taken place in Germany on October 15, although judging by the lack of detail provided in the paper, GI participation was probably minimal. In very vague terms the editors reported on sit-ins participated in by black and white soldiers in Munich and Frankfurt. According to the article, the protesting GIs were wearing "black armbands, flashing peace and power hand signs, and rapping about the War and the Army." In Berlin some GIs reportedly wore black armbands and black gloves on their left hands.[49] Demonstrations in Kaiserslautern and Grafenwöhr involving forty to one hundred people found mention as well.[50] The references to black power symbols indicate once more that protest actions involving issues of racial pride or racial discrimination were the most prevalent form of dissent among

GIs. The writers accompanied their reports on past GI activities with suggestions on what to do November 15. GIs were to ask their COs for a base meeting during which COs were supposed to explain GIs' constitutional rights under the new DOD (directive on dissent). Other suggested measures included a mess hall boycott, a petition to end the war, changing insurance beneficiaries to include peace organizations, sending telegrams to elected officials, and canceling savings bonds.[51] Reports on GI movement activities in the United States took up a large part of the paper. Under the heading "GI Struggles," WIA reported on the stockade rebellion at Fort Dix involving the ASU and the arrest of two soldiers in Texas who had distributed copies of *Your Military Left*.[52]

By the early 1970, efforts to involve the soldiers had, to some extent, succeeded. At that point soldiers were the main contributors to the newspaper. The increased participation of soldiers was reflected in a name change; *Where It's At* was now called *Up Against the Wall*. The paper reported on and supported protest activities in the army. Activists from the paper tried to coordinate efforts to exert pressure on the army to stop transferring soldiers to Vietnam. Naturally their efforts met with little success. The editors recruited Vietnam returnees to speak out against the war. Several soldiers associated with the paper participated in activities surrounding the Vietnam moratorium. Of course, the protest activities of black GIs, such as the riots at the Mannheim stockade, the Fourth of July demonstrations in Heidelberg, or so-called riots at McNair barracks in Berlin, received coverage as well.

The editors also tried to establish a GI coffeehouse, but their efforts ultimately failed. Like most underground newspapers, *Up Against the Wall* had difficulties sustaining momentum because of membership turnaround. Soldiers and civilians working for the army were eventually transferred back to the United States, depriving the newspaper of active contributors. The publication of the paper lagged in late 1970 because the remaining activists were unable to recruit enough new contributors to keep publishing regularly.[53] In 1971 the paper reformed once more. The remaining publishers decided to change their approach in reaching soldiers. The civilians among the activists realized that they had to take the daily concerns of soldiers more seriously. They deemed *Up Against the Wall* too aggressive and counterproductive, partially because it revealed the intent behind the paper too readily. The publishers adopted a more neutral title that still hinted at their political leanings, *Forward*.[54] With the new concept, local concerns of soldiers featured more prominently, although larger issues such as Vietnam or racism did not disappear from the paper. *Forward* reported extensively on the trial against two black GIs who had gone AWOL for six months after the riots at McNair barracks in August 1970. By writing articles in their paper and organizing events, *Forward*'s publishers were able to persuade four hundred soldiers to request permission to be present at the trial.[55] In 1972 the paper supported George McGovern's presidential campaign. Among the activities to support the concerns of soldiers locally was the opening of a GI counseling center in 1974. During that year the center and *Forward* became strongly involved in supporting GIs who wanted to let their hair grow. The history of *Forward* displays the difficulties encountered by civilian activists in organizing resistance within the army. The name changes reflect a growing realization among the civilian editors that revolutionary rhetoric and references to class solidarity were insufficient to winning GI support.

Max Watts published two papers during his time in Heidelberg. The first, *Graffiti,* appeared in 1969 and 1970. Just like *Where It's At* out of Berlin, the second issue of *Graffiti* was devoted to Moratorium Day. The editors themselves referred to it as a "moratorium collage concocted as tribute to that day of participatory democracy which (we hope) blew Nixon's mind!"[56] Accordingly the paper featured excerpts from stateside magazine and newspaper articles. Most articles dealt with the war in Vietnam or protest activities at Fort Dix. Several items stressed soldiers' right to own such underground publications as *Graffiti* and called on soldiers to demand their First Amendment right to free speech. The final item of the paper described the precarious situation the papers found themselves in due to lacking manpower and financial support. The item was a call for help. The paper needed "writers, artists/cartoonists, layout men, news, and money." Money was a particularly urgent concern as the editors feared they would be unable to pay the cost of printing the third issue. *Graffiti* claimed to represent the viewpoint of the regular GI: "This paper is our paper. It tells what's happening—not what the Brass *say* is happening. It's written by GIs for GIs."[57] However, as was typical for papers initiated by civilians printed at the height of the antiwar movement, events on the bases in the Heidelberg or Mannheim area received little coverage.

The other paper out of Heidelberg that enjoyed a more substantial run was *Fight Back*. It first came out in 1971. Those responsible for the newspaper wrote that *Fight Back* was a newspaper produced "by a group of GIs and other folks in Germany. It exists to help unite and inform GIs and their families who are fighting for their rights," thus repeating the usual claim made by such newspapers.[58] In reality, however, the papers' longevity, well beyond the peak of protest activities, was due to the efforts of "other folks" involved in the paper such as Max Watts and Karen Bixler.[59]

Both *Forward* and *Fight Back* stayed in print until 1978. Most other underground papers such as *The Witness, Venceremos*, or *FTA* did not survive as long. By 1975 all other papers had faded out.[60]

Despite RITA's best efforts to broaden the movement, black soldiers and issues of race discrimination dominated protest activities within the military. Some of the rhetoric employed by black activists touched issues that went beyond mere discrimination. Activists would draw parallels between the plight of the Vietnamese and other Third World peoples and that of the working-class and black GIs.[61] In some instances, protest activities of black soldiers and white antiwar activists overlapped as in the disturbances in Nellingen where both white and black GIs came into conflict with their overzealous base commanders. Protest activities there became explosive. After a soldier of the 903 Company was arrested on July 21, 1970, a Molotov cocktail detonated in front of the company offices. On August 10 and 24, soldiers tried to burn the office of the company commander. Protest activity in Nellingen culminated on September 21 when two hundred GIs broke an order confining them to their barracks and marched through the barracks. The march disbanded after the commander of the MPs assured protesters that no action would be taken against them.[62]

Another example of black protest that went beyond issues of racial discrimination was the founding of the "Black Baptist Religion" by SP4 Lunnie Smith. In early 1970 Smith, who was stationed in Hanau, decided to found his own religion. The two main features of his faith that bought him into conflict with the army were its pacifism and the admonishment to its followers to let their hair grow. The new faith drew about twenty-five followers. Smith became the "First Minister" of his religion, and in accordance with his new faith he refused to cut his hair and turned in his rifle as an expression of his pacifist stance.[63] The army court-martialed Smith for refusing an order to cut his hair. The trial took place in early May, and the court decided that the army had not violated Smith's rights, and it found him guilty of disobeying an order. Smith took the discharge offered because his refusal to bear arms made it impossible to perform his duties.[64] After Smith left the army, some of his followers continued to resist army regulations on hair length. In August authorities placed three black Baptists in pretrial confinement and forcibly cut their hair.[65] Hair length was an issue that actually transcended race. Many GIs at the time felt that the army's regulations on hair length amounted to unnecessary harassment, a regulation that had nothing to do with their ability to do their jobs.[66]

Despite the incident in Nellingen, cooperation between white and black activists was not necessarily the norm. As a matter of fact, despite their public claims to the contrary, the RITA activists repeatedly appeared to tag on to black activist actions for lack of a widespread revolutionary movement. Underground publications such as *Forward* frequently ran articles describing and supporting racial protests. RITA and the underground presses readily took on causes such as the Darmstadt 53. One flyer appearing before the Darmstadt trial explained that, at first, when "the black brothers started standing up for their rights a lot of white GIs got up-tight." This initial reluctance to support their fellow black soldiers, RITA argued, was fading as evidenced by white soldiers coming out in support of the Darmstadt defendants. The flyer also referred to a court-martial in Kaiserslautern where a case against eight out of nine African American soldiers had to be dismissed because the white witnesses refused to testify against them.[67]

RITA was also involved in the protest activities in support of the Ramstein 2. A flyer from June explains the incident from RITA's perspective and demands the release of the two Black Panther activists. RITA claimed that the trial was political in nature and that the "German Puppets and their American Bosses" were railroading Lawrence Jackson and William Burrel "to stop brothers and sisters in Germany from getting organized, from waking up to the oppressive system that enslaves them."[68] The language used, referring to the two Panthers as beautiful brothers, for example, indicates how strongly RITA tried to link the struggles of African Americans to a broader struggle for freedom.

A further example of RITA's support for race-related protests was a flyer from September 1971 that outlined a racial disturbance in Kaiserslautern on June 27, 1971. After a mess hall brawl, fourteen black GIs spent four weeks in pretrial confinement before they were released by an order issued by Davison. Only six of the fourteen went to trial, and five of the trials resulted in acquittal. RITA referred to the group involved in this incident as the K-town 14 and used it as an example to prove how racist an institution the army was.[69]

Forward devoted an entire issue to the trials against two black GIs, Spec 4 Samuel Robertson and Sgt. Ronald Bolden for going AWOL. During Robertson's trial, the defense successfully claimed that because of the racial prejudice and violence prevalent in that particular unit, Robertson had feared for his life and saw leaving the unit as his only option. The jury acquitted Robertson, and the authorities dropped the charges against Bolden before he even saw trial.[70] The writer commenting on the trial in *Forward* basically tried to explain why the trial had not become a great rallying point for protest. The reasons he gives provide valuable insights, showing that the army was becoming more adept at maintaining a low profile in politically charged cases and illustrating the problems that political organizers within the army faced in mobilizing support for their causes.

According to the writer, one major reason why the trial had been a disappointment as a political showcase was because the lawyer and his two defendants had decided to concentrate their arguments on their own individual cases and their specific unit instead of putting the entire army system on trial. They had chosen this strategy out of necessity. "Any generalizations about the army" and accusations of racist thinking "would have turned the jury away from a 'not guilty' verdict."[71] The lawyers had made a choice between "a political trial and freedom for the two brothers." The writer shows awareness of the difficulty activists faced in presenting their message. An overly ideological stance by the defendants would have antagonized the jury. Activists faced an uphill battle persuading soldiers to take up their causes.

However, aside from the defendants' choice to pursue a strategy that would bring them freedom rather than public political exposure, the army also pursued a strategy that made it difficult for activists to steer public attention toward the trial. While only a year before Berlin Brigade commanders had come down hard on protesters at McNair barracks, according to the *Forward* article, they had chosen to handle this trial much more discreetly. One way in which the army limited the amount of publicity given to the trial was by limiting access to the courtroom. When four hundred enlisted men signed up for seating at the trial, the army assigned seats to only twenty-five by means of a lottery system. Thus brigade leadership was able to prevent activists from staging any protest inside the courtroom. *Forward* lamented the fact that activists were unable to react to the lottery in time to organize the four hundred applicants to demonstrate and demand a more open trial. While *Forward* expressed disappointment that no major protest actions had been mounted, its authors expressed some satisfaction that there had been an unspecified number of black and white soldiers as well as civilian activists who had assembled at the main gate of the Berlin Brigade headquarters to express their solidarity with the two soldiers on trial. The fact that the article provided no figures indicates that the crowd was small. So *Forward* stressed the significance of black and white GIs protesting together.[72]

Because the Robertson trial was over after only one day and the army dropped charges against Bolden, activists were unable to organize any more substantial demonstrations. *Forward* argued that while the army had been successful in limiting the negative effects of the trial, it had done so at a price: "The Bolden and Robertson trial is over and the army thinks it has successfully played off EM solidarity with the brothers paying the heavy price of legally admitting racism in the army." *Forward* called upon its readers to use this admittance as solid evidence of the army's racism. The final two pages of that third issue included a rap in which the author calls upon enlisted men of all colors to unite and fight their oppression by the army. The coverage and commentary of *Forward* on the trial represents a typical attempt by activists to turn racial grievances into part of a wider class struggle, in which black and white enlisted men, as the "workers" in the military system, were supposed to unite against their officers as representatives of capitalist oppression.[73]

White activists were encountering difficulties in closing the gap between black and white soldiers. In an editorial of the sixth issue of *Forward* published in December 1971, writers once again stressed that African American GIs were part of a broader struggle. The authors called on black and white activists "to tear down the wall" that came between them. Black and white GIs shared a common struggle "against the system that controls the army and our lives, the war of aggression in Vietnam, and for our rights." As long as the two remained separate and fighting each other, the army retained control. The authors argue that the problems GIs faced were systemic, transcending race. The editorial further called upon combat vets to carry over the unity and solidarity achieved during combat to the political organizing activities in Germany and admonished GIs of both races to overcome their own reservations about working with each other. White GIs needed "to accept Black Power: the demolishing of racism" addressing the widespread discomfort white GIs felt toward African American displays of black power or pride. To the editors of *Forward*, all activists had to believe in equality for "all oppressed masses and self-determination for all minority peoples in the country and in the barracks." Black GIs needed to accept that "due to such situations as relate to the war, Attica, Soledad, and other Amerikkkan penal colonies, that our revolution is a people's revolution, a truly socialist revolution."[74] The editor also invoked Malcolm X's experience in Mecca to convince black activists that their struggle needed to be more inclusive.

Civilian antiwar activists were supportive of African American efforts to fight discrimination in the army. In their difficulties connecting with GIs and inspiring a successful and continuous antiwar movement within the army ranks, black GIs offered to civilian organizers an example of successful activism. Efforts by RITA to wed their agenda to black causes, however, met with little success. Black protests did not spread into a wider struggle against U.S. imperialism and capitalist society. The disconnect between civilian organizers and GIs remained.

In December 1971 and early 1972, protest activities died down. This was partially due the "Early Out" program thanks to which thousands of draftee veterans could opt to leave the service, an indication that their activism was fueled more by their negative view of army life than by a strong commitment to a more general ideological struggle.[75] The number of activists who joined the army for the express purpose of organizing political activities from within was small. Ironically, soldiers who joined RITA while already in the army tended to want to leave it exactly because of their involvement with RITA. Few soldiers were dedicated enough to the cause to "re-up to organize."[76]

During the second half of 1972, protest activity picked up again. However, all events and activities remained localized, much to the chagrin of the civilian organizers.[77] On Memorial Day, May 29, 1972, a group of eighty to one hundred protesters including GIs and dependents staged a protest walk against the Vietnam War in Schweinfurt, Bavaria. The group gathered at a park in Schweinfurt. After an hour of passing out leaflets and discussing GI rights, the group marched to

Ledwood Barracks, where people gathered around the front gate for ten minutes and then proceeded to Conn Barracks. At the entrance to Conn Barracks, the demonstrators read their demands, which included calls for the right for soldiers to refuse to obey illegal orders, the election of officers, and an end to saluting. The protection of minorities was a concern as well as the need for a guarantee that troops could not be used against civilians, be they antiwar demonstrators or striking workers. Finally, the demonstrators demanded rank-and-file control of court-martial boards, the right of free political association, federal minimum wages, and the right of collective bargaining. Military police dispersed the demonstrators soon after they had read their demands. They arrested one demonstrator. The following day they placed John Walsh, a soldier suspected of organizing the event, in custody.[78] Authorities placed all GIs identified as being present at the demonstration on barracks restriction. Most of those soldiers (more than fifty, according to RITA) took Article 15 punishments.[79] At least two GIs went before a court-martial. In separate trials Pvt. William Burke and Pvt. Frederick Ellison were convicted of violating USAREUR regulation 632-10, paragraph 25: active participation in a public demonstration. Burke received only a reprimand, because the presiding judge deemed his confinement prior to the trial excessive. The judge in Ellison's case was less generous and sentenced him to a demotion to E1 and one month of hard labor.[80]

After this Memorial Day, demonstrators came together at the same park every Saturday in June. The first meeting on June 3 drew about twenty participants. Military police and German police dispersed the group.[81] To avoid further interference from the German police, one GI applied for and received a permit for these meetings, an act that RITA touted as an extraordinary "first." However, the number of GIs participating diminished steadily, and the meetings were discontinued in July, leading an author of the RITA Notes to conclude that "frontal sustained attacks against the green machine were not the bag of most of the Schweinfurt GIs—who judged that the best method was to hit them when they weren't looking."[82] Despite the bravado of the quotation, it is clear that the revolutionary fervor among troops was not as strong as civilian activists wished and on other occasions had claimed it to be.

In the RITA Notes, spontaneous acts of violence committed by GIs became signs of the inner disintegration of the army. One RITA Note described an incident in Neu Ulm. Members of the Eighty-First Artillery set fire to a garbage dumpster after they were refused an appointment with their CO.[83] The soldiers harassed German firemen rushing to the scene, throwing bottles and rocks at the firemen and military police.[84] Another incident reported by RITA involved violence between black GIs and the German police in Stuttgart. Black GIs felt harassed by the German police and started a fight with the police. Like the American journalists, they interpreted this as a sign of the rapid disintegration of the army. Unlike the journalists, they also interpreted these incidents as a sign of a growing class consciousness among soldiers.

One incident shows that while RITA was exaggerating the degree of class consciousness soldiers had attained, race consciousness was well developed and African American soldiers continued to mount effective protests. In Ludwigsburg, a group of black GIs took over the gate at Grabenloch Caserne and complete control of the traffic going in and out of the barracks for six hours. This demonstration led to a violent confrontation with the military police. However, the GIs were also successful in getting the CO removed whose refusal to hear their grievances had caused the action in the first place.[85]

Despite the best efforts of the civilian RITA organizers, resistance inside the army never became a mass movement. However, organizing efforts and sporadic acts of protest did continue throughout the 1970s. As the Vietnam War subsided as an issue in 1973, at least as far as American participation was concerned, RITA members shifted their attention to other matters. Soldiers' civil rights, always an important theme, now became the major focus.

Military trials were often used as a major staging ground for protests. In August 1972 the Lawyers Military Defense Committee, an organization that had been active only in Vietnam up to that point, set up an office in Heidelberg. The LMDC had opened an office in Saigon in July 1970 with the purpose of providing free civilian counsel for GIs in Vietnam.[86] Howard DeNike had been part of the three-member team in Vietnam in 1971 and had been asked to serve in Germany for a year. According to DeNike, Max Watts had played a crucial role in persuading the LMDC to open an office in Heidelberg. Watts would remain an important asset to the LMDC's activities. Through Watts, DeNike was able to obtain office space with a Heidelberg law firm, Becker, Laubscher, and Becker, which would later attain notoriety for its legal defense of the Baader-Meinhoff Gang. Robert Rivkin joined DeNike in November 1972. The aim of the LMDC in Heidelberg was to focus on high impact cases, meaning cases with a chance of making headlines with political implications. However, in absence of such "high impact" litigation, DeNike also took on more mundane cases.[87]

Working with *Forward* editor Dave Harris, DeNike took on the case of SP4 Dave Wolter. Wolter was scheduled to appear before a court-martial for "assaulting an acting NCO" and disobeying an order given by the acting NCO. An officer had left another soldier lower in rank than Wolter in charge of the barracks one night. This soldier, as the acting NCO, had ordered Wolter to remain in the barracks, but Wolter had ignored the order and shoved the acting NCO out of the way so that he could leave the barracks. Wolter claimed that he had not realized that the other soldier was in charge, and therefore he was unaware that he was disobeying an order. He also believed that command had singled him out because they saw him as an agitator. *Forward* used the trial as an example of the army's intolerance toward politically active soldiers, arguing that such petty charges would not have gone to a court-martial otherwise. DeNike was successful in getting a "not guilty" verdict on the assault charge and getting the other charge reduced to negligently disobeying an order. The judge lowered Wolter's pay one grade and placed him on thirty-day restriction. DeNike declared this outcome to be a legal victory.[88] The fact that a fairly petty incident such as this became the focus of activists' attention indicates that "high impact" cases were not easy to come by for the lawyers.

A case that actually did have greater repercussions was the court-martial against Pvt. Raymond Olais. Olais sought out DeNike after his captain had ordered him to take down a poster of Che Guevara that hung above his bunk and featured the motto "Hasta la Victoria Siempre!" (Victory will be ours!). After receiving advice from DeNike on the consequences of refusing the order to take down the poster, Olais went ahead and refused the order and opted for a special court-martial presided over by a military judge without a jury. Olais's superior argued that he gave the order because the poster featured a controversial image unlike the other posters displaying rock stars. DeNike argued that this line of reasoning could lead to forcing soldiers to remove images of Jesus Christ hanging on the wall and represented an infringement of a soldier's right to free speech without providing any proof that the poster endangered the discipline and morale of the troops. The judge found Olais not guilty, and the poster remained above his bed.[89]

At approximately the same time as the Olais trail, DeNike took on the case of Pvt. Larry Johnson. Johnson was a black GI working as a desk clerk at the Strasbourg Kaserne in Idar-Oberstein. After reading an article in *Jet* magazine about the colonial war in Mozambique and the brutalities that Portuguese soldiers committed against the guerillas, Johnson became concerned about his government's support of Portugal. He expressed his concern to his captain, but felt that the officer's recommendation that he write to his congressman was an inadequate and disappointing response. After consulting with Howard DeNike, Johnson decided to unilaterally resign from the army. He failed to report for work, refused orders to muster in the morning, stopped saluting his superiors, and stopped wearing his uniform.[90] Accordingly, the authorities charged him with four violations of the Uniform Code of Military Justice.[91] DeNike and his client harbored no illusions that he could escape conviction. Johnson's stated purpose was to turn the trial into a political demonstration against U.S. support for Portugal in Mozambique. To help him in his endeavor, Max Watts contacted a Catholic missionary whom the Portuguese had expelled from Mozambique for protesting the slaughter. DeNike called upon the priest as a witness at the trial on June 19, 1973.[92] While Johnson received the political trial he had wanted, the jury found him guilty on three of the four charges and sentenced him to a month of hard labor and a forfeiture of pay.[93] In July 1973, the army eliminated Johnson from service, deeming him unfit to serve.[94]

A comparison of these cases illustrates the fact that the use of military trials as an activist strategy often had very divergent goals, and the success of the strategy varied accordingly. In the case of Olais, the goal was to clarify to what extent individual freedoms were granted to soldiers in the army. The trial demonstrated that GIs had a right to express their political opinions within certain boundaries. The Johnson trial was a political demonstration exposing one of the darker sides of U.S. foreign policy. In the first trial the activists actually succeeded in carving out a little space in which GIs could express themselves. It is doubtful that the Johnson trial achieved its goal. Despite the bravery with which Johnson faced his trial and certain conviction, the trial did not generate much publicity or heighten awareness of U.S. participation in Portugal's colonial war. Johnson's conviction was eventually revoked. However, this had nothing to do with the merits of his political stance, as will be seen further below.

One issue that provided the Lawyers' Military Defense Committee with similar traction as the Olais case was the plan developed by the army leadership to combat the growing drug abuse problem in their commands. In their efforts to identify drug users, local commanders at some bases reverted to questionable methods even in the eyes of military lawyers. The use of surprise inspections, referred to as "full court press," to locate drugs and identify drug abusers was controversial. Not all military judges accepted evidence against an alleged drug user gained during such so-called health, safety, and welfare inspections.[95] Activists argued that the "full court press" was a search without cause, a clear violation of soldiers' civil rights.

Methods like this and a drug program instated by the community commander at Nellingen Barracks gave the Lawyers' Military Defense Committee an opportunity to put the entire Seventh Army on trial. As part of the "Nellingen Anti-Drug Movement," suspected drug users could be restricted to barracks or lose privileges, such as pass privileges or permission to wear civilian clothes while off duty. Furthermore, officers could remove the door of a suspected drug user's room and take his possessions.[96] DeNike and Rivkin collected affidavits describing the worst abuses. They filed the lawsuit on behalf of the Committee for GI Rights representing the members' interests in a class action suit. According to DeNike, the committee existed more on paper than in reality.[97] With the help of Robert Rivkin and the ACLU, the committee filed a suit against the secretary of the army and the entire leadership of USAREUR before the U.S. District Court in Washington DC.[98] The lawsuit ultimately failed. However, Rivkin and DeNike had been successful in forcing USAREUR to clarify its drug abuse policies and to curb excessive behavior on the part of its commanders. Of the different strategies expressing dissent, trials were the most viable. They did not require large numbers of dissidence to be effective. As in the case of Olais or the GI Committee, the trials did force the military leadership to review or change policies and behavior.

To Rivkin and DeNike, the significance of the antidrug policies exposed during the trial proceedings extended beyond encouraging officers in USAREUR "to institute a multitude of illegal measures to terrorize the troops into foregoing drugs and informing on their buddies." The program unleashed commanders "to exercise the harassing tactics of their choice against all those men in their units whom they merely suspect of being users or pushers." Thus USAREUR had officially authorized and encouraged "illegal punishment without trial."[99] To antiwar activists, as expressed in the *Bond*, an underground paper, the crackdown on drug abuse was just an excuse used by a "Brass" growing "panicky over the politicization of GIs in Germany and the rapid growth of underground newspapers."[100] While the chapter on the drug abuse problem will show that drug use was more than just a pretext to excuse a crackdown on perceived deviants, the *Bond's* characterization of the USAREUR commanders' response to protest activities as panicky is not entirely out of place.

The anxiety that the activism of Max Watts and the Lawyers' Military Defense Committee provoked in some commanders led them to implement countermeasures that would lead to a major scandal in the summer of 1973. In July 1973 SP4 John M. McDougal, normally referred to as Mike McDougal, approached Howard DeNike to inform him that some of his phone discussions concerning his client Larry Johnson had been wiretapped.[101] McDougal was working for military intelligence at the time and had run across reports on such phone conversations. DeNike was not the primary object of the wiretap. In May 1971 USAREUR military intelligence had asked German authorities to conduct telephone surveillance of Max Watts. The phone conversation that McDougal had alerted DeNike to had been between the lawyer and Watts.[102] McDougal in working for military intelligence had apparently suffered from a pang of consciousness in the wake of the Watergate scandal and felt compelled to go public with what he knew.[103]

The German *Verfassungsschutz* conducted the wiretaps, sending typed transcripts to the "Military Intelligence Group" in Kaiserslautern. In addition to conversations between Watts and DeNike, the German agents had also recorded talks between Watts and an editor of the *Frankfurter Rundschau*, a daily newspaper, the editor of the *"Berliner Extradienst,"* Rudi Schwinn, and the pastor who had worked in Mozambique.[104] The USAREUR leadership initially refused to publicly comment on the surveillance, but promised an inquiry into the matter.[105] After the *New York Times* published a report on the matter, obviously using information from Max Watts, the Defense Department confirmed that there had been surveillance of civilian antiwar organizations in Germany.[106] A Senate investigation conducted that summer indicated that the military had been engaged in a more comprehensive intelligence operation. Army intelligence, headed at the time by Maj. Gen. Harold R. Aaron, had infiltrated radical dissident and pro-McGovern groups. The broader intelligence effort was justified by the Pentagon with a reference to two bomb attacks on army installations in Germany in May 1972.[107] Army leaders further contended that the low morale engendered by the GIs' weak economic position and the post-Vietnam malaise made soldiers "an easier target for subversive propaganda from the outside."[108]

That the army wiretapping scandal came to light in the summer of 1973 at the height of the Watergate affair was not a coincidence. Mike McDougal claimed that it had been the revelations gained from reports on Watergate that had caused him to approach DeNike and later the media.[109] The Watergate panel also took an interest in the army's surveillance activities. One member of the panel, Republican senator Lowell P. Weicker Jr., headed an investigation into the matter. As a member of the Watergate panel, Weicker was primarily interested in the surveillance of U.S. citizens abroad, particularly civilians supporting Democratic presidential candidate George S. McGovern.[110] Twenty members of this group of supporters would take the army to court over the illegal surveillance and win a ruling against the army at the Federal District Court in Washington DC two years later.[111] One year later the staff of the Senate Select Committee on Intelligence Activities concluded that the army had indeed conducted a widespread surveillance program both at home and abroad.[112]

Despite the promise to conduct its own inquiry in 1973, the army leadership's main concern was to make the story go away. Howard DeNike and Robert Rivkin sent several letters to military leaders demanding an investigation into the wiretaps. At first their demand was part of their efforts to appeal the conviction of their client Larry Johnson.[113] It had been Johnson's case among other matters that DeNike and Watts had been discussing when the military intelligence was listening in.[114] Two years later, evidence would emerge that army intelligence had not only wiretapped conversations carried on by the lawyers but had actually placed an informant in the lawyers' office.[115]

The U.S. and German press continued to cover the issue of army surveillance of dissidents with the LMDC and Max Watts feeding journalists information on army activities.[116] During a press conference on August 10, 1973, a spokesman denied that USAREUR was "conducting an intensified counterintelligence drive against the GI underground." However, in the same announcement, the spokesman disclosed that a division-level anti-dissidence program had been rescinded, a somewhat paradoxical claim.[117] The spokesman issued the denial two days after the *New York Times* had published an article describing exactly that program. The army's Eighth Infantry division had issued the program on June 23, 1973. As in the case of the wiretapping a soldier, SP4 Wayne W. Sparks, who believed the army's actions to be illegal, provided civilian activists, in this instance Max Watts, with evidence proving that program against dissidence had been conducted.[118]

The reason provided for rescinding the program was that "the document was determined to be inappropriate." The "guidance on dissent contained in Army regulations" was deemed sufficient. Furthermore, according to the spokesman, soldier dissent within the command was at a very low level at the time.[119] The assertion that dissent was at a *very* low level was maybe a little exaggerated, but not entirely inaccurate. Non-race-related protest activities remained scattered and disorganized. However, this did not prevent some military commanders from overreacting to any sign of dissent in their units.

The Eighth Division counterdissidence program shows that the threshold of tolerance was low. Mainly the document reiterated USAREUR regulations dealing with dissidence, but it also provided commanders with instructions on what to look out for in regard to dissidence activity. The purpose of the program, as stated in the introduction, was to coordinate information gathering efforts on dissidence within the Eighth Infantry Division. The assistant chief of staff had the responsibility to ensure coordination with SSA, PM, CID, EOSO, and MI. Furthermore, he was to ensure "the accurate and timely reporting of dissident incidents throughout the division" and "complete division-wide reports for analysis to aid in pinpointing potential trouble areas and prevent further dissident activities." Finally, he was to guide commanders in handling problem areas of dissident activities. On the brigade and battalion level, the intelligence officers were in charge of implementing the program. These responsibilities included compiling and analyzing dissident activities and keeping their immediate superiors aware of the "dissident climate."[120]

The intelligence officers were to report on all acts of sabotage or vandalism, theft of weapons, ammunition, or explosives, or penetration of secure areas. Measures against offenses in these areas were not particularly controversial, but other areas were more problematic. Officers were to report on "demonstrations, teach-ins, and other activities with anti-American themes engaged in by local nationals or military personnel," as well as on "unauthorized meetings with controversial topics." Characterizations such as these led to the surveillance of civilians and provided groups such as the Lawyers' Military Defense Committee with ammunition for their struggle to preserve soldiers' civil rights. Officers were required further to report on "efforts by dissident or subversive influences (military or civilian) to promote disaffection or dissidence among military personnel," as well as the "distribution of unauthorized publications" and the "formation of groups with controversial purposes or racially exclusive membership." This latter point indicates that the leadership of Eighth Division was particularly concerned about racial dissidence. The regulations included a request to report "serious incidents and crimes with racial overtones or motives, including assaults by members of one racial group upon members of another. Finally, officers were to report the full names, SSAN, ranks, units, and *races* of individuals who were involved in any of the cited activities.[121]

The regulation also contained a list of indicators of dissidence. The threshold was not high. "Complaints to NCO's, officers, IG, news media, or Congress about living conditions, harassment, unfair treatment etc." were the first indicators. The next level included the "frequent circumvention of chain of command or use of extra–chain of command vehicles such as 'spokesmen' to voice grievances." Other indicators mentioned were unauthorized meetings and formation of groups intended to address grievances, demonstrations, and frequent minor acts of insubordination or insolence. Officers needed to be wary of the presence of civilian extremists on their posts or of their personnel attending extremist meetings off post. The regulation offered no definition of an extremist. The distribution of underground newspapers and dissident graffiti were further signs of dissident activity as well as other forms of vandalism. Finally, the list included "confrontations with symbols of authority," the "escalation of minor incidents, exaggeration of incidents to provoke troop reaction, the circulation of rumors," and "agitation by military personnel or by civilians."[122]

Annex D of the regulations provided additional clarification of the laws and regulations concerning dissidence. Many of the laws and regulations cited dealt with the distribution of political flyers and underground newspapers. Another major concern was servicemen's participation in political rallies and demonstrations, the possession and use of privately owned firearms, or possession of destructive devices. Commanders were "not authorized to recognize or to bargain with a servicemen's union." However, the guidelines acknowledged that commanders could not constitutionally prohibit mere association with or membership in such a union.[123]

The Eighth Division quickly rescinded the antidissidence program. Nonetheless, it does point to a low degree of tolerance among commanders for any type of dissent. The fact that intelligence officers were in charge of countering dissidence shows an unwillingness to engage with dissidence in a more public manner. The covert attitude toward dealing with the problem stands in marked contrast to commanders like Davison publicly acknowledging that the army still had ways to go to end discrimination in its ranks or, as will be seen later, that the army had to do more to help drug-addicted GIs. The surveillance program against Max Watts and the LMDC was not the only instance in which army leadership tried to counteract civilian organizing.

In September 1973, city authorities in Heidelberg ordered civilian activist Karen Bixler, a U.S. citizen and a student enrolled at the university, to leave the country. The rationale for her expulsion was her involvement in the underground GI paper *Fight Back.* The city officials alleged that she had been mainly responsible for the contents of four issues of the paper that had appeared in 1973.[124] The three most objectionable items from the city's viewpoint were an article comparing Nixon and Hitler, a cartoon depicting Nixon as the "Pig of the

Month," and an article titled "Sailors Show How to Fight Back," which called upon readers to sabotage the U.S. armed forces. According to the Heidelberg authorities, the articles published threatened the constitutional order of the Federal Republic of Germany. German law prohibited the sabotage of Allied troops in Germany.[125] Sedition among American troops was endangering the safety of West Germany. Seditious activities were a burden to German-American relations.[126]

The expulsion order elicited protests from *Fight Back* as well as from students and faculty members at the University of Heidelberg.[127] Press accounts reveal that the city did not take action unilaterally but that the state government of Baden-Württemberg had prompted the actions. The government in turn admitted at a press conference that a third party brought Bixler to its attention.[128] There seemed to be little doubt among contemporaries that the third party was the U.S. Army.[129] Bixler saved herself from deportation by marrying her German boyfriend and father of her child.[130] *Fight Back* hailed the withdrawal of the deportation order as a victory of the GI movement and simultaneously tried to downplay the significance of the marriage in preventing Bixler's deportation.[131] The army leadership's tactics in this matter mirrored similar efforts in the United States where civilian authorities were encouraged to seek legal means to stop civilian activists from engaging in their work around military bases.

While press coverage forced the army to publicly renounce some of its harsher antidissidence measures, it had other means of limiting the influence of activists. Probably one of the more effective measures was to transfer "troublemakers" to other bases and assignments. This strategy was employed after the Darmstadt 53 trial. Another instance occurred when, in January 1973, six GI activists, the majority of whom had worked on the Wiesbaden underground newspaper *FTA with Pride,* were transferred back home to the United States early. Howard DeNike was able to delay and eventually cancel the reassignment of one of the activists, Terry Botts, but he was not able to prevent the departure of the other five.[132]

Overall dissident activities not related to racial issues received less public attention. General Davison did not mention antiwar activism within the ranks as a major problem area, despite its frequent invocation by the press, although he certainly expressed concern about race-related issues. When asked during an oral interview whether he had considered dissent in the command a problem, General Persons responded negatively. He acknowledged that there had been some groups, but that they had not been effective.[133] While Persons's opinion of activists' effectiveness was not inaccurate, fellow officers did not necessarily share his lack of concern at the time. The counterdissidence program and even more the counterintelligence efforts brought to light by the scandal show that army leadership was indeed apprehensive and far less accommodating in their response than on issues of race.[134] Despite the relatively small number of actual GI activists, commanders displayed little tolerance toward dissidents. However, when the army faced public scrutiny on its treatment of dissidents and civilian activists as in the case of the wiretapping or the counterdissidence program, army leadership retreated.

After 1973, activists found it increasingly difficult to find issues around which to organize soldiers. Few troops remained in Vietnam, taking away the most powerful issue for organizing protest. The topics covered in *Fight Back* appearing after 1974 broadly fit into three categories: attempts to raise soldiers' political awareness, attempts to educate soldiers on their rights and personal freedom, and reports on incidents of dissidence on bases in Germany.

In an attempt to raise political awareness, the editors of *Fight Back* wrote articles contextualizing current events within their ideological convictions and trying to make enlisted men more conscious of class differences. One example was the energy crisis. The editors of *Fight Back* argued that oil corporations had manufactured the crisis to obtain further concessions and tax breaks from leaders of the U.S. government with whom the corporations had a cozy relationship. According to *Fight Back*, the issue was important for soldiers not only because they were taxpaying citizens but also because the oil companies' desire to lower costs of Middle Eastern oil could lead to a military intervention. Playing with Woodrow Wilson's famous quote, they speculated that GIs might be called upon "to keep the Middle East safe for Standard Oil, Esso, etc."[135] After the oil embargo ended, *Fight Back* saw its analysis validated because the energy crisis had not ended. Instead, they told soldiers that the energy crisis was just part of a greater economic crisis brought on by the corporations and their efforts to control wages and curb unions. The recent strikes by truckers and coal miners in the United States were signs that "the people of America are building a powerful movement to kick Nixon out and let all the rulers know that we are fed up with all their corruption and lies."[136]

One issue that was gaining new prominence was women's struggle for equal rights. Up until 1974, activist organizing among GIs had made no mention of women's struggles. The March issue of *Fight Back* was devoted to International Women's Day. The cover of the issue featured the picture of an African woman's face surrounded by smaller pictures of women of different races raising their fists or holding guns underlined by the subtitle "Sisters."[137] Inside the issue the editors explained the significance of March 8, linking women's struggle against oppression to more general struggles against racism and capitalist oppression.[138] However, the editors also tied women's issues to military life. One article describes the everyday sexism prevalent among officers and very apparent in basic training where recruits were "feminized" as a form of humiliation and then built up to be "men." These sexist attitudes made life difficult for the 50,000 women in the military at the time.[139] The status of women in the army was quickly changing during this period. By 1974 U.S. Army, Europe had dissolved its one remaining Women's Army Corps company. Women in USAREUR now served alongside men.[140]

However, the problem of sexism extended to the wives of soldiers in Germany whose classification as "dependents" characterized their treatment by the army, which viewed wives not as individuals but as the property of their husbands. If a wife did something wrong, her husband would get punished.[141] Spouses provided much of the cheap civilian labor on the bases, because families could not subsist on the father's income alone. The woman writing in *Fight Back* felt that army doctors did not treat spouses well. She felt isolated and powerless.

In order to connect what was happening in the army to the host country, *Fight Back* also reported on a group of civilian American and German women occupying a house in Heidelberg scheduled for demolition that they wanted to save and turn into a women's center. Initially the women were successful in remaining in the house and turning away the police, but after a week the German police returned with reinforcements and removed the women by force. Even though the women had to yield in the end, the editors of *Fight Back* argued that the fact that the demonstrators had been able to occupy the building for a week showed that collective action could be effective in bringing about change.[142]

After the publication of the issue devoted to International Women's Day, *Fight Back* continued to treat the women's struggle as a major topic. Issue 19 featured an article from a stateside underground paper where a woman enlisted in the air force related her frustrations about her treatment by the military.[143] Issue 23 featured an article on attempts to recruit more women into the new all-volunteer army. The author argued that while the army had been taking advantage of liberation by advertising the military as a place where women could gain their independence, the reality for women in the army was quite different. According to *Fight Back*, the women were merely filling slots opening up because more and more men were realizing that the army had little to offer beside drudgery. Instead of receiving job and leadership training, women were performing the same "Mickey Mouse" chores as the men and receiving even less respect. Many service men saw them as little more than "government paid prostitutes." At the same time, recruiters seduced young men "with promises of increasing numbers of women."[144] The Library of Congress interview with Beverly Jean Brown corroborates the paper's depictions. As a captain in USAREUR, Brown had to deal with male superiors asking her about the "lesbian problem" among her female soldiers, revealing her superiors' biases regarding both gender and sexuality. The article concluded that providing volunteers with training and the means for becoming independent was not the army's primary goal. It trained men and women for war, be it as combatants or support. Women's liberation meant not sharing responsibility for making war but resisting war by "resisting the militarization of womanhood."

While discussions of women's liberation could sit uncomfortably with coverage of the new all-volunteer military, the prominence of the issue and articles on matters such as the oil crisis marked a new trend in *Fight Back*. From 1974 onward, coverage of activism in USAREUR decreased. Fewer and fewer articles appeared on racial incidents or on enlisted men facing court-martial for resisting orders. Most issues provided information on the personal rights of soldiers in the army and gave soldiers advice on how to protect their rights and resist violations. The paper repeatedly informed soldiers about Article 138 of the UCMJ. Article 138 was a provision of the UCMJ that allowed any soldier who believed himself wronged by his superior to complain to any superior officer. Any complaint filed under the article had to go up the chain of command all the way up to the secretary of the army, and the investigation of such a complaint by the authorities was obligatory.[145] The LMDC had put the provision to very effective use.[146] DeNike and Rivkin liked using the provision because nobody had "any clear understanding of its scope, since it had almost never been tested in scope." Soldiers could claim that their commanding officers had deprived them of "a property right, or abused his command discretion, or otherwise dealt with him unjustly in a field other than discipline." The only shortfall of the provision was that discipline tied in to almost all aspects of military life.[147] The LMDC was able to put the provision to good use because the prospect of an investigation alone could scare officers seeking a career into compromising on a legal action.[148] *Fight Back* provided readers with a step-by-step guideline as to what constituted an Article 138 complaint and how to file it.[149] The article also listed the contact information for the LMDC. *Fight Back* reprinted the advice in later issues.[150]

Another provision that *Fight Back* discussed was Article 139, Injuries to Property. The article urged soldiers whose superiors had confiscated their property to file a grievance. The activist emphasis was, of course, on political literature or posters. If the complaint procedure led to no results, the paper advised GIs to press charges. Pressing charges could result in court-martial for officers or NCOs who had wrongfully confiscated a soldier's personal property. Even without conviction, getting superiors into this kind of trouble would "be fun."[151] The main point of providing this legal advice was to encourage soldiers to disrupt army routines and aggravate superiors. Judging from the content of the available papers printed in 1974 and beyond, the advice did not lead to major disruptions worth reporting on.

The issues of *Fight Back* published in 1974 and thereafter provided little coverage of protest activities on bases. One of the few topics that appeared to still get some traction was the length of soldiers' hair. The February issue carried two articles. In one article African American GIs expressed their frustration about prohibitions against wearing their hair in braids even though they believed this did not violate army regulations on hairstyle. The article pointed out that the army was once more discriminating against black soldiers by ignoring their cultural preferences. The second article related an incident in Gelnhausen near Frankfurt where a captain performing inspection not only ordered two-thirds of his company to get haircuts but actually marched them to the post barbershop. When some of the men claimed to have no money with them and insisted on going to a barber of their own choosing, the lieutenant in charge ordered them to get the haircut immediately. The soldiers were able to successfully resist the order because their CO deemed the matter too trivial. To *Fight Back* this proved how much power a group of soldiers resisting could wield if they stuck together.[152]

Fight Back covered two court cases centered on hair length. The first case was that of an airman in England who refused to have his hair cut. The judge sentenced him to four months of hard labor, loss of pay, loss of rank, and a bad conduct discharge.[153] In September 1974 an enlisted man named Louis Stokes faced trial for his refusal to cut his hair. To prove that the army's regulation infringed on Stokes's rights, his lawyer called upon female soldiers and soldiers from the Dutch army, which at the time had no hair length regulations, to prove that long hair interfered in no way with a soldier's duties. The lawyer also called upon an even more prominent resister in the hair length struggle, 1st Lt. Matt Carroll, who was also refusing to cut his hair but who had not up to that point been court-martialed, an oversight the army would soon correct.[154]

Carroll's case was probably the most famous hair length case in Germany. Carroll had originally been an engineer officer, but his last assignment before his involvement in the hair length matter had been as an equal opportunity officer. Working in this function Carroll became convinced that the army was treating its soldiers unfairly and started growing his hair in protest. The official reaction was to reassign him to an engineer battalion and to order him to cut his hair. Carroll refused the order and an Article 15 punishment. The matter would have gone to trial if Carroll had not resigned from the army.[155]

Fight Back asserted that the army was engaged in a losing battle when it came to GIs' hair length. The recent trials had shown that individuals were willing to go to jail, if necessary. The army had to accept that long hair had become normal both in the United States and Europe. Soldiers would no longer accept the military cut.[156] Hair regulations according to the writers of *Fight Back* were just an instrument of oppression, a means to keep soldiers separate from the population.

The *Fight Back* articles of 1974 indicate that the GI movement, never a mass movement to begin with, had lost its driving issue, the Vietnam War. Efforts to get GIs involved in greater ideological issues and struggles, such as capitalism or women's liberation, had little effect. Daily grievances and frustrations of enlisted men were covered and tied to a wider class struggle. One of the most popular features of *Fight Back* was the nomination of a "Pig of the Month" in every issue. The "Pig of the Month" was usually an officer or senior noncommissioned officer who had a reputation for harassing his troops.[157] Such harassment was an expression of the class struggle taking place within the military with the officers and NCOs as lackeys or the fascist or capitalist oppressors. While the letters to the editor in the papers show that individual soldiers were grateful that the paper allowed them to vent some of their frustrations about military life, this did not inspire them to participate in greater protest movements.

By 1978 protest activities in USAREUR had petered out completely. The publication of *Fight Back* and *Forward* ceased. During its ten years of existence, RITA had not managed to bring about a revolution within the army ranks. As long as the Vietnam War lasted, civilian and GI activists had managed to voice soldiers' dissent against this endeavor. While the protest culture within the army never became a mass movement, activists had succeeded in bringing publicity to various problem areas and had contributed to the general perception of declining morale and discipline in the Seventh Army. Army leadership never publicly addressed the specific grievances of antiwar activists. Instead army intelligence started a massive counterintelligence program that ultimately proved to be out of proportion to the threat posed by dissidents. However, army leaders did address the general morale problem that these protest activities exemplified.

In their efforts to turn the army into an all-volunteer force, Army leaders recognized that they needed to make the army attractive to volunteers. In preparation for the switch, the army implemented a program named VOLAR (Volunteer Army Field Experiment).[158] As part of the program, selected bases in the Unites States and Germany eliminated certain irritants of army life such as reveille and nonmilitary duties, such as KP (kitchen patrol) duty, window washing, or grass cutting. The army permitted soldiers more privacy and freedom on base. This included the relaxation of hair length standards, individual partitioning of barrack rooms, and permission to buy and consume beer on the barracks ground. Overall Davison deemed VOLAR a success in Germany. Particularly successful was the part of the program that let the army hire civilians to take over the unpopular additional duties. It provided army dependents with employment and freed up the soldiers for training. Davison also reported that the freer lifestyle arrangements had no adverse effect on the discipline of the troops.[159] While the army did not develop VOLAR as a direct response to the morale and discipline in USAREUR, it did play a role limiting dissent. As civilian activists found out, few GIs responded to their more ideological arguments to organize political resistance within the army. The issues that gained traction among soldiers included frustration over additional cleanup duty, lack of privacy, or officers overly concerned with military etiquette. The VOLAR program as a precursor to the all-volunteer army addressed some of those issues treating enlisted men as responsible individuals. Just as with race relations, programs designed to take soldiers' concerns seriously helped in reducing tensions, while attempts to maintain a hard line or to suppress soldiers' grievances backfired. This pattern would repeat itself in the army leadership's handling of the drug abuse problem.

BETWEEN PUNISHMENT

AND REHABILITATION

On July 4, 1971, the *Baltimore Sun* published an article voicing concern about the wide use of hashish among troops in Germany. According to the *Sun*, 70 percent of the soldiers below age twenty-five had tried hashish and at least 10–15 percent were habitual users. While the use of heroin was not widespread, "amphetamines, barbiturates, tranquilizers, LSD, and especially hashish" were "cheap and easily obtainable in Western Europe."[1] Such articles shifted public attention on drug abuse in the military from Vietnam to Germany.

Unlike the issue of racial discrimination, drug abuse did not have a long history as a prominent issue in the U.S. military. This is not to say that there had been no drug abuse. But prior to 1969, it had never been a major concern, and it had certainly never been connected to the military in the same way as during the Vietnam War.[2] Use of opium, marijuana, or heroin did not emerge as a major social or political issue in the United States until the first half of the twentieth century. That half century saw a growing consensus in the government and society that the use of such drugs was a crime. This assumption informs much of the debate to this very day and was a major stumbling block in establishing programs in the military that were aimed at rehabilitating drug users.

Struggles within the army in regard to dealing with drug abuse were informed by the debates of the 1960s, when the consensus on the criminality of drug use was challenged not only by members of the so-called counterculture but also by health experts and officials who defined drug use and addiction to drugs as a public health issue. While the U.S. military's drug programs were informed by the public debates, the military was also an important factor in bringing concern for the addict into the equation. The perception of widespread drug abuse among GIs in Vietnam and returning veterans, men who had served their country, made it difficult to criminalize all users. While rehabilitation would not replace law enforcement as the primary means to combat drug use and addiction, it would become an increasingly important part of government policy. The initiatives of the Nixon administration in its War on Drugs are an important prerequisite to discussing drug abuse in the military. Not only were many measures a direct response to the growing abuse in the military, but the government's approach framed the military's.

Chapter 7 provides the historical background needed to contextualize the army's approach to drug abuse and will then outline the army's response to the growing drug use in its ranks, focusing particularly on Vietnam, which was an important precursor to events and measures taken in Germany.

7

Drug Abuse Prevention in the U.S. Government

Before 1900, the United States had shown very little interest in the regulation of drugs. Substances such as cannabis or opium and its derivatives morphine and cocaine were legal and widely used for prescription medication as well as for over-the-counter medicines.[3] Elements of the Progressive movement concerned with health issues and combating perceived vices such as drinking, gambling, and prostitution also became concerned about the addictive properties of other substances.[4] While the prohibition of alcohol remained the main focus, "mind-altering" substances became an increasing concern throughout the first three decades of the twentieth century. Veterans' addiction to morphine and the accessibility of opiates to soldiers and sailors serving in the Far East was one of the concerns that fueled reformers' desire to control narcotics.

The Harrison Act of 1914 was the first major legislation on narcotics in the United States. However, its aim was the control, not the prohibition of drugs. It required "every person who produces, imports, manufactures, compounds, deals in, dispenses, sells, distributes, or gives away opium or coca leaves" to register with the collector of internal revenue in his district.[5] The passage of the bill went almost unnoticed by the general population, which was far more interested in the debate over alcohol prohibition.[6] Narcotics remained an afterthought.

However, the consensus among lawmakers, physicians, pharmacists, and prominent newspapers was that opiates and cocaine "predisposed habitués toward insanity and crime." The public imagination most often linked the evils of such substances with minorities or foreigners. Opiates were linked to the Chinese population while the image of the "cocaine crazed Negro" was also prevalent.[7] These preconceptions helped foment a consensus among white Americans about the moral evil that narcotics posed. Groups and individuals involved in the prohibition movement also denounced the consumption of opiates and cocaine as the equivalent to drinking.

In the heated atmosphere created by the movement, officials from the Treasury Department charged with enforcing the Harrison Act increasingly interpreted the act as a prohibitive rather than a regulatory law. These officials would arrest addicts and the doctors who prescribed narcotics to them. After 1919 the Supreme Court handed down decisions that supported the Treasury Department, which in 1920 had formed a Narcotics Division.[8] Prohibition also began in 1919. A series of national scares helped the prohibitionist cause from the anti-German propaganda during World War I to the Red Scare of 1919–20. Americans were afraid of succumbing to foreign influences. The number of addicts and the drug-related crime rate were widely exaggerated by prohibitionist crusaders, such as Richmond P. Hobson, who claimed that there were a million heroin addicts in the United States in 1928.[9]

Awareness of narcotics abuse as an issue in the armed forces mirrored developments in society. The armed forces had recognized drunkenness coupled with some types of conduct as a military offense. It had even recognized that substances other than alcohol could cause "drunkenness." However, not until 1917 did the army specifically address habit-forming narcotic drugs in the *Manual for Courts-Martial* and a year later in a general order by the War Department prohibiting the wrongful possession of habit-forming drugs.[10]

By 1930 the U.S. government had established a predominantly punitive rather than regulatory or medical approach to narcotic drugs. In this year the Narcotics Division of the Treasury Department became the Federal Bureau of Narcotics, and the Hoover administration appointed Harry Anslinger as its director.[11] He would dominate federal drug policy for the next thirty years and continue the trend to make drug abuse a law enforcement issue. He conducted an aggressive media campaign to reinforce antidrug attitudes and argued against the notion that drug abuse was a disease rather than a crime. He successfully lobbied with state governments to adopt a Uniform State Narcotic Law that was mainly punitive in nature. His activities played an important role in forging a public consensus against marijuana. Anslinger repeatedly linked marijuana to criminal actions and lobbied to delete the substance from the annals of legitimate medicinal substances. The FBN assisted in writing and passing the Marijuana Tax Act of 1937.[12]

Once again developments in military law mirrored those in society. During World War II, marijuana was treated as a "habit-forming drug," the use, possession, and introduction of which was prohibited, because marijuana produced a "deleterious effect upon human conduct and behavior" that was inconsistent with the "requirements of military efficiency and discipline."[13] By 1949 marijuana offenses were included in the *Manual for Courts-Martial*. With the enactment of the Uniform Code of Military Justice in 1950, military authorities no longer deemed the distinctions regarding the type of drug involved in an offense relevant.[14]

By the late 1940s a broad public consensus had emerged that drug abuse was a menace to society that called for a punitive approach rather than a therapeutic/medical one. The FBN was successful in using the political atmosphere of the beginning Cold War to establish harsh mandatory sentences for drug possession. Fear of Soviet aggression, communist subversion, and the Mafia aided the FBN. Between 1900 and the 1950s the perception of drug abuse had gone from a mostly ignored medical problem to a serious criminal problem requiring stiff punitive measures.[15] Distinctions between the use and the abuse of drugs or between more or less harmful drugs became blurred. Despite these developments, overall drug abuse remained a minor political and social issue in the 1950s. The debate that did begin to develop late in the decade "among medical and legal professionals over how best to deal with what was mostly a problem of inner-city heroin addiction was at first a fairly low key affair."[16]

During the 1960s, drug abuse would become a growing concern. The resignation of Harry Anslinger in 1962 and the emerging health bureaucracy within the federal government brought drug abuse as a medical problem back into the larger debate.[17] That same year the Supreme Court ruled that addiction was a disease, not a criminal act. Psychiatrist-administrators from the National Mental Hygiene Division, which had been created in 1946 and had grown into an agency whose budget dwarfed that of the FBN, argued that addiction was a physical and psychological disease requiring treatment by medical professionals.[18]

In 1964 drug abuse was still a minor concern among the general public. But the issue rose to prominence as drug consumption among middle-class youth increased dramatically in 1966 and 1967. The negative public attitude had not softened significantly. The Johnson administration made drug control part of its agenda, not purely out of necessity but also because of the perceived political gain. With growing middle-class drug consumption, the public felt increasingly threatened by drugs. These fears were disproportionate in relation to the actual extent of the problem that was far from critical. The erroneous reasoning among some officials was that acting decisively on such a problem would garner support but would require only a small expenditure of money and interest.[19]

The Johnson administration maintained the primacy of law enforcement, but put greater emphasis on treatment and rehabilitation. Johnson formed the Advisory Commission on Narcotic and Drug Abuse. Its goal was the complete termination of drug and narcotic use through law enforcement and medical treatment rather than just law enforcement. In reaction to the Advisory Commission's report, Johnson issued a statement calling upon all federal units involved in antidrug activities to work toward "(1) the destruction of the illegal traffic in drugs, (2) the prevention of drug abuse, and (3) the cure and rehabilitation of victims of this traffic." On November 8, 1966, Johnson signed the Narcotic Rehabilitation Act (NARA) into law. The administration had introduced the act as a measure to provide addicts with means to rehabilitate themselves. However, the bill remained limited in scope partially because Johnson did not want to appear weak on crime and partially because Congress changed the provisions weakening the rehabilitative aspects of the bill even further. NARA would prove too complex to put into effect. The passage of the Comprehensive Drug Abuse and Control Act in October 1970 essentially replaced the previous bill.[20]

If the 1940s and 1950s were a period when the broad consensus among the American people was that narcotic drugs posed a moral evil that needed to be defeated through tough law enforcement, the presidencies of Kennedy and Johnson functioned as a mild corrective. The validity of the earlier consensus was not really questioned, but medical treatment was added to the formula as a necessary supplement to law enforcement.[21] The rising Health Bureaucracy had brought the medical aspects of drug abuse back into focus. Striking the right balance between punishment and rehabilitation would continue to characterize the debates over the issue during the Nixon administration. It would also become an important question in the army's struggle with drug abuse. The Johnson administration would set patterns for drug control policy that Nixon would pick up and expand, creating a coherent approach to the issue combining interdiction, law enforcement, and rehabilitation.

During his campaign for the presidency, Richard Nixon used the issue of drug abuse as a vehicle to portray himself as a candidate who was tough on crime.[22] Until then, crime had been a difficult issue for presidential candidates to tackle, since primary responsibility for law enforcement lay with states and municipalities. The issue of illegal drugs offered an opportunity for the federal government to get more involved. In a statement on September 17, 1968, Nixon expressed his concern over the rising crime rates connected to narcotics. Nixon called narcotics "the modern curse of youth" that his opponent, Hubert Humphrey, was doing little to address.[23] He proposed five steps the federal government would take if he became president. Because most drugs were not manufactured in the United States but smuggled into the country from abroad, the federal government could claim the issue as its responsibility, since it involved foreign policy, border protection, and interstate traffic. When Nixon took office in 1969, drug control immediately became important. In April 1969 the administration prepared a message to Congress outlining its policy.[24]

Nixon's strategy was effective because awareness of drug use had grown in the 1960s. Statistics presented by government officials on the increase of abuse were alarming. Rates of abuse were doubling and tripling. This led to the widespread perception that drug abuse was an important issue that the government had to deal with. However, the actual extent of drug abuse in the United States was hard to quantify despite the official statistics. Numbers varied wildly.[25] The often-confusing statistics led critics to argue that the Nixon administration had consciously inflated the numbers of users with its estimates from 1969 to 1971. The numbers had conveniently reached their peak in 1971 and started dropping in the election year 1972.[26]

Whether the government's estimates were inflated or not, public awareness and concern increased considerably during Nixon's first term. In May 1969 drug abuse had ranked comparatively low among respondents to a White House survey. When respondents were asked to name the most important problems facing people in the United States aside from Vietnam and foreign affairs, most named the "racial problem" (39 percent), "student unrest" (34 percent), or "crime/lack of law and order" (15 percent). Only 3 percent included drugs and alcohol abuse on the list. The Gallup Poll did not include drugs on its list of national fears until 1971, even though it used it in other contexts. By 1970 the issue had gained importance, according to polls. Of the six issues cited as the most important facing the United States, drugs moved from fifth place in January to third place in December.

When they were included in the list of national fears in 1971, drugs ranked seventh.[27]

The Nixon administration also became more involved in stopping the domestic drug traffic than previous governments, strengthening federal law enforcement agencies through new legislation. On July 14, 1969, Nixon announced a national "war on drugs." The announcement was a prelude to the introduction of the Controlled and Dangerous Substances Act of 1969.[28] On October 13, 1970, Congress passed the Comprehensive Drug Abuse Prevention and Control Act.

During the negotiations over both measures, debates ensued between administration officials in the Justice Department and the Department of Health, Education, and Welfare. The primary question was whether the government should treat drug abuse as a crime or as a disease. Agency rivalries partially motivated the debate. The agencies vied for overall responsibility for narcotics control efforts. Ultimately the Justice Department would win and maintain control of most aspects of the issue.[29] The inclination of the Nixon administration to treat the drug abuse primarily as a law enforcement issue was not surprising considering that Nixon wanted to appear tough on crime.

The Comprehensive Drug Abuse Prevention and Control Act contained some provisions indicating that the administration and members of Congress were also aware of drug abuse as a health issue. Congress abolished the death penalty for the sale of heroin to minors. First possession of narcotics and dangerous drugs became a misdemeanor rather than a felony, and Congress removed mandatory minimum sentences. Marijuana was no longer in the same category as heroin. Congress granted community mental health centers more money and authorized a number of grants for research and education.[30]

Once it had established the primacy of law enforcement with the passage of the Drug Abuse Act of 1970, the administration felt it had sufficient credibility to develop rehabilitation and treatment policies without looking soft on the issue. Prior to 1970, most emphasis in drug control policies outside of law enforcement had been on education, but the growing visibility of drug abuse among Americans forced the administration to consider rehabilitation and treatment. Growing public concern about addicted soldiers played an important role in rethinking programs.[31] The government could not dismiss men risking their lives for their country as mere criminals or lost causes. Accordingly, the administration had to find alternatives to a purely punitive approach.[32] The administration expanded federal oversight of and spending on treatment and rehabilitation at an unprecedented level.[33]

Government activity in regard to drug abuse peaked in the election year 1972. On January 28, 1972, Nixon announced the creation of the Office for Drug Abuse Law Enforcement within the Justice Department.[34] The White House held an antidrug conference for celebrity athletes in February and created a "Heroin Hot Line" in April, where citizens could anonymously tip off federal authorities on drug-trafficking activities they had observed.[35] In July three high-ranking officials overseeing the government law enforcement efforts reported that federal arrests for drug violations had nearly doubled since 1969. Nixon claimed that the public enemy was "on the run," and also took credit for what it described as a heroin "drought" on the East Coast.[36] He touted successful negotiations with France and Turkey as evidence that the supply was drying up.[37] Reports by government officials on the situation in the military also became increasingly optimistic.[38]

However, other reports indicated that the government's outlook was too optimistic. *The World Opium Survey, 1972*, published by the Cabinet Committee on International Narcotics Control, reported that while "the efforts of the U.S. government and others to interdict and eliminate the international traffic in heroin" were "beginning to have an impact on international trafficking," it also appeared that the international market had "adequate supplies to meet the demand in consuming countries."[39] The pronouncements on success in the military also appeared premature. This was partially due to the fact that reports on successes dealt primarily with Vietnam, where the number of active servicemen was steadily decreasing.

After 1972 the Nixon administration treated drug abuse with less urgency. On September 12, 1973, Nixon declared that the country had turned a corner on addiction.[40] As attention to the issue declined, however, attitudes hardened within the government. When the National Commission on Marijuana and Drug Abuse reported its findings, administration officials considered the conclusions to be too complex and too compromising. The commission, for example, recommended decriminalizing the possession of marijuana for personal use but maintaining that production and distribution should be illegal. Nixon argued that such a separation was not feasible. Marijuana could not be "half legal and half illegal." In March 1973, the government moved to revise the penalty structure on drugs. Nixon called for mandatory minimum sentences for heroin trafficking offenses and for restoring the death penalty for certain federal crimes. Introduced on March 20, at the height of the Watergate investigations, the legislation died without a vote.[41]

Under Nixon, the U.S. government did not fundamentally change its outlook on drug abuse, always retaining the primacy of law enforcement. However, treatment and rehabilitation became a greater concern, at least during Nixon's first term. The army's growing drug use problems strongly influenced this new emphasis. The perception of the problem had become more complex, and so had the approaches of the government to solve it. The military's drug abuse control programs reflected these changes. But the military went even further in the direction of rehabilitation and treatment. It continued this policy during the second Nixon administration and the Ford administration, despite hardening attitudes and waning interest in other branches of the government.

Drug abuse in the army was not an entirely new phenomenon when it rose to prominence in 1970. Cases of abuse and trafficking had occurred earlier. In November 1964, thirty-three American servicemen stationed in the Rhineland Palatinate were seized in a narcotics raid. German and American military police had conducted raids in Hanau and Kaiserslautern, arresting one hundred people, among them thirty-three GIs believed to be users.[42] In May 1966, Representative James R. Grover Jr. asked the House Armed Services Committee to investigate drug use in the military. Grover wanted Congress to determine whether servicemen were "receiving preventive education concerning the hazards as well as the adequacy of existing regulations and rehabilitative treatment."[43] One expert testified before Congress that he estimated that at least "10,000 to 15,000 heroin and barbiturate addicts" and "100,000 marijuana smokers" were serving in the military. The Pentagon, however, denied the allegations claiming that in Vietnam there had only been 44 cases of drug abuse involving 81 men. This, according to the Pentagon, amounted to 0.05 percent. The Pentagon further claimed that "widespread use of marijuana or narcotics by members of the armed forces could not go undetected" in either the United States or overseas because of the very nature of military service, which required a high degree of close supervision.[44]

Two years later, the Pentagon seemed to be less confident about its ability to identify drug users. On February 16, 1968, the *New York Times* reported that the Pentagon had "stepped up efforts to stem the use of marijuana and other drugs by servicemen in Vietnam." Investigations into the use, possession, and sale of marijuana among servicemen in Vietnam had increased drastically, from a little more than 40 in 1965 to 503 in 1966. During the first six months of 1967 alone, the number had risen to 549, and preliminary tallies quoted in the *Times* indicated a total of 1,267 marijuana investigations in 1967. That amounted to an incidence rate of 0.25 percent. Worldwide there had been 3,391 investigations compared with 3,096 in 1966 and 522 in 1965. More than half the investigations occurred in the United States. The Pentagon reacted to this increase by stepping up its education and law enforcement efforts. Rehabilitation did not yet figure greatly in its response.[45]

As military lawyer Maj. Charles G. Hoff Jr. pointed out, when it came to law enforcement, the military approach was "humane, responsive, responsible, and adaptable, in comparison with the federal system." According to Hoff, the *Manual for Courts-Martial* only prescribed a maximum sentence, no minimum, giving judge advocates more discretion than their civilian counterparts. The army also changed regulation 600-50, which dealt with drug abuse, to include depressant, stimulant, and hallucinogenic drugs in recognition that barbiturates, amphet-amines, and LSD were increasingly finding their way into the army.[46]

While the Pentagon conceded that there had been an increase in drug abuse investigations, officials also claimed that the higher figures were "a result of greater efforts to stem the use of the drug." This was a somewhat dubious claim, since that only indicated that the number of investigations and arrests did not reflect the rate of abuse in the military services. The question remains open whether the heightened interest in the issue of drug abuse after 1968 was a result of the increasing number of cases or whether the increased numbers reflected the heightened interest. However, ultimately the perception that drug abuse had become a critical threat to the effectiveness of the armed forces pushed the Pentagon into a more active engagement with the problem. Investigated drug cases in the armed forces tripled from 1968 to 1969 in regard to hard drugs and doubled in regard to marijuana.[47] Of the four services, the army and the marines had the highest rate of investigated personnel. In 1969 the army investigated more than fifteen per thousand soldiers for marijuana abuse in Vietnam and more than nine per thousand worldwide. Again, the numbers had nearly doubled since 1968.[48]

In June 1970 the *New York Times* published a report claiming that drug abuse and addiction were far greater problems than acknowledged by the armed forces.[49] In August of the same year Senate hearings drew further public attention. Members of a Pentagon task force on drug abuse admitted when questioned by senators that drug abuse in the armed forces was growing at an alarming rate.[50] In October the *Chicago Tribune* reported that 89 GIs had died of overdoses during the previous ten months in Vietnam.[51] A CBS broadcast from November 10, 1970, showed soldiers of the First Air Cavalry Division smoking marijuana at the fire support base Aires. A survey conducted by army psychologists in Vietnam showed widespread marijuana use among soldiers.[52]

The Nixon administration reacted to the public's concern. Nixon directed Secretary of Defense Dean Rusk to begin identifying drug users among the servicemen slotted to leave Vietnam within seven days in June 1971. He also ordered the establishment of detoxification and rehabilitation programs for identified abusers.[53] Hard drug use was a particular concern. In 1970, military services investigated more than 700 members for their involvement with hard drugs. The number rose to 800 in 1971. Under a new amnesty program, 6,700 members of the military forces in Vietnam asked for help and claimed their dependency. Heroin became the most popular hard drug. The heroin available in Southeast Asia was very potent because it was 95–98 percent pure.[54] So heroin tended to be smoked or inhaled rather than injected. Heroin could be obtained very easily in South Vietnam because the trade with opium, out of which heroin was derived, was an important factor in the power struggles and the corruption among many South Vietnamese officials. The opium was smuggled into South Vietnam from Laos and then shipped to other parts of the world.

The heroin from the Golden Triangle region increasingly found its way to GIs in South Vietnam.[55] GIs could buy 95 percent pure heroin on the street. Accordingly reports on heroin use were alarming. Of 3,103 soldiers of the American Division surveyed, 11.9 percent had tried heroin since they arrived in Vietnam and 6.6 percent identified themselves as regular users. By mid-1971, army medical officers estimated that between 25,000 and 37,000 junior enlisted men in Vietnam were using heroin.[56]

Until 1970, drug abuse efforts in the army had been mainly limited to prevention through law enforcement. The DOD launched its first effort in drug abuse education in 1968, but only started to develop a more comprehensive strategy in 1970. Under the impression of steadily increasing use of drugs among military personnel, a task group chaired by Vice Adm. William P. Mack formed in April 1970 to review the DOD's drug abuse policy.[57] The group recommended considering "recent trends in research, changes in social attitudes, and changes in administration policy." The task force maintained that the military had to deal with abusers quickly, firmly, and fairly. But it also suggested using enlightened methods that served "the best interests of the Government and the individual." The group agreed that rehabilitation of the individual should become a policy goal and proposed amnesty programs as a measure that would encourage soldiers to seek treatment and give them a chance to rehabilitate themselves. Amnesty meant that a commander would not criminally prosecute the soldier for possession or use of illegal drugs if the soldiers sought treatment voluntarily.[58] The argument was that medical treatment, education, and training could develop individual discipline.

The task force's recommendations led to the revision of the DOD directive 1300.11 on drug abuse in 1970. The directive recognized "both the necessity for curtailing drug abuse by service members and the varied nature of the military's obligation to respond to the problem." The armed forces had to curtail drug abuse because it could have a "seriously damaging effect" on a soldier's "health and mind." It could also "jeopardize his safety and the safety of his fellows" and would ultimately lead to criminal prosecution and a dishonorable discharge. The directive acknowledged the responsibility of the military services to counsel and protect their members against drug abuse and to restore them to useful service.[59]

As the number of troops in Vietnam steadily decreased after 1968, policy makers and military leaders realized that they would have to treat and rehabilitate more and more troops in the United States. Directive 1300.11 outlined the Pentagon's Drug Abuse Control Program. The overall responsibility for the program was assigned to the assistant secretary of defense for manpower and reserve affairs. He received advice from the Drug Abuse Control Committee, which consisted of two members of each military service and additional advisors chosen by the secretary or the committee chairman. The two main tasks were to develop a program to screen out drug addicts or potential drug addicts before they entered the military service and to develop a drug education program. As part of the education effort, the secretary had to procure and develop educational material including films, pamphlets, posters, and radio and television programs. The materials had to emphasize the dangers of drug use, stress the "inconsistency of their use with military responsibility and national security," and explain the disciplinary actions for a soldier discovered using drugs.[60]

The secretary and his committee also oversaw the education efforts made in the different departments and branches of the armed forces. Drug abuse prevention education had to extend to "all military educational levels from basic training to the senior service schools and joint colleges." The armed forces had to particularly train medical officers, judge advocates, and chaplains in "the identification, treatment, discipline, rehabilitation, and counseling on drugs and their abuse." The assistant secretary and the committee also had to make sure that information was widely disseminated and that orientation, refresher training, and supplemental programs were devised for all military and civilian personnel as well as reservists. Military personnel departing to overseas stations had to receive extra orientation. Apart from overseeing drug education, the committee reviewed, evaluated, and monitored existing programs through on-site inspections, recommended policies, and ensured exchange of information between departments on drug abuse.[61]

Despite installing the committee, most details of the drug abuse control programs were left to the individual branches of the military. They were asked to develop additional procedures "to prevent trafficking and shipping of drugs by civilian personnel and military members" of the armed forces, "especially members traveling from one country to the other." Departments were to instruct commanders on identifying areas and businesses where illegal drugs were sold and declare them off-limits. Commanders in foreign countries were to work closely with local law enforcement agencies. The departments were encouraged to "develop programs and facilities to restore and rehabilitate members who are drug users or drug addicts when such members desire and are willing to undergo such restoration." However, rehabilitation programs could replace "appropriate disciplinary or administrative actions." This was a directive not always remembered by officers, who often used rehabilitative measures as means to punish their soldiers.[62]

The three military branches had different programs in the United

States and Vietnam. The army had the most problems in regard to drug abuse, partly because it had to deal with a far larger number of men. Consequently, unlike the navy and the air force and against military tradition, the army had a decentralized treatment and rehabilitation system. The army leadership further justified its decentralized approach with the argument that it was more flexible and left more room for experimentation. As they would later in Germany, army leaders in the United States emphasized community-based programs. Post commanders were central to providing an atmosphere within their community that encouraged soldiers to seek rehabilitation. When the congressional staff analyzed the drug programs in the United States, it gained a positive impression of the army's approach, deeming it more effective than the more centralized programs of the navy and the air force.[63]

Despite these positive observations, the staffers also noted deficiencies. Drug programs on army bases differed greatly, particularly in terms of how addicts were regarded. Reports reaching the congressional staff indicated that the army's attitudes about drug abuse had not changed significantly. One such report described bases where an addict returning from Vietnam found himself caught between "straights" and "junkies." The former despised users, and the latter tried to pull them back in. Despite problems, the decentralized approach extended to bases in Europe. Not surprisingly, similar problems would appear, particularly when it came to the varying attitudes of community commanders and their subordinate officers.

In its recommendations to the Senate Subcommittee on Drug Abuse in the Military, the investigating staff touched on issues that would recur as the new decade progressed, particularly in Germany. The very first recommendations concerned alcohol abuse. The staffers argued that so far, the armed services had paid insufficient attention to the problem, despite the fact that alcohol was the most widely abused substance. The staff report argued that the armed forces could not expect "to deal effectively with other forms of drug abuse and bypass the one that is most common and does the most damage."[64] In subsequent years the armed services followed this advice at least nominally. Almost all programs and initiatives included alcohol abuse in their titles. Nonetheless, drug abuse received greater attention.

The congressional staff's second recommendation was that the army needed to bridge the communication gap between young enlisted men and their superiors, both officers and senior NCOs. The staffers called for the army to educate its leaders on the issue, a recommendation that would prove difficult to fulfill. Other measures such as unannounced urinalysis spot checks and constant evaluations of the testing program worked more smoothly.[65]

The congressional report was particularly concerned with the fate of rehabilitated soldiers. It expressed the opinion that the army should not discharge soldiers from service because of their drug use or dependence unless they had chronic health problems that prevented them from carrying out their duty or they wanted to leave. Members of the armed services who had been treated successfully "should be eligible for reenlistment or for otherwise continuing in service." Even members convicted under the Uniform Code of Military Justice should receive treatment for the duration of their enlistment. The army had to reinstate any member whose job qualifications or pay advantage it had withdrawn because of their drug use if considered fully rehabilitated.[66] Soldiers could not be subject to disciplinary action or dishonorably discharged because they were drug abusers or had sought treatment.

The decriminalization of drug users marked an important shift in the Defense Department's drug policy. It now emphasized rehabilitating the soldier. Commanders were asked to consider "all the facts and circumstances of each case" before taking disciplinary and administrative actions. They were to consider whether the soldier was an experimenter, an addict, or a supplier. If a soldier's rehabilitation was feasible, commanders needed to make use "of such administrative and judicial tools as will ensure that the service member is not prematurely and permanently precluded from participation in service sponsored or other government agency rehabilitation programs."[67]

Directive 1300.11 outlined the so-called amnesty program. Under these programs the services could suspend action under the UCMJ for "a person who is sincere in seeking help to eliminate his drug dependence and who voluntarily comes forward before he is apprehended or detected as a drug abuser." A member of the armed services seeking treatment received amnesty and medical assistance in recognition of his "personal moral responsibility for his actions and their consequences." If such an individual could not be rehabilitated and restored to full duty, the services could give him an honorable discharge. The "amnesty" only remained effective as long as the individual fully cooperated in his own rehabilitation.[68]

Prior to the DOD directive, in September 1970, the army had already published regulation 600-32, which contained similar points as the directive.[69] The regulation provided guidance to field commanders on how to establish amnesty programs. They could not punish a soldier who presented himself voluntarily as a drug user to his commander, chaplain, surgeon, or other designated official if he requested rehabilitation assistance. This was only possible if command had not been previously aware of the soldier's drug use.[70]

The amnesty program represented a policy shift. The army recognized "that in a period of widespread drug abuse, the value of identifying drug users so that they could be treated and returned to duty out-weighed the deterrent effect of criminal sanctions in most cases."[71] Realizing that rehabilitation programs would differ in various parts of the world, the army permitted major overseas commanders to supplement AR 600-32.[72]

However, AR 600-32 did more than introduce the amnesty program. It announced the overall army policy and assigned responsibilities for the prevention of drug abuse. The stated policy was "to prevent and eliminate drug abuse and to attempt to restore and rehabilitate members who evidence a desire and willingness to undergo such restoration." The army acknowledged that it had "a particular responsibility for counseling and protecting its members against drug abuse and for disciplining members who use or promote the use of drugs in an illegal or improper manner." The newly formulated regulation also left no doubt that soldiers involved with drugs were committing an illegal act.[73] However, commanders had to consider even soldiers punished or disciplined for their involvement with drugs for rehabilitation. They needed to treat each case individually and to take into account the specific circumstances of each case. This admonition would prove difficult to put into effect in Europe.

With troop levels in Vietnam decreasing, Germany became a new focal point of concern regarding drug use. Factors specific to the country aggravated the problems. When discussing the morale problems in Germany, observers noted the abysmal conditions of many of the barracks. The army had taken over most of the barracks from the Wehrmacht after World War II. The Germans had built them in the 1930s or even before World War I.[74] A newspaper in Heidelberg in August 1968 called quarters in Mark Twain and Patrick Henry Village "dirty dark American Heidelberg." The article mainly called attention to the bad exterior conditions of military housing. The responsible army engineer explained that he did not have sufficient funds to do renovations.[75] But the disrepair of the soldiers' quarters went beyond the exterior. The *Overseas Weekly* published reports about barracks without functioning heating systems. The freezing conditions in the barracks led soldiers to buy and run electric space heaters. This practice led to a power shortage in barracks in the Heilbronn area and to the electrocution of a soldier who had tried to repair a broken heater in the Frankfurt area.[76] An army engineer claimed that heating systems all over USAREUR were antiquated and inefficient. The commentary went on to claim that the lack of funds was not merely a result of the war in Vietnam and that the neglect had been going on for the last twenty years. As a result, troops occupied housing "that would be condemned in any stateside ghetto. Generations of enlisted men have suffered overcrowding, crummy plumbing, and broken-down heating plants."[77]

Another *Overseas Weekly* from January 1970 described barracks in Camp Eschborn. Mold was growing on bathroom walls, many walls had fist-sized holes, lights were not functioning, and the roof was leaking. The motor pool latrine had had no glass in its windows since

November. The article was entitled "Welcome to the 'Snakepit.'"[78] Later editions of the *Overseas Weekly* contained similar reports. In June 1970 the paper reported on bad conditions in a mess hall in Wackernheim, and in September a German contractor refused to complete a latrine renovation because he wasn't receiving any payments from the army.[79]

During a hearing of a subcommittee of the House Committee on Appropriations, one representative stated that he felt "ashamed we have to have military personnel in some of those barracks."[80] Polk had introduced the so-called Stem to Stern program in 1970 to improve the living conditions. In 1970 he had been able to allocate $34.6 million in an effort to make the plumbing, electrical systems, heating, sanitation facilities, flooring, painting, and lighting conform to DOD standards.[81] The money allocated was not sufficient. Estimates for renovating facilities in Germany stretched between $150 million and $200 million.[82] Polk had already expressed his concern over the deteriorating conditions of the barracks and the scarcity of funds to renovate them in 1967 albeit not publicly. Because he believed USAREUR would deplete the reserves of the welfare and morale activities programs by the fiscal year 1968, he advised the deputy commander in chief of the European Command to request loans rather than grants for improving the officers' club. While Polk saw the need for improvements, he prioritized fiscal discipline over barracks improvement.[83]

The scarcity of funds and resources contributed to the low morale among the units in Germany. Throughout the second half of the 1960s, Vietnam had taken priority in the allocation of resources. In many ways USAREUR had become "a replacement depot for Vietnam," according to Lt. Gen. Arthur S. Collins, who became deputy commander in chief of USAREUR when Polk left. Because Vietnam had also had priority in assignments, USAREUR lacked experienced NCOs and officers. The army would reassign soldiers to Vietnam just at the point when their experience would have made them valuable to their unit in Germany. At the same time many of the soldiers in Europe who came from Vietnam were there merely to serve out the remainder of their tour, often only a few months. Few of these veterans were motivated to receive new training in Europe. Apart from renovation funds, USA-REUR also lacked the funds to sufficiently support its training.[84] The lack of training meant soldiers either did menial duties or nothing at all. The boredom was exacerbated by the declining economic status of GIs. The devaluation of the dollar during the 1970s, paired with rising prices in Germany, meant that GIs could not afford to spend as much of their leisure time outside the bases.

The lack of a comprehensive drug abuse control program in the army prior to 1970 was evident in USAREUR. General Polk, who was not prone to discussing social problems in his command publicly unless forced to do so, never mentioned it in public speeches or publications. However, despite the lack of acknowledgment, drug use had already become a familiar problem in USAREUR barracks as shown by the raids in Hanau and Kaiserslautern in November 1964. The *Overseas Weekly* reported several incidents in 1969, such as a drug raid involving GIs at a German apartment in October or a GI driving a tank while high on LSD.[85] Such reports increased in 1970. Always trying to reflect the common soldier's point of view, the *Overseas Weekly* often reported on the work of CID informants and undercover agents in an unfavorable manner to the authorities.[86] While articles in the *Overseas Weekly* would normally take up an understanding stance toward users, they would also warn soldiers of the dangers of drugs.[87] In some cases, reports on racial unrest would also mention drug abuse as a further source of tension. In September 1970 the *Wall Street Journal* and the *Overseas Weekly* ran stories on the First Battalion, Eighty-First Artillery in Neu-Ulm. While the articles focused on the racial unrest, drug use found mention as another problem area in the unit.[88]

Polk showed little initiative in regard to controlling drug use among the soldiers. Although he did briefly allude to drug abuse during the opening speech for the twenty-ninth session of the Interservice Legal Committee, a meeting of military lawyers in Berchtesgaden in June 1970, he provided no further detail on how he planned to resolve it.[89] Similarly the response letter from the deputy commander of EUCOM,

Air Force Gen. David A. Burchinal, in which Burchinal advised Polk on how to use the military media in dealing with both race issues and drug use, indicates that Polk was certainly aware of the problem.[90] Polk's papers at the U.S. Army Military History Institute contain one letter from an anonymous soldier complaining about the rampant drug abuse and low morale at First Battalion, Eighty-First Artillery in Neu-Ulm.[91] Polk instructed Brig. Gen. Patrick W. Powers to look into the matter.[92] Mostly he implemented those measures outlined in the new army regulations.

USAREUR introduced the amnesty program in December 1970. Originally soldiers had to seek amnesty in writing. When commanders discovered that this requirement was a deterrent, USAREUR switched to an informal verbal agreement between the soldier seeking amnesty and his commanding officer. As in all other commands, "exemption" replaced the term "amnesty" in September 1971. Military health clinics, division mental hygiene consultation services, and fourteen military hospitals provide most of the support for soldiers seeking to end their involvement with drugs. Psychiatric facilities provided inpatient and outpatient care, which included detoxification as well as individual and group counseling. USAREUR also began to open "street clinics" where "drug abusers could discuss their problems and receive information and treatment from professionals." The exact methods employed by these clinics varied from location to location. By the fall of 1971 USAREUR had established seven such clinics.[93]

Two examples of street clinics would be Now House and Attic. Now House offered the services of a physician, a psychiatrist, ex-addicts, a chaplain, and a volunteer trained in psychiatry. Enlisted men seeking rehabilitation at Now House initially went there three times a week. As their condition improved, they would go twice and then once a week. The Now House provided "a lesser degree of rehabilitation for more abusers."[94] The Attic, which was aimed at so-called hardcore users, provided "a lot of help for a few drug abusers." The clinic was open twenty-four hours a day. It offered help to individuals experiencing a "bad trip" or suffering from withdrawal. For rehabilitation, the Attic offered weekly rap sessions, twice weekly group-therapy sessions, and if necessary private counseling from an ex-addict, a doctor, or a chaplain.

As in Vietnam, amnesty was at first a hard sell among troops in Germany. Although it was advertised through many channels, such as the enlisted men's advisory council, division newspapers, and radio programs, soldiers often did not fully understand it. Not all soldiers comprehended that participants were not excused from illegal possession of drugs. Other soldiers did not understand that no therapeutic program existed, at least during the first year of amnesty. The lack of a rehabilitation program was one of the main reasons why so few soldiers joined the program. Participants could seek counseling from the field hospital's psychiatric unit. If they were in VII Corps they could also seek help at Now House and Attic. In V Corps six mental hygiene clinics staffed by trained enlisted social work technicians provided counseling and treatment. The clinics received weekly visits from psychiatrists and social officers.[95] However, counseling was not a mandatory part of the program. It depended entirely on a soldier's initiative.

Drug abuse more than either of the other two problem areas indicated the strain that a quarter-century military presence abroad put on a unit like USAREUR. GIs were living and working in old and outdated facilities. In a foreign environment, their declining economic status isolated them even more. The lack of resources due to Vietnam left soldiers with little to do and few opportunities to improve their living conditions. Despite growing evidence of widespread drug use in his command, Polk barely acknowledged it and did little other than implement armywide measures. As with race relations, his successor's approach differed significantly.

8

Drug Abuse in
USAREUR, 1970–1975

When Davison assumed the command of USAREUR, drug abuse control became his second priority after race relations. It would develop into the number one priority by 1973. Davison had already encountered drug abuse problems among his troops in Vietnam, where he claimed heroin abuse was rampant. Davison believed that the use of heroin was "beginning to make its appearance" among the troops in Germany as well. What concerned Davison in particular about the use of heroin was that it was hard to detect: "A guy could be on it with light to moderate addiction and you'd never tell because he could still fly an airplane or do a complicated task. It's a very insidious thing."[1] After only a few weeks in Germany, Davison outlined his approach to drug abuse in the yearly *Army Green Book Report*.

The report listed three areas of concentration: education, law enforcement, and rehabilitation. Education on drug abuse was probably the area that Davison stressed most during his tenure in command. Information on the dangers of drug use were to be disseminated through lecture seminars, workshops, spot announcements and programs on the Armed Forces Network, and the distribution of posters and pamphlets or similar educational materials. Davison addressed three separate audiences. The first category included those soldiers and officers concerned with drug education, counseling, and rehabilitation, namely, doctors, chaplains, and selected enlisted specialists. The second category consisted of officers and noncommissioned officers who required "in-depth information on the drug problem in order to enable them to understand its nature and underlying causes as well as to equip them to instruct and counsel their subordinates concerning the dangers of drug abuse."[2] The third category consisted of enlisted personnel, young men under the age of twenty-five who were considered the most likely to become users or addicts.

His initial approach to drug abuse was similar to his approach to race relations. Davison stressed the importance of candid communication and sensitivity. He believed that officers and NCOs had to be "infused with the desire to protect their men from the consequences of drug abuse" and to help those already involved with drugs. Such help was only possible if such leaders dealt with their subordinates in "a compassionate and sensitive manner." The education of the young soldier could only succeed if they received factual information in an honest, persuasive, and innovative manner.[3] Davison reiterated his message of compassion and education during a lecture he gave in Washington DC. In a speech to scholars of the Woodrow Wilson Center, Davison argued that "the most important factor in drug abuse" was the abuser, not the drug. Accordingly, "a humane and compassionate concern for each man as an individual" had to be the basis of USAREUR's program.[4]

Davison demonstrated his concern over the issue by turning the Drug Abuse Control Office staffed by two officers into the Discipline and Drug Prevention Division with sixteen staff members. The staff included one doctor and three enlisted men who made up the Drug Information and Education Team. The team had five major objectives: "(1) assist commanders at all levels in identifying the nature and extent of drug abuse and in developing programs to combat their problems, (2) develop and conduct educational programs on drug abuse at all command levels, (3) develop, collect, and furnish statistical data on drug abuse, (4) formulate and make recommendations concerning drug education and rehabilitation programs, and (5) advise the Chief, Discipline and Drug Prevention Division, of effectiveness of current drug policies." With the creation of the team and the division, education efforts in USAREUR became more coordinated. Davison published a *Commanders' Notebook on Drug Abuse*. It provided guidelines to commanders on how to establish a prevention and control program.[5]

Moreover USAREUR published three flyers on drug abuse targeting the three groups Davison had outlined in his letter to Willard Pearson.[6] The *Mind Expander* was a periodic publication targeted at army physicians, chaplains, and counselors. *Everything You Wanted to Know about Fighting Drug Abuse, but Were Afraid to Ask* was the title of a series of flyers designed to assist commanders and other leaders in controlling drug abuse. Finally, the *Cosmic Flash* was a periodic flyer for lower-grade enlisted personnel using drugs. This publication tried to use a contemporary style and the language of the drug subculture.[7] In October 1971 USAREUR conducted workshops for counselors and doctors to exchange ideas.

Despite the increase in pamphlets on drug abuse, the main emphasis in education was on workshops and seminars. The experiences of the previous two years had shown that written materials and education through other media such as the press or movies "had little, if any, influence on drug users." Especially educational movies were unpopular with GIs, because they were often outdated, contained nonfactual information, used scare tactics, and did not resemble the contemporary drug scene in Germany.[8] VII Corps had analyzed its soldiers' response to various drug education efforts by letting them fill out questionnaires. The conclusion drawn from these questionnaires was that the enlisted men were most receptive to lectures and skits presented by former addicts who "told it like it is."

The law enforcement efforts in the fall of 1971 did not change significantly. In his *Green Book Report*, Davison gave a very general summary of USAREUR's efforts in this area. USAREUR directed law enforcement efforts primarily at identifying and eliminating illicit drugs. Davison claimed in the report that the military police and the criminal investigation division were working closely with the local authorities to interdict the international traffickers.[9] Davison did not mention the frictions between the army and local authorities in regard to the drug traffic. At this point the law enforcement efforts concentrated on stopping the influx of drugs into the barracks. A year later these efforts would become a lot more far-ranging.

In the same *Green Book Report* published in October 1971, Davison cited only one effort undertaken within his command in regard to drug rehabilitation, an effort that had begun under his predecessor. As mentioned earlier, the Third Infantry Division had established a drug clinic named New House.[10] However, by December 1971 USA-REUR was setting up drug counseling facilities called "rap centers" in military communities all over Germany. The rap centers counseled and educated soldiers who were experimenting with drugs or were frequent users but who were not drug dependent. When approached by Pearson with the idea of creating a resident rehabilitation facility, the Freedom House for V Corps, Davison was open to the idea, but he felt disappointed that such facilities were even needed. The facility he argued was an indication of failure: "failure to educate our leaders and soldiers in the dangers of drug abuse, and failure to counsel those with drug problems before the problems become overwhelming." The main effort of the army, Davison believed, had to be devoted to stopping the men from ever becoming dependent on drugs. Therefore, efforts at counseling and education had to be increased. The rap centers offered the most cost-efficient solution to that goal.[11]

Davison claimed in March and April 1972 that increased drug education had already met with some success. He claimed that drug abuse had leveled off in 1971 and had been decreasing so far in 1972.[12] Reports later the same year would contradict Davison's assertions. But even at this point he conceded that so far, the drug abuse control programs of some of his commands had more form than substance: "Time is running out for those commanders who claim they have no drug problem or who give lip service to the drug programs." In June 1972 Davison had to modify his optimistic pronouncements in regard to the level of abuse. He still maintained that drug use had leveled off, but now it was doing so at a high level. What Davison found particularly disquieting was that the use of opiates such as heroin seemed to be increasing.[13]

Despite the efforts made in the fall of 1971 and the concern he had expressed publicly, Davison had no coherent strategy on how to deal with drug abuse for the first year of his command. He tried to provide guidance to his subordinate commanders, but wanted to let them set up their own programs. As the drug problem failed to subside by the summer of 1972, Davison became convinced that there would have to be a more structured program that would be applied uniformly throughout the command and that would make use of all available resources in the military communities, from "the medical people, the chaplains, the social workers, the law enforcement people" to the commanders.[14]

Davison stepped up his efforts in August 1972 when he formed a special committee with senior members of his staff, among them his JAG, Wilton Persons. The Alcohol and Drug Abuse Panel was to "gather information about the threat and recommend actions to be taken to control it." The panel met once a month and provided the commander in chief with status reports on drug-related incidents and the progress of the various programs.[15]

Despite Davison's increased involvement in the second half of 1972, the actual operation of the program remained decentralized. The rational was that different units required approaches that had been adapted to the specific environment. A unit in Frankfurt required a different emphasis from one in a more isolated environment. Commanders were supposed to develop programs that met their particular needs. Of course, they had to stay within the framework laid out in the relevant army regulations and the guidelines provided by Davison. He tried to direct his subordinates toward an understanding that the situation required both a high standard of military discipline and concerned leadership.[16] As the different drug control programs implemented in Germany would show, the second goal remained elusive.

Davison's appointment of the Alcohol and Drug Abuse Panel reflected his growing concern as his earlier pronouncements that drug use was leveling off turned out to have been inaccurate. Between 1971 and 1972, commanders in Europe registered a 30 percent increase in drug abuse cases requiring medical treatment. One doctor surveying drug usage in nine military communities in Germany found a steep increase in hard drug usage in six months.[17] Conducting his research in early 1971, the doctor found "that the self-reported incidence of illegal drug use . . . among 3,553 soldiers was 46 percent." This number included individuals who had used drugs only once. Of these 46 percent, over 95 percent reported using hashish. Sixteen percent admitted that they were using drugs more than three times a week. Four percent used "hard drugs," such as LSD, amphetamines, barbiturates, and inject-able more than three times a week. When the same doctor conducted another survey later that same year, he found that the percentage of self-reported incidents had stayed the same, but the use of "hard drugs" had gone up from 4 to 8 percent within six months. Another survey of 1,270 military personnel found that almost 60 percent of the eigh-teen- to twenty-year-old soldiers reported some use. This percentage declined progressively the older the soldiers were. Soldiers at the age of thirty or older reported almost no drug use at all.[18] USAREUR sur-veys conducted between October 1970 and April 1972 showed similar results. Of the 16,700 people surveyed, 40 percent claimed to have used drugs. Twenty percent claimed they had used drugs other than alcohol and cannabis at least once; 10–15 percent claimed that they used cannabis products on a daily basis; and 1–2.5 percent claimed that they were using drugs other than alcohol and cannabis products on a daily basis.[19] In 1972 the Senate Subcommittee on Drug Abuse in the Military sent a staff member to Germany to "examine aspects of the problem of alcohol and drug abuse among military personnel and their dependents."[20] In his report Julian Granger claimed that 50–60 percent of military personnel and dependents used hashish.

In a deposition for the U.S. District Court, Washington DC, Maj. Christopher R. Robbins, until August 1972 chief of the annual general inspection division of the V Corps Inspector General's Office, testified that drug abuse had become an ever-growing concern in 1972. He saw a growing number of soldiers "who had serious problems with drugs" and who displayed "the obvious physiological indications of drug abuse."[21]

Such physiological indications would include scabs and puncture marks. Most of these addicts came to the inspector general's office to obtain a release from the army. The major did not address whether soldiers faked their addiction to obtain a release, nor is there any other data that would indicate that this occurred.

A survey of 25,000 soldiers conducted in V Corps between April and July 1972 found that of the 19,844 soldiers "who answered the question concerning the use of drugs," 36 percent admitted that they were "using hashish or marijuana on an occasional or regular basis; 17 percent out of 18,454 were using opiates on an occasional or regular basis. Robbins, who in August 1972 became V Corps's drug control officer, estimated that in the fall of that year drug abuse had gone up by 60 or even 80 percent. Robbins believed that the major influx of hard drugs only started in the fall of 1972.[22]

Prior to Davison's arrival, USAREUR had no established method of detecting drug users. On September 1, 1971, urinalysis testing began. Initially soldiers submitted to testing fifteen days before they returned to the United States or their discharge from the service. The period extended to sixty days in November 1971. Soldiers were also tested fifteen days before departing on ordinary leave to the United States or within ten days after requesting an extension of their foreign service tour of duty. The initial number of soldiers detected through these urinalysis tests was much lower than other statistics on drug abuse. Of 8,793 urine samples collected between September 1 and October 21, 1971, about 106, or 1.2 percent, tested positive. The best means of identifying individuals or units with drug problems was by monitoring hospital admissions. If a unit was flagged as having a serious drug problem, the drug abuse officer was sent to the unit to present the education program. According to the comptroller general's report, hard drug use in problem units dropped after such visits.[23]

The numbers of soldiers detected through urinalysis testing also increased in 1972. The numbers went up from 1.2 percent of those tested in March to 5.7 percent in September. The increase was partly due to improved testing procedures, but observers considered the increase substantial nonetheless. In October 1972 USAREUR began fully randomized testing procedures. Randomized testing meant that USAREUR picked units by chance. The aim was that a unit's chances for testing would "remain relatively constant throughout the year and be invulnerable to prediction based on historical analysis." Thus each individual had "an equal probability for selection" regardless "of the size or unit of assignment, or number of times" he had been selected previously.[24] During that same month, 6.4 percent of the soldiers selected at random tested positive for the presence of amphetamines, barbiturates, or opiates. Approximately 13,300 V Corps soldiers were tested. The detection level remained above 6 percent in November and December but decreased to 4 percent by March 1973. Between January and May 1973, random or regular testing identified about 1,200 individuals per month. Most of the confirmed drug users were under age twenty-five. Since 93 percent of the lower enlisted ranks (E1–E4) were under twenty-five, USAREUR considered drugs a major threat to its mission and functionality.

The number of soldiers treated at hospitals because of their drug use also increased from 1971 to 1972. In 1971, USAREUR evacuated 490 soldiers to the United States for drug and alcohol abuse. Twenty-five percent of the evacuees reported using hashish alone, and 50 percent reported using both hashish and LSD. In 3,197 drug abuse cases, the soldiers required medical treatment. The number rose to 3,995 in 1972. The number would rise dramatically to 4,422 during the first six months of 1973.[25] House members from the Committee on Foreign Affairs issued a similar report on March 21, 1973. A brigade commander estimated that 60–65 percent of the lower five grades had used hashish occasionally and 40–50 percent used it on a regular basis. About 10 percent of the lower four grades had used heroin. The numbers reached through the evaluation of urinalysis testing were somewhat lower. According to those statistics, 6.3 percent of the soldiers under twenty-eight had tested positive. Forty percent of these "were using opiates such as heroin. The remainder was using amphetamines, barbiturates, and hashish."[26]

Despite the discrepancies between the tests and the various surveys, observers were convinced that USAREUR had a major drug problem. Davison and his subordinate commanders agreed with that assessment. The army leadership in Europe believed that drug use was a major detriment to the army's efficiency. Officers argued that soldiers on drugs lost interest in maintaining the equipment that belonged to their unit and became negligent in their duties. Commanders spent resources on monitoring them because they could not easily replace these highly trained individuals, especially in a foreign country. Drug abuse was draining the army's medical resources. Cases of serum and unspecified hepatitis, connected to drug abuse, had increased. Moreover, there had been seven drug-related deaths in 1972, and by mid-1973 there had already been six. The crime that accompanied the spread of illegal drugs such as theft, assault, and robbery damaged morale and eroded trust between soldiers.[27] Drug abuse was part of a vicious cycle. The crime and petty theft surrounding the drug use contributed to the already substandard living conditions. Morale suffered, making the escape that drugs offered attractive.

In the fall and winter of 1972, a number of local commanders in Germany produced new drug and alcohol abuse control and prevention programs. On November 30, 1972, Lt. Gen. Willard Pearson, commander of V Corps, sent a letter to his subordinate commanders in which he outlined V Corps's drug abuse control policy. To Pearson, drug abuse was the "number one problem in V Corps." He believed that "much of the crime, dissidence, and racial incidents" were rooted "in drug abuse and the economics of the drug traffic."[28] Pearson wanted his commanders, community leaders, officers, and noncommissioned officers to start a counteroffensive against drug abuse. Pearson proposed "a three phased attack." The goal of Phase I was to eliminate the environment in barracks that stimulated and encouraged the use of drugs. Phase II was aimed at the "cleaning out of a drug pocket," and in Phase III wholesome alternatives to drug abuse were to be provided.[29]

To eliminate the environment that encouraged the use of drugs, V Corps implemented a number of measures. Pearson prohibited the painting of windows because he saw dark and murky billets rooms as conducive to abuse. Moreover, soldiers could not pull heavy curtains or "other such drapery" over windows "to prevent the passage of light." He prohibited black lights and encouraged leaders to ensure that lighting in rooms was "adequate to provide good visibility for inspections and supervisory checks." Soldiers could not burn scented candles or incense or excessively divide their rooms into small compartments with closed or restricted access. These measures allowed officers and noncommissioned officers the greatest amount of access and soldiers as little room for secrecy as possible. Accordingly, soldiers could not lock their rooms from the inside. If soldiers did lock their rooms, commanders had the authority to remove the locks. Locking the back door at a set hour limited access to barracks after duty.[30]

To further discourage soldiers from secret drug use, V Corps heightened the visibility of officers and noncommissioned officers in the barracks. At least two noncommissioned officers had to live in every barrack. Pearson introduced constant and flexible inspections. Officers and NCOs could check soldiers for needle marks and inspect their billets, including their lockers, on a monthly basis.[31] If possible, most unmarried personnel were supposed to live in the barracks to allow for greater supervision. Officers in charge of pass rosters closely monitored anyone who might be smuggling drugs.

Phase II of the V Corps Drug Control Counter-Offensive described how a commander was to "marshal available resources for an intensive, full scale detection operation." What followed was the description of a "full court press," even though the term did not appear in the instructions. The instructions advised commanders to provide the drug abuse education session after the inspection was completed. The V Corps program was also more specific on rehabilitation measures. Commanders had to refer detected or suspected abusers "to the supporting Community Assistance and Social Counseling Center."[32] The commanders were to work closely with the centers in developing a rehabilitation program and monitor each man until he was "either determined to be rehabilitated or discharged from service."[33] The program manual did not mention punishment at all. The emphasis was on cleaning out the drugs. This was also evident in the instruction to set up an amnesty box on the day of the inspection. Individuals could dispose of drugs or drug paraphernalia not discovered during the inspection.

A memorandum from the community leader of the Friedberg/Bad Nauheim community, home of the Third Brigade, Third Armored Division, outlined in detail the responsibilities of officers in regard to inspections. Apart from the commanding officer and community leader, who established and operated the program, and the assistant community leader, who administered it, the key officers were the brigade surgeon, chaplain, and commander of the military police platoon supported by the division surgeon, provost marshal, and the division judge advocate.

Aside from defining the key officers' role in the program, the memorandum also provided detailed instructions on how to conduct a "full court press." Once a commander picked a unit for such an inspection, he removed its soldiers to a central location away from their barracks, where they had to undergo urine testing. After the testing they attended a refresher training presentation while the military police secured the barracks. The presentation addressed the local drug situation and outlined what rehabilitative and counseling services were available at Ray Barracks. After the refresher training, the troops went back to the barracks to participate in a health and welfare inspection. Overall the Friedberg/Bad Nauheim program was mainly concerned with inspections as a way to eliminate the sale, transfer, storage, or use of illegal drugs. While rehabilitation was a stated goal, the memo offered little guidance as to how officers could achieve this. Under "additional efforts to reduce drug and alcohol abuse," the memo listed improving liaison and coordination with local German and U.S. criminal investigation personnel, increasing refresher training, conducting presentations for dependents, and conducting random searches of organic military vehicles (ambulances, ration trucks, etc.).

Phase III offered instructions on how to provide alternatives for drug abuse. Among the things discussed was intensified training, which was supposed to contribute to the "professional development of the soldier, to satisfaction on the job." Such training was also physically and mentally taxing and had "a liberal amount of hard challenge, adventure training, and night activity." Physical exercise could be a useful alternative. The program recommended "a strenuous on and off duty sports program" that was "physically tiring" Soldiers were to be encouraged to qualify for the German Physical Fitness Sports Award (Sportabzeichen) and the German military shooting medal. Soldiers were also encouraged to participate in German-American social and sports activities such as KONTAKT, the V Corps Friendship through Sports and Hobbies Program, Project Partnership, and Volksmarches. They were also to take advantage of the off-duty graduate and undergraduate classes provided by the U.S. Army Service Schools, or complete German I and II at the University of Maryland or the *Volkshochschule*. Participation in these programs would not only enhance "the professionalism of the individual soldiers" but would also provide "alternatives to accepting the boredom of the kasernes and possibly turning to drugs."[34]

The V Corps's program mirrored Davison's early attitude about drug abuse in that it emphasized prevention above all else. Neither punishment nor rehabilitation was fully considered. However, many preventative measures such as inspections and limits on room decorations could easily be turned into punitive measures as some commanders on the community level proved. One of the most notorious drug control programs in USAREUR was the so-called Nellingen Anti-Drug Movement. In December 1972 Brig. Gen. Anthony F. Daskevich was the community commander in charge of Nellingen Barracks. Daskevich issued a memorandum to his subordinate commanders, "Nellingen Anti-Drug Movement: Put Pressure on Drug Abusers."[35] The document listed the policies that Daskevich had developed together with his subordinate officers to combat drug abuse in the Nellingen facility. These policies would become the focal point of a lawsuit filed by GIs against the secretary of the army, Davison, and other commanders in USAREUR.

After moving his headquarters to Nellingen in July 1972, Daskevich gained the impression that drug abuse at the facility was rampant. According to him, 8 percent of the installation's total troop strength had had "a brush with the law over drugs." A survey of soldiers living in the barracks concluded that 60–75 percent of the soldiers were using drugs and that 30 percent were probably using or experimenting with hard drugs.[36] After USAREUR and VII Corps issued their directives implementing the Department of the Army Drug Control Program, Daskevich and his subordinates developed a policy for the community. Daskevich claimed later that the "Nellingen Anti-Drug Movement" had been the briefing notes for a meeting with the commanders of Nellingen Barracks, not a directive. He insisted that he never intended for the "notes" to circulate outside of Nellingen Barracks. That the document did circulate through the "grapevine" both inside and outside the army Daskevich ascribed to "a concerted effort on the part of some individuals to mislead other soldiers and the public about this document."[37]

Directive or briefing notes, the policy outlined in the paper was aggressive and emphasized pressure and enforcement. This seemed out of step with Davison's publicly stated policy. The document did not mention rehabilitation. The paper called upon officers to "identify and maintain a list of suspected and known drug pushers and users." In order to monitor and keep known "drug pushers and users" under control, commanders were to consider seven measures: removing an individual's door to take away his privacy, taking away his driver's license, confiscating his civilian clothes, removing all except essentials from his room, and referring him to a Center for Drug and Alcohol Abuse Control (CDAAC) for counseling and urine testing. Married men should be required to move into the barracks to be monitored. The only potentially rehabilitative measure among the seven was counseling. The paper advocated frequent shakedown inspections, especially of suspected and known drug pushers and users. Commanders needed to reduce known users to the lowest rank possible. If the CDAAC could not help, they needed to eliminate users from the army's ranks. The paper further called for night antidrug control teams to patrol the barracks.

Commanders needed to report the names of suspected and known drug pushers to the Law and Order Section, VII COSCOM. They also had to inform individuals that they were suspected or known drug pushers or users. Troops were encouraged to turn in dealers. Users were promised leniency if they were willing to provide information.[38]

In a memorandum Daskevich told his officers how to brief their troops. He called upon them to enlist the help of the "good" soldiers, those not involved with drugs: "The movement is aimed at the drug abusers (users/pushers). The 'good' soldier has NOTHING to fear. He should be encouraged to join the movement."[39] The distinction made by Daskevich between abusers and "good" soldiers was revealing. In both memos Daskevich mentioned pushers and users as virtually the same category of undesirable soldier. Compassion and rehabilitation were not priorities in his drug abuse control program, despite the emphasis placed on it by Davison and the Department of the Army. Daskevich admitted before the U.S. District Court that the policy outlined in the "Nellingen Anti-Drug Movement" might appear overly aggressive to those who were not present at the meeting. He claimed that he had made it clear to his subordinates that the actions listed "were to be used in accordance with the regulation governing the particular area in question." Commanders were to use their good judgment in applying these actions.

Daskevich claimed that the Nellingen movement had "substantially reduced drug abuse" at Nellingen Barracks and that it had ended "much of the fear that gripped the Kaserne, and restored a sense of military discipline to the post." Within the first few days, 11 soldiers had turned themselves in to the hospital for detoxification. By June 1973, the program had identified 177 individuals as "hard" drug users. Of the 177, 66 were on the way to rehabilitation. Only 44 people had to be eliminated. The percentage of "hard" drug users had declined to an average of 2 percent.[40]

Nellingen exemplifies how difficult some commanders found making their drug control programs appear compassionate. Speeches given by Davison in early 1973 indicate that he himself struggled to find a balance between compassion and suppression. At a commanders' conference that month Davison admonished his subordinates to interdict the drug traffic in the barracks more effectively. While he did not yet believe that drug abuse had increased over the past year, he was certain that drugs were "more available now than they were then." With no indications that the international trade in drugs could be eliminated any time soon, commanders had to look at other ways to improve the situation: "The place where you can attack drugs and have a high probability of success is in the barracks and caserns which all too often have become the breeding ground for the drug subculture." Davison's attitude appeared to have hardened if compared with earlier pronouncements. His goal was still to reach out "to the soldier who can be saved" and restore him "to useful soldiering and citizenship." The emphasis in drug abuse control programs was compassion rather than vengeance. However, Davison warned that compassion did not mean softness. The key to ending drug abuse was self-discipline. Self-discipline, Davison argued, best emerged in a disciplined environment: "Any effective rehabilitation program must have as its foundation a firm and disciplined attitude."[41]

Davison felt the need to point out to the other commanders that they also possessed the means to put pressure on the drug dealers and users. Despite the fact that he had earlier encouraged his subordinate commanders to treat first-time offenders lightly, that did not mean that those first-time offenders caught with large amounts of illegal drugs could not be charged to the full extent of the law. He now asked commanders to make use of the judge advocate assigned to their command as well as the military police and the CID. Constant communication between the commander, the Center for Drug and Alcohol Abuse Control, and the provost marshal were necessary to identify and apprehend pushers as well as identify drug users. Davison suggested that his commanders make use of the "full-court press." This was "an attic-to-basement shakedown for contraband, including drugs." It also included an inspection of private vehicles as well as work and recreation areas.[42] While Davison did not abandon the principle of rehabilitation as the main priority, his speeches of January suggest that he felt he had overemphasized compassion and rehabilitation.

Despite the stronger emphasis on discipline, Davison never abandoned his concept of a concerned leader motivated by compassion rather than vengeance. Even in January he described a good leader as somebody who had to be "concerned for the welfare of his men." Such a leader had to recognize his men as "warm, live human beings with individual hopes, beliefs, aspirations and problems." Soldiers had to "see themselves as important contributing members of the unit." Enforcing discipline was a way to demonstrate concern. Interest in a soldier's welfare "was not shown by laxity of purpose, eye-wash training, slack discipline, and a laissez-faire atmosphere in the billets." A commander was responsible for making the barracks secure and drug-free. Davison wanted "maximum effectiveness in reaching out to the soldier who can be saved," but at the same time he made clear that any officer had to "be willing to take prompt and vigorous action in the discovery, apprehension, and disposition of drug offenders."[43] This latter message seemed to resonate with many officers. While Davison tried to guide his subordinate commanders to find a balance between compassion and discipline, they often understood the second better than the first. "The Nellingen Anti-Drug Movement" was just one example.

In February 1973 VII Corps revised its Circular 600-3 on Alcohol and Drug Abuse Prevention and Control. This listed six functional areas of the program: prevention, identification, detoxification, rehabilitation, evaluation, and research.[44] Unlike V Corps's policy earlier, VII Corps heavily emphasized enforcement, but it also discussed rehabilitation efforts in more detail. Prevention consisted of education, law enforcement, and community action. Commanders needed to ensure that "factual educational classes" were conducted "for every member of his command." Commands through division level were required to have a Drug and Alcohol Information and Education Team. The team used two curricula, one for officers and senior noncommissioned officers and one for ranks E5 and below. Classes needed to omit "scare tactics" and had to offer "an adequate question and answer period." The teams should provide additional information using handouts, pamphlets, booklets, books, and newsletters. Each battalion and separate company had to have at least one drug education specialist, who could be either an officer or an enlisted man.[45]

The circular advocated the use of overt and covert law enforcement operations conducted jointly with the local law enforcement agencies. The purpose of overt operations was to disrupt the drug subculture. Covert operations aimed at securing convictions against illicit drug manufacturers, traffickers, or users. Aside from law enforcement operations, commanders received a long list of other actions they were to take "to discourage trafficking and illegal use of drugs at the installation/community level and to assist in the identification of drug abusers." Commanders were to gather as much information as possible by instituting a program that would encourage and protect personnel who volunteered information on drug abusers and traffickers. Officers were to maintain a list of suspected and known drug traffickers and abusers and circulate it to all commanders on a military installation or in a community. They needed to periodically review lists of unaccompanied personnel living off-post with a view toward identifying suspected drug traffickers and abusers. Private discussions were to be held to solicit information from soldiers who were about to depart from USAREUR.[46]

Constant checks were another aspect of the program. Officers and noncommissioned officers needed to become more visible during nonduty hours. Access to each installation needed to be controlled. Commanders conducted spot checks of vehicles. Other measures included requiring a charge of quarters to be on duty in each barracks during nonduty hours to control visitors to the barracks and to conduct monthly or more frequent health and welfare inspections. The circular also contained detailed instructions on how to conduct a "full court press." Aside from a search of the entire barracks, the circular also recommended that soldiers be ordered to strip to their underwear and that the soldiers should then be examined by medical personnel for signs of drug abuse.[47]

One major goal was creating an environment that made drug use more difficult. Many of these measures were similar to the "Nellingen Anti-Drug Movement" and the measures taken in V Corps. Establishments that tolerated the use or sale of illicit drugs were placed off-limits, as were specific locations, such as streets, alleys, parks, etc., that were known to be places where drugs were sold. The circular prohibited the use of black lights in barracks rooms or painting over windows. Soldiers could not excessively partition rooms with wall lockers or other furniture. They could not burn candles, incense, or other odor-producing material. Just as in Nellingen, individuals suspected of drug trafficking or abuse could be deprived of certain privileges. Commanders could remove the doors to their rooms and suspend their driver's licenses and the registration to their privately owned vehicles. They could require identified or suspected abusers to wear their uniforms during off-duty hours, making it harder for them to obtain drugs outside the barracks. They could require them to move into the barracks if they lived off-post.

Compared with the sections on law enforcement and creating a drug-free environment, the section on community action was short. The purpose of community action was "to improve the quality of life in the military community, especially in those areas that provide meaningful alternatives to drug use," such as noncommissioned officers' and enlisted men's clubs, Special Services, and Army Community Services. The section provided no specific instructions on how commanders were to accomplish this. The circular identified the community Drug and Alcohol Assistance Center and the Alcohol and Drug Dependency Intervention Council as the institutions through which drug- and alcohol-related problems were to be handled.[48]

According to the circular, it was VII Corps's objective "to identify abusers of alcohol and other drugs as rapidly as possible," since "the earlier an individual with a problem is identified, the more receptive he is to rehabilitative efforts." The circular distinguished between voluntary and involuntary means of identification. The exemption policy represented the main means of voluntary identification. Involuntary identification normally occurred when MPs arrested a soldier or when soldiers came into a medical facility because of a drug-related emergency.

The exemption program of VII Corps was similar to the army's program. By 1973 the policy had evolved somewhat from the earlier amnesty program. Exemption provided an individual immunity from punishment, if someone volunteered for help or was identified through urinalysis testing. Commanders could only grant exemption for past use or incidental possession. The policy was not applicable to soldiers who already were the subject of a drug abuse investigation, had been apprehended for a drug offense, had received official warning that they were suspected of a drug offense, had already been charged with a drug offense, or had been offered nonjudicial punishment for such an offense. The immunity was only for possession or use, not for sale or transfer of drugs.[49] Exemption became effective for a soldier as soon as he asked a doctor, chaplain, officer, or noncommissioned officer for help. Once in effect, commanders could not vacate or withdraw it. If commanders had to discharge a soldier under the exemption program because of his addiction, they could not discharge him under less than honorable conditions *solely* as a result of that addiction.[50]

After volunteering for treatment, the soldier underwent a medical evaluation to determine whether his commanders had to flag him or revoke his security clearance. Commanders could revoke the security clearance if a "competent medical authority" indicated that "the individual's judgment or reliability" had been impaired and the individual had been "subjected to and failed every reasonable rehabilitative effort." The commander would consider the removal of administrative flags and the restoration of security clearance once a "competent medical authority" attested that the individual had not developed or no longer had "an impairment in judgment and reliability."

Involuntary identification could occur when a soldier got himself arrested for disorderly conduct with drug involvement, possession of illegal drugs, or possession of illegal paraphernalia, such as needles, syringes, smoking pipes, etc. Admission to a military hospital or other medical treatment facilities for drug intoxication, drug detoxification, emergency treatment for a drug overdose, medical complication with drug involvement, suspected serum hepatitis, or injuries resulting from drug misuse could also lead to involuntary identification. A commander could label a soldier a suspected drug abuser if the commander received credible information that an individual had been using drugs or he displayed an inability to perform assigned duties due to the misuse of drugs or evidence of drug intoxication. Commanders could also label a soldier found to associate with known drug dealers or users or regularly attending locations known to be points of drug use or sale. This could also occur if a soldier paid frequent visits to the medical treatment facility for sick call ailments that were difficult to diagnose.[51]

Annex C of the VII Corps circular discussed the rehabilitation of soldiers. The stated objective was "to restore soldiers to full duty status." If rehabilitation was not possible, a soldier was discharged. The responsible commander and a medical professional (a physician, psychologist, or psychiatrist) determined the rehabilitative capability of an identified abuser. VII Corps would help those they deemed capable of rehabilitation. The assistance varied from frequent counseling for those soldiers whose drug or alcohol involvement was considered minimal to detoxification and placement in a resident rehabilitation facility for heavy users.[52] The authors of the circular recognized that it was difficult "to establish a clear point which determines that rehabilitation has or has not occurred." Occasional lapses could occur. Commanders should not judge the success or failure on the basis of an absolute "cure." Instead "the soldiers' attitude, performance of duty, and his estimated potential for further improvement" were to be "the primary criteria."[53] Commanders should consider transferring soldiers from one unit to another in order to enhance their chances for rehabilitation. Soldiers who failed the rehabilitation process or were deemed incapable of rehabilitation from the start were discharged. Such soldiers received an honorable discharge unless they had committed previous offenses "not directly attributable to alcohol or drug abuse."

Many of the measures adopted in various locations as part of the USAREUR drug control effort became controversial among GIs and even officers. In February 1973 a group of GIs formed the Committee for GI Rights.[54] In a flyer the GI committee called upon enlisted men to complain openly about the excesses of the drug abuse control programs implemented in the various units in Germany. The committee objected particularly to infringements upon their rights to personal privacy. The removal of doors was one of the most criticized measures. The committee also objected to the removal of interior locks on doors, the removal of posters, and the impoundment of personal property. They argued that the programs did not sufficiently distinguish between drug users and individuals who were only associated with drug users: "In carrying out these policies, innocent men are being injured; because of this policy, people are now being found guilty with suspicion alone."[55] The current measures adopted to control drug abuse were destroying "the morale and basic understanding between commanders and those serving under him." With the help from lawyers of the Military Defense Counsel, Rivkin and DeNike, the GI committee brought a suit against the secretary of the army and the entire leadership of USAREUR before the U.S. District Court in Washington DC.[56] The trial took place in 1973. During the course of the trial, numerous GIs testified about abuses they had endured because their commanders suspected them of using drugs.

Rivkin and DeNike listed a number of incidents in which officers had violated the soldiers' rights as individuals. The plaintiffs' lawyers argued that many of the provisions in various drug programs in Germany themselves violated GIs' rights. Many officers had added more stringent measures to their programs, which resulted in even greater restrictions on the rights of soldiers serving under them. The plaintiffs stressed particularly that commanders imposed punitive measures not only on known drug users but also on suspected drug users or associates of users.[57] The criteria that the commander used for the designation were often vague. Close association with known drug dealers or users or the regular attendance at places known to be points of drug sales or use often seemed to be sufficient criteria for labeling a soldier a suspected drug user. One of the programs identified the following "common symptoms of drug abusers:

a. Marked changes in conduct, attitude, and general mood.
b. Lack of motivation and a change in the character of work performed.
c. Poor physical appearance and lack of pride in personal appearance.
d. Unusual flare-ups or outbursts of temper.

. . .

h. Association with known drug abusers.
i. Borrowing money frequently (i.e., to buy drugs).
j. Lack of valuable possessions (i.e., stereo, camera, good civilian clothes).[58]

These criteria described a broad spectrum of individuals, many of whom were most likely not using drugs. The plaintiffs argued further that commanders were arriving at their knowledge about drug use mainly through hearsay. Once they labeled a soldier as a suspected or known user, commanders could subject him to a variety of punitive actions.[59]

Soldiers provided sworn testimonies that they had been subjected to punitive measures solely based on suspicion. Pfc. Ron G. Borolov testified that his superior ordered him to remain on base so that the military police and the German police could search the off-base apartment of his girlfriend. Even though the search turned up no illegal drugs, the superior ordered Borolov to move into a billets room without a door for two days, restricted him to the post, and prohibited him from wearing civilian clothing on the post for those two days. Subsequently Borolov's commanding officer had his bed, locker, and work area searched. The search party found one pipe with hashish residue in Borolov's locker.[60] The measures described by Borolov came straight out of the V Corps drug control program and the Nellingen anti-drug movement. Borolov was trying to argue in his testimony that his officer had picked him out arbitrarily and punished him out of mere suspicion.

Borolov's superior, Lt. Vernon L. Lyght, claimed in his testimony that he had legitimate reasons to impose restrictions on his subordinate. Lyght maintained that Borolov was living off-post without permission and that he had therefore counseled him to resume living in his billets room. The lieutenant explained convincingly that he had probable cause for suspecting that there would be drugs in the off-post apartment. He argued that the evidence he had accumulated had been enough to convince the German police to obtain a search warrant for the apartment. He also insisted that the door to Borolev's room had only been removed after the pipe had been found, arguing that at that point Borolev was no longer merely a suspected drug user.[61] The testimony of the two soldiers shows the difficulties the army faced when it tried to introduce a drug abuse program that was rehabilitative while maintaining discipline at the same time. Judging from the two testimonies, Borolev likely had used drugs at some point or other, but whether he was an addict remained unclear. Lyght was probably right to suspect his subordinate, and the search Lyght initiated was probably legitimate. However, Lyght's conduct toward his soldier demonstrated little concern for Borolev's well-being. Neither of the two indicated that they had ever discussed rehabilitation. Removing Borolev's door for two days was hardly a rehabilitative measure, considering that Lyght had labeled Borolev merely on the basis of hashish residue in a pipe.

Other GIs gave similar testimony. Sgt. Dennis C. K. Puccia accused his commanding officer, Lt. Col. Daniel R. Zenk, of searching his room without probable cause.[62] Another soldier whose room was searched at the same time supported his testimony.[63] In his statement Zenk insisted that he had had probable cause in Puccia's case, but conceded that he might have exceeded his authority in searching the second man's room, and he received a reprimand. The reprimand was a further indication that he had had no probable cause. His superiors directed him to conduct searches only in the presence of the individual concerned and only after consultation with the staff judge advocate.[64]

Pvt. Gary D. Henderson also claimed during the trial that his superiors had searched his room without probable cause. After they found a pipe containing hashish residue, his commander ordered Henderson to move out of the billets and "to live in an empty, heatless room, located directly over the company orderly room." He further ordered him to turn in his civilian clothing. When he refused to turn them in, the commander threatened him with disciplinary action, but never followed through. Henderson lived in the empty room for three to four months.[65] Henderson's commander responded not entirely convincingly that he had not moved the private because of the pipe but because of disciplinary problems and the overcrowding of the billets.[66]

All of the cases above occurred within the context of the Nellingen movement. The class action suit was filed not only on behalf of the plaintiffs who had testified in court but on behalf of all soldiers in USAREUR under the grade of E5. During the trial the plaintiffs' lawyers had tried to show that the drug control efforts in USAREUR were systematically flawed. The defense lawyers, on the other hand, tried to show that in each example of a violation of a soldier's rights, the plaintiffs had either misrepresented the case or the incident represented an individual excess. The judge advocate general of USAREUR believed that the military's lawyers were able to demonstrate that these actions were the result of "an excess of zeal on the part of a commander," not the intended outcome of the commandwide program. The defense argued further that considering the responsibility soldiers in USAREUR were holding, drug use was intolerable. Despite that, the army's approach remained compassionate, making every effort to avoid "disciplinary or court-martial proceedings, and elimination, or trial, or imprisonment." Those were only measures of last resort.[67]

The army's arguments did not convince the presiding judge, Gerhard Gesell of the U.S. District Court for the District of Columbia. In January 1974 he ruled that the USAREUR drug control program was unconstitutional. Gesell could not see any reason why a drug control program in the U.S. Army, Europe had to be any different from such a program for high school students in the United States. Gesell believed the drug control program to be "interlaced with constitutional difficulties." The sanctions allowed in the program could restrict a soldier's immediate liberty and reduce his eligibility for promotion. Some of the sanctions could lead to discharges under less than honorable conditions that carried a serious stigma. The judge argued further that the characterization of the drug situation in Germany as epidemic was an exaggeration. He acknowledged the problem, but denied that it warranted disregard for constitutional safeguards.[68] Judge Gesell's ruling never took effect. The U.S. attorney was able to get a stay, and the Court of Appeals reversed his ruling eighteen months later.[69] The judges determined that the army had acted reasonably in its response to the growing drug abuse problem.

The testimonies at the trial suggest that most of the plaintiffs testifying had used drugs or had been in contact with drugs. In many cases the commanders had good reason to suspect them. At issue in the case was whether the measures and the actions they imposed on those suspects were legal. However, beyond the legality issue, the testimony is revealing in that it shows how difficult Davison's concept of concerned leadership was to implement. Whether their actions were actually legal or not, many of the lower-level commanders displayed a preference for disciplinary action over rehabilitation. This was evident in such programs as the Nellingen movement and in the way the officers used the measures suggested in the different guidelines. One of the most prominent examples of an officer who did not fully support Davison's "understanding" attitude toward drug abuse was his own deputy commander. In an oral history interview he gave after retiring from the army, Lt. Gen. Arthur S. Collins indicated that he disapproved of many of the "liberal" measures taken in regard to drug abuse. He did not agree with exemption policy becoming a permanent program, but believed the army should have set a cutoff date once everybody had become familiar with the problem and the army's policies. To Collins the amnesty program and measures, such as the halfway houses, were a sign of an overabundance of softhearted liberals in the Department of Defense who pushed "understanding."[70] He argued this was mainly a matter of lower-level commanders not being able to get rid of troublemakers in their units.

That many commanders were overzealous in punishing drug users was not just the perception of the members of the GI committee. Davison and his JAG, Wilton Persons, shared some of their concerns. Three months before the trial, Davison had Persons review the Nellingen movement. While Davison and Persons generally approved of the program, they made some notable exceptions. Persons warned that a commander could not take away a soldier's civilian clothes, even though he could prohibit the soldier from wearing them. Similarly, a commander could not remove an individual's personal belongings from his room unless they constituted contraband. Persons cautioned Daskevich about frequent shakedown inspections. A soldier did not lose his Fourth Amendment rights upon entering the military. A commander needed "probable cause" to conduct a search. The Fourth Amendment prohibited "a general exploratory search" for a matter that was not directly connected "with commission of a suspected offense." A commander could not use inspections "to determine the fitness and readiness of the person, organization, or equipment" as a subterfuge to seek contraband, thereby turning the inspection into a search.[71] The original version of the Nellingen movement in effect mandated illegal searches.

Persons also objected to the paragraph advising officers to tell suspected and known abusers and pushers that they were after them. Persons considered this inappropriate because it was the declared policy of the Department of the Army "to make a sustained effort to prevent abuse and dependency on drugs and to attempt to restore to effective and reliable functioning all individuals with problems attributable to drugs." Helping an abuser was mandatory. Commanders needed to turn pushers over to the responsibility of the proper investigative agency. Persons also strongly objected to the instruction that commanders should reduce all pushers and users to the lowest rank possible if there was any evidence that they were involved with drugs. Such an action constituted unlawful command influence. A superior officer could not direct or recommend the type and degree of punishment that a subordinate commander used to discipline or punish his troops. Similarly, commanders could not legally influence the judicial acts of the military courts.[72]

Finally Persons recommended the addition of a paragraph that reminded commanders to view every case individually: "It is not suggested that in each case, every drug offender or every participant in the rehabilitation program should feel the full brunt of the command's administrative and judicial powers." Commanders were required to analyze each situation on a case-by-case basis and only take actions that were absolutely necessary to ensure a positive and effective rehabilitation.[73]

Persons's legal objections to aspects of the Nellingen movement apparently did not spread. Programs developed after January 1973 still contained provisions that were legally objectionable. The commander of the First Support Brigade distributed a memorandum among his officers containing guidelines on drug abuse control. He termed his drug control effort "Operation Hardline." Among the measures suggested were many that Persons had objected to in the Nellingen program. The guidelines also demonstrated that the commander of the First Support Brigade held a contemptuous view of drug abusers and gave little thought to rehabilitation. The memo advised commanders to inform all potential and known users that they were after them. Commanders were to reduce identified users to the lowest rank. Moreover, commanders were to conduct frequent health, welfare, and safety inspections focusing their attention on potential and suspected abusers. As with the Nellingen program, the commander intended to scare soldiers away from drug use. In his oral history interview, Persons referred to a commander who called units under his command into a movie theater. He then had the soldiers strip down for full cavity searches.

Persons believed that many commanders were misusing the inspections to harass drug users, even if they did not charge soldiers they had found possessing drugs. Neither Davison nor Persons condoned these measures.[74] They believed that commanders had sufficient means to find drugs and their users. As long as commanders stayed within the legal definition of what constituted an inspection, they had the authority to look into people's belongings in a way that was not possible in civilian society.

Legal officers reviewed the legality of inspections, specifically the "full court press" on two further occasions. One memo to Persons outlined the legal difference between a health and welfare inspection and a search. The "full court press" was still "a form of military inspection and corrective activity, not a search in the legal sense."[75] Commanders could not violate a soldier's right to privacy unless the military mission of a unit was threatened. A "full court press" was only acceptable if the inspection met "the generally accepted standards of a true health, safety, welfare, and operational readiness inspection."[76] The goal of such an inspection was "to inspect for those areas, the identification of drug users, the rehabilitation of drug users, administrative separation of non-rehabilitative drug abusers, and establishment of a drug-free environment." A criminal prosecution could not be the goal of such inspections. The government's right to conduct such inspections depended in part "on its decision not to use evidence so discovered in criminal prosecution." Another aspect of the "full court press" that made it legally problematic was that unlike the standard inspection, commanders did not conduct it randomly. A "full court press" was triggered "by a commander's generalized knowledge of his unit." If a commander suspected an individual in such a unit of possessing drugs, he needed to consult the judge advocate's office before conducting an inspection or a search.[77] A soldier had the following rights during an inspection:

(1) a right to be examined in a segregated and semiprivate area by a trained physician under conditions approximating a normal medical examination; (2) a right to be present when his room and belongings are inspected; (3) a right to have the inspection conducted during duty hours and not in the middle of the night; (4) a right to have personal items such as letters, pictures, wallets, etc., only cursorily examined for presence of illegal items; (5) a right to be inspected no more thoroughly than anyone else, regardless of prior suspicion of drug or alcohol use; and (6) a right to be treated with dignity.

By March 1973 Davison was growing concerned over the heavy emphasis some of his subordinate commanders were placing on monitoring and disciplining drug users. In a backchannel communication to the other commanders, Davison stated that a few commanders had "abused their discretion and exceeded the limits of their authority." These commanders had used "techniques authorized as rehabilitative tools" as punishment. Commanders were not looking at the individual soldier but using all techniques against all abusers. They did not seek adequate confirmation of an individual's involvement with drugs and were using the hardest techniques indiscriminately. This indiscriminate use of authority by a few, Davison warned, undermined the credibility of the program and was counterproductive. Davison asked his commanders to consider "the limits on our authority to compel rehabilitation, and of the effects that some programs have on the majority of soldiers who are not abusers." However, despite his warnings Davison did not condemn most of the measures the GI committee had highlighted in its lawsuit. Davison only advocated a more measured use. He made clear that suspicion of drug use was only a valid basis for further inquiry. Commanders could not take disciplinary action against a suspected user, nor could they initiate a treatment program for such an individual. They could send a suspected user to a Center for Drug and Alcohol Abuse Control for further evaluation. They could suspend their access to classified material or their flying status while the centers evaluated them. Any other administrative action was only valid against identified abusers. Davison cautioned that "not every administrative corrective action is appropriate in every case." Commanders had to evaluate the individual and apply the program according to his needs in consultation with the CDAAC.[78]

In his backchannel Davison went through most of the procedures that commanders had developed since the fall of 1972. Every action taken had to aid directly in maintaining a safe and drug-free environment for the individual soldier. It had to be relevant to the individual's case. Davison considered the prohibition on wearing civilian clothes a useful measure, but he cautioned commanders against actually removing civilian clothes from a soldier's room. Commanders could order a man who violated an order not to wear his civilian clothes and not to keep them in the barracks area. However, they could not confiscate his clothes. Suspension of an individual's privately owned vehicle for sixty days was a reasonable measure, because intemperate use of alcohol or drugs bore a reasonable and substantial relationship to the licensee's qualifications as a vehicle operator. However, Davison cautioned that such an individual was entitled to present his side of the story.[79] Commanders could order an identified abuser, married or not, to move into the barracks for part of the rehabilitation cycle. But a commander could not force a soldier to terminate his lease on an off-base apartment. Commanders only had the power to curtail an individual's use of the residence temporarily when the individual's living off-post was contributing to his abuse. Such off-base living quarters could only be searched with probable cause and only "in conjunction with host country bearing a warrant." Asking soldiers who wanted to live off-post to sign a "consent" form to search before giving the approval for the move was illegal.

Searches were another area in which Davison, like his JAG, cautioned his subordinates. Health and welfare inspections could function as a subterfuge to perform a search in absence of probable cause: "If the shakedown follows a tip and its object is contraband that an individual is thought to possess, the shakedown is a search, bringing into play the requirement for 'probable cause.'" A commander who conducted a search which he knew to be illegal was subject to criminal prosecution. Health and welfare inspections were a tool to ensure the fitness and readiness of the troops. Similarly, Davison insisted that while officers and NCOs should increase their visibility in the unit areas during off-duty hours, the appearance of harassment was to be avoided: "What is needed is to make our presence and concern felt while preserving, so far as possible, the individual's privacy." While Davison encouraged commanders to seek confidential information about drug abusers from their troops, he cautioned them to act only upon information from sources known to be reliable.[80]

Davison repeatedly warned his officers about inflexible policies that treated all drug users as the same. Such policies were counterproductive in his view. Commanders were to avoid blanket reductions in rank of the identified abusers, as recommended in the Nellingen movement. Instead each case had to be "considered on its own merits in light of job performance and likelihood of successful rehabilitation." Reduction could never become a forgone conclusion. Directives stating that identified drug abusers would receive a court-martial or punishment under Article 15 were blatantly illegal. Equally illegal were orders for identified abusers not to accept, buy, or take items of personal property from other members of the unit. The order represented an attempt to remove users from a drug culture. However, this was an unlawful invasion of the individual's property rights and was unenforceable. Similarly, blanket prohibitions against hanging pictures and posters in an identified abuser's room Davison considered too broad. Such a measure did not "bear any reasonable relationship to the rehabilitation effort."[81] Commanders could not advise a soldier's parents or wife of his drug use without his consent. Moreover, commanders could not have the names of identified abusers read at company formations or post them on the unit bulletin boards. An identified drug user could only be restricted to his quarters when a commander intended to take disciplinary action, not as a preventative measure.

If Davison had stressed the need for discipline in his January speeches, he now went back to an emphasis on the concern for the individual soldier: "Our rehabilitation policies and programs should foster a desire to seek treatment and encourage individuals to continue in a treatment program." Certainly, those unwilling to accept treatment were to be discharged promptly, but the emphasis remained on rehabilitation. Commanders needed to avoid implementing antidrug programs that negatively affected "clean soldiers." No policy or drug program could threaten morale or "violate any legal right of any soldier."[82]

The document does not give away whether Davison's backchannel was in any way inspired by the pending trial in which GIs from USAREUR asked the U.S. District Court to declare USAREUR's drug abuse control program to be in violation of the soldiers' rights as individuals. The references to the legal rights of the soldiers seem to indicate that Davison was trying to avoid any impression that the program was punitive in nature and that officers in his command were unconcerned about their soldiers' rights. The backchannel also shows that Davison's attempts to make the concern for the individual the main focus of the program had not fully succeeded.

Concern for the welfare of the individual soldier was not the only reason Davison issued his memorandum. Marijuana cases were clogging up the military justice system. So far, the CID had been required to open investigations in every case of possession of marijuana. Davison and Judge Advocate Persons concluded that in order to free up the system, the priority in law enforcement should be hard drugs, since the JAG office did not have the resources to try all marijuana cases. Aside from efficiency, Davison and Persons also believed that going after every marijuana case was detrimental to the soldiers' faith in the military. To equate marijuana possession with more serious crimes was counterproductive, because it lowered soldiers' respect for the justice system.[83] Davison believed that while the army could not condone drug use, commanders had to accept that many men did not view drug use as a social evil. Moreover, there was "no logical corollary between the personal use of marijuana, hashish, and the commission of a more traditional criminal offense." If both were treated the same, it destroyed the soldiers' respect for the military justice system and caused resentment against the entire disciplinary structure.[84] Once again Davison and Persons argued that a differentiated approach was the key to solving USAREUR's social problems.

When the lawsuit was filed in April 1973, many of the drug control programs were already being adapted to the demands of the commander in chief and the judge advocate general. The trial sped up the process but did not the trigger the turnaround. While many of the lower-level commanders seemed reluctant to make the needs of soldiers a priority in dealing with drug abuse, the highest levels of command demonstrated a consistent concern for the welfare of the individual soldier.[85]

In reaction to Davison's backchannel, the commander of V Corps, Pearson, also sent a memo to his subordinates warning them that in a few instances commanders were taking actions that were possibly infringing on their individual rights or dignity. Pearson specified that commanders could not categorize any soldier as a drug abuser, require him to enter a rehabilitation program, or subject him to administrative sanctions simply on the basis of suspicion or association. Rehabilitation measures were not a form of punishment. For any administrative measure taken, there had to be "a reasonable basis for the action," and it had to "bear a reasonable relation to the purpose for which it was taken." Inspections could not function as a subterfuge for a search. Pearson instructed his commanders to avoid measures that would "cause unnecessary degradation, embarrassment, or harassment of soldiers."[86] While USAREUR's top leaders would admit that excesses were taking place in regard to the drug abuse control efforts, the leadership always denied the GI committee's central claim that the overall program itself was flawed. However, Davison did have USAREUR circular 600-85 revised.[87] The timing of Davison's and Pearson's responses does suggest that they were concerned about the complaints documented in the court case.

Command emphasis on motivating soldiers to seek rehabilitation voluntarily continued. In the summer of 1973, V Corps leadership started an effort to include military dependents in its rehabilitation program. Soldiers weren't the only ones experimenting with drugs; their teenaged sons and daughters sometimes did so as well. A survey conducted among 557 high school students in Germany found that 30 percent of fifteen-year-olds reported using drugs. The number rose to 67 percent for male and 50 percent for female students who were eighteen years old.[88] A congressional report put together in 1972 estimated that as many as 50–60 percent of the military dependents used hashish. This was not the result of a survey but the estimates of dependents interviewed in Germany. In trying to identify such dependents, USAREUR leaders faced a dilemma. They did not have the legal right to require urinalysis tests of the dependents. Even a voluntary testing program was fraught with legal and logistical difficulties. Among the logistical difficulties was the fact that USAREUR lacked the facilities to treat dependents using or addicted to drugs.[89]

To change that situation, V Corps established the Frankfurt Youth

Health Center (YHC) in May 1973. While primarily founded as a means to combat drug use among teenagers, the facility's capabilities exceeded that narrow mission. Services included "medical care short of hospitalization and psychiatric and psychological services short of residential care." Adolescents, ages thirteen through eighteen, were the target group. The center handled other problems as well, including family dysfunction, behavior problems, or school difficulties. The center was very successful at identifying venereal diseases and pregnancies.[90] A comprehensive health care facility also carried less of a stigma than a facility expressly set up to handle drug abuse or just metal health or family counseling problems.

By the summer of 1973, USAREUR had completed its administrative overhaul of its drug abuse program and policies. Davison had rewritten circular 600-85. Rehabilitation was now a major priority. All major commands within USAREUR had established their own programs in accordance with circular 600-85. Centers for Drug and Alcohol Abuse Control now existed in most military communities. Davison and his subordinates had been successful in setting up an infrastructure within USAREUR to handle drug abuse among its soldiers. However, the trial before the U.S. District Court indicated that at the community level, commanders still struggled with finding the balance between vigorously enforcing discipline and showing concern for the soldier suffering from addiction. Many officers did not fully embrace Davison's concept of concerned leadership.

Reports from the USAREUR Drug and Alcohol Abuse Assessment Team visiting military communities all over Germany indicated that administrative changes alone were not solving the problems. The reports showed that many of the Centers for Drug and Alcohol Abuse Control (CDAAC) lacked staff and support from the local commanders.[91] Counselors and commanders were often lacking in knowledge of the USAREUR guidance on drug abuse. The medical staff kept incomplete records and handled urinalysis testing samples sloppily. Addicts hoodwinked overworked counselors into believing that they were no longer using drugs. When visiting the CDAAC at Flak Kaserne in the

Ludwigsburg area, the assessment team found that the center was six months behind in its paperwork. The case records they had kept provided no histories of drug use and no urinalysis testing results. The center placed soldiers in a follow-up program after one session with the counselor. The team conducted interviews with soldiers who admitted that they had continued using drugs after seeing a counselor but had been declared rehabilitated.[92] Officers on some bases retained a punitive attitude toward abusers, trying to keep them in the unit until they could obtain a discharge under less than honorable conditions.[93]

On other bases, commanders took little interest one way or the other. During a visit to Böblingen, the assessment team described a drug abuse problem of almost epidemic proportions. A private on leave in the United States triggered the visit to Böblingen. PFC David C. Coffey refused to return to his unit in Germany. He claimed that drug abuse was widespread, alleging that 80 percent of the post personnel were using drugs and smoking hashish, 50 percent were using downers, and that heroin and cocaine were also widely used. Coffey also claimed that users were beating and robbing non-users for "fix money." They had to pull extra guard duty and suffered intimidation by drug users. Officers and NCOs were aware of the problems but apathetic.[94] Multiple interviewees in the Library of Congress's Veterans History Project describe similar scenes regarding drug use in Germany.[95] During its visit to the Panzer Kaserne, the assessment team found that Coffey was afraid not so much of the harassment he faced from drug users but of the consequences of his own use of drugs. The team found out that Coffey was a frequent user of hashish and amphetamines. The team suspected that Coffey had bought a large amount of drugs on credit before he left and was afraid of his creditors.[96]

Despite Coffey's somewhat suspect motives, the team also found indications of widespread drug use and a failure by command to cope with it. Coffey's unit had a particularly high number of users. Fifteen members of E Company of the 701st Maintenance Battalion used needles, 40 used speed, and 130 smoked pot. During the visit one of the team members actually found a man "nodding out" from heroin on the steps of the company barracks. The commander of E Company had been unable to get urinalysis tests from the dispensary the day after pay day because the medics refused to do any tests on that day. The team found out that 26 of the 32 medics running that dispensary were drug users themselves. A random survey of units at the Panzer Kaserne members of the headquarters and C Company, 116th Infantry Division estimated that approximately 80 percent of the men in their respective units were using hashish and 20–25 percent were using hard drugs. The assessment team member visiting these units had talked with 27 enlisted men and 12 NCOs. None of the soldiers interviewed had any confidence in the programs run by the Center for Drug and Alcohol Abuse Control.[97]

Soldiers and commanders alike lacked confidence in the CDAAC. Lower-level commanders were not ensuring that abusers in their units kept their appointments for counseling and urinalysis. They often took their time in referring abusers to the CDAAC, and the CDAAC itself was slow in reacting to new cases. Individuals would not receive interviews until months after their initial referral. Some soldiers went for their interview a month after they had gone through detoxification. The counselors kept vague and incomplete records, making it difficult or impossible to pass a case from one counselor to the other.[98] The report showed that the newly created institutions were not yet functioning as intended, because lower levels of command did not pursue the drug abuse control program with the same vigor as their commander in chief.

Both Böblingen and Ludwigsburg were part of VII Corps, which had been slower in developing a policy than V Corps or USAREUR command. The VII Corps circular came out in February of that year.[99] Böblingen had only established a CDAAC in April 1973. The assessment team conceded in its report that this might have been a contributing factor. But reports from other facilities indicate that V Corps bases had difficulties as well despite the fact that V Corps had formulated its policy in the fall of 1972 and that the commander in chief, General Pearson, had been very active in formulating the policy. In the fall of

1973, some commanders still retained a punitive attitude toward drug users. A battalion commander in Bad Kreuznach published a circular in which he claimed that permissiveness and clemency could not solve the drug problem. Commanders had to balance the pleasure derived from drugs with corresponding displeasure and pain. Commanders could only keep drug users from using if they feared detection and punishment. Users had to enroll in an eight-week program during which they were under constant supervision and had to undergo intensive drill and training. The commander discontinued the program after the *New York Times* took an interest.[100]

When an assessment team visited the Mainz community and three facilities in the surrounding area in August 1973,[101] they found a fragmented program that was not fully functional. The CDAAC was not "the focal point for the management of drug and alcohol abusers in all units." Commanders showed a punitive attitude toward abusers and urinalysis collection, and reporting had proven unreliable. They had not taken any visible actions to eliminate the drug traffic in the area.[102] Notorious locations such as the Kings Club in Frankfurt where GIs could obtain drugs continued to operate without command interference.[103]

The CDAAC kept incomplete case records and was not conducting frequent interviews with the enlisted men who were being referred there. In Mainz the CDAAC lacked the support not only of the lower-level commanders but also of the community commander, who had actually barred the CDAAC personnel from contacting unit commanders directly. As a result, the center and officers exchanged little information on drug abuse cases. The assessment discovered that one unit, First Battalion of the 509th Infantry Division, had actually set up its own center for drug abuse control, bypassing the CDAAC entirely. Staffed by the battalion drug education specialist, a sergeant, with three full-time counselors, this center did not coordinate with the CDAAC, the ADAPCT, or with the medical professionals in the command. The fragmentation of control efforts and the lack of communication led to inadequate treatment and monitoring of drug users.[104] As one particularly egregious example, the report cited the case of a soldier whose urine had tested positive on several occasions but who after four months without improvement remained in the service.[105]

The urinalysis program was deficient. Commanders were not placing their personnel in the urinalysis program. The program also had history of false results. Individuals with positive urine test results turned out to be clinically negative. The CDAAC at Finthen was the exception among the Mainz facilities, as it received high marks despite some problems with record keeping.

Mainz was not the only community where the implementation of a drug abuse program proved difficult. Commanders in the Giessen community also demonstrated little enthusiasm.[106] The Third Medical Battalion stationed in Aschaffenburg actually became the focus of a congressional inquiry by Representative Shirley Chisholm of New York. Chisholm had received reports of a deplorable drug situation in that battalion. The indifference on the part of the superior officers was causing enlisted men "to seek escape through drugs and drug abuse discharges." More and more, non-users were supposedly becoming involved, and increasing numbers of people were applying for the rehabilitation program.[107]

When the assessment team came to the battalion, they found the situation to be less alarming than Chisholm had indicated. However, they did find low morale within the battalion. According to the assessment team, the Third Medical Battalion had effectively implemented the USAREUR drug control program. The community center was functioning, and a majority of the officers and NCOs "were familiar with and effectively implementing USAREUR circular 600-85."[108] A somewhat surprising finding was that despite a functioning drug control program, morale was low for reasons not directly attributable to drugs. Instead, the unit had been in the field for three months and had been working on weekends since its return. Because of billets renovations, soldiers were living in a gym with no privacy or security, and they were complaining about their leadership. Superiors were not showing any interest in their men and tended to talk down to them. Pay problems remained unresolved, and the battalion leaders gave a general impression of disorganization. According to the report, "Approximately 95 percent of all the men interviewed complained about some morale factors, expressed little faith in the organization, and displayed little loyalty toward the unit."[109]

While the army in Germany struggled with the implementation of an effective drug control program throughout 1973, the situation started to improve in the following year. Despite the refinement of the urinalysis program, fewer users were being detected. . Davison interpreted the decline that started in September 1973 as a sign that the program was finally taking effect. Hepatitis levels, which had peeked in August 1973, were also declining. During the first half of the year, 5,200 soldiers (2.9 percent of the command) were in active rehabilitation. During the second half, the number went down to 3,400 (or 1.9 percent). Eighty percent of those soldiers had used drugs and 20 percent overindulged in alcohol. USAREUR had a 48 percent success rate returning soldiers to active duty after undergoing the 60-day rehabilitation program. Thirty percent of the soldiers failed. Twenty-two percent never completed the program. The army interpreted this as progress. While the problem would not disappear anytime soon, the army had ameliorated it to a degree that it was not a threat "to the command's discipline, professionalism, and readiness."[110]

The assessment teams sent to various posts in Germany generally reported an improved situation. Their reports tended to list as many favorable aspects as deficiencies, and many of the deficiencies noted were minor compared with the reports filed a year or six months earlier. In most reports the assessment team found "a keen awareness" of the Alcohol and Drug Abuse Prevention and Control Program.[111] Commanders, first sergeants, and drug and alcohol education specialists were knowledgeable about drug abuse and the program. The CDAACs were now functioning properly and were coordinating their efforts with commanders. Education efforts were ongoing and believed to be sound. Among the common deficiencies noted was a lack of diligence on the part of company or battery commanders. These commanders were responsible for ensuring that facilities conducted urinalysis as prescribed. Some commanders were negligent in ensuring that soldiers in rehabilitation were keeping their appointments for testing and for counseling. Some company and battery level commanders also showed a reluctance to identify and refer drug abusers early before an overt act.[112] These were probably the most serious deficiencies. Most others were concerned with administrative processing of abusers.

The assessment team revisited the Nellingen and Böblingen communities in the summer of 1974. Unlike a year earlier, both received positive evaluations. In the case of Böblingen, the team reported now that command emphasis on the drug abuse program as a top priority permeated throughout the entire community. Commanders and drug and alcohol education specialists were very knowledgeable about their responsibilities and duties. The CDAAC was located in a new building and was functioning effectively. The staff was competent, motivated, and dedicated. Officers were properly referring affected soldiers to the CDAAC. Commanders were conducting periodic health and welfare inspections. The urine testing procedures had been implemented properly and were functioning smoothly. The report on Nellingen made similar positive observations, but the assessment team was even more enthusiastic about the work of the CDAAC. The deficiencies noted in both cases were similar to other communities during this period. Command had not set up the ADDIC council properly. Soldiers were not always keeping their counseling appointments, and minor glitches in the urine testing procedures persisted.[113] Of course, not all of the communities had improved their drug control programs as much as the ones cited above. Davison admonished the Kirchgoens/Butzbach and the Bad Kreuznach communities to step up their efforts.[114] Despite these exceptions, the overall perception was one of an improving situation.[115]

When asked during his oral history interview whether the drug control efforts undertaken between 1970 and 1974 had any noticeable effect, Persons gave a cautiously positive answer. He believed that the programs in USAREUR had been successful in getting drugs out of the barracks. Increased command attention and command presence had been an important factor in that effort. USAREUR now had a comprehensive and clear policy on drug abuse, which had not been the case before. Many of the policies developed in USAREUR became DA and DOD policy. General Hayward, who had been the deputy chief of staff responsible for personnel in USAREUR would become the assistant deputy chief of staff for personnel at the Pentagon. He was also a member of a DOD task group in charge of developing the DOD's policy on drug abuse.[116]

A very important improvement for Persons was the change in the leadership's attitude toward the problem. They now considered drug use mainly as a medical issue, not a moral or ethical problem, and they treated it as an illness, not a crime. As in the case of discrimination, the army started moving toward a solution when it put the problem in terms of efficiency and practicality. Drug abuse was unacceptable because it interfered "with the physical ability of the soldier to do his job." On the area of law enforcement and interdicting the supply, Persons was less optimistic. He did believe that USAREUR had been successful in convincing German authorities of the importance of the problem. German authorities had become much more active in their law enforcement efforts in regard to the traffic of illegal drugs. However, Persons concluded that as long as selling drugs remained lucrative, people would be smuggling and selling it.[117]

When a task force of the Select House Committee on Narcotics Abuse and Control held hearings on drug abuse in USAREUR in November 1978, two years after Davison had left his command, the task force members gained the impression that the situation had not improved much since 1976. In his opening statement, Representative Benjamin A. Gilman of New York claimed that surveys and inquiries conducted by the task force among the troops in Germany indicated a high rate of abuse. According to Gilman, 75 percent of the troops were using soft drugs and more than 15 percent were using hard drugs.[118] The chairman of the task force, Glenn English of Oklahoma, expressed the opinion that the situation among troops in Germany was more alarming than in civilian society: "I don't believe that there is any question that there are more hard drugs used in Germany than there are among comparable young people in the United States, and that is particularly true . . . of young soldiers in the United States."[119] Throughout the proceedings, the members of Congress present at the hearings expressed their concern over the situation.

Their reaction to what they had observed in Germany seemed to indicate that little had changed in USAREUR since the beginning of the decade. However, the responses and analyses of soldiers in Germany differed from the politicians and indicated that things had changed even though drug use had not diminished. While officers questioned by the committee were willing to admit that there was a drug problem, they were not willing to admit that the military was not ready to face it or that the problem was interfering with the readiness of their troops.

During the hearings Brig. Gen. Grail L. Brookshire, spokesman for the headquarters, European command (EUCOM), emphasized the increased communication between the branches of the military in Europe. The army, navy, and air force had been exchanging ideas on a regular basis since 1976. Now two years later European command had developed methods to identify the magnitude of the drug problem in a comprehensive manner. European command had published a directive that standardized "definitions for common drug use terms, standardized methods for drug abuse reporting," and required "that component commands, using the new standardized procedures," provided headquarters with quarterly reports. According to Brookshire, the first two reports showed that the European command had a drug problem. The command considered the problem serious, just as it would "anything that adversely impacts upon the ability of this command to fight and win." Command was concerned about "the exploitation of young Americans and the destructive effect of drugs on their lives." Despite the seriousness of the problem, Brookshire stressed that the military in Europe was taking action to counteract it. The general was admitting to a problem, but he was stressing that procedures had been set up to analyze it and deal with it.[120] His reaction is not much different from other commanders in previous hearings on drug abuse. Such commanders would always stress when admitting to a problem that they were already working hard to solve it. What had changed was that the army had put procedures and institutions in place to deal with the problem, providing a sense of administrative control. The military was now capable of quantifying and defining the problem.

When Brookshire listed the areas where the military had to intensify its efforts to suppress drug abuse, those areas were not much different from Davison's enumerations in the first half of the decade. Commanders were to intensify their efforts to keep their subordinates productively occupied, particularly during their off-duty hours. The depressed value of the dollar was "making virtual prisoners" of many young GIs.[121] Commanders had to make their presence felt in the barracks and eliminate peer pressure. Brookshire put greater emphasis on law enforcement than Davison and other commanders had. He called for the removal of legal and regulatory constraints that were currently inhibiting corrective efforts. The army needed to attack the sources of illegal drugs more vigorously.

Davison's successor as CINCUSAREUR was his former subordinate, commander of VII Corps, George S. Blanchard. Like Brookshire, Blanchard acknowledged a drug problem in Europe. Blanchard was particularly concerned about the availability of high-grade, inexpensive heroin. When asked by the task force whether drug abuse had increased or decreased since his arrival in Europe as commander of VII Corps in 1973, Blanchard said he believed that it had increased.[122] Nonetheless, Blanchard's overall assessment was much more positive than the assessments of Davison and other commanders in USAREUR at the beginning of the decade. He based his relative optimism on two factors, the level of awareness about the drug problem and the high readiness of his troops.

Blanchard believed that awareness was higher than ever before: "Never in my five years in Europe have I witnessed the degree of awareness of the problem and the intense desire to do something about it which prevails today." Awareness implied readiness to deal with the problem. Blanchard and his staffers stressed that they were capable of reliably quantifying and measuring drug abuse and the combat readiness of the troops. In assessing the present effect of drug abuse on the readiness of his troops, Blanchard concluded that at this point drug abuse was not a major detriment to the overall readiness. Blanchard based his conclusions on five factors. According to USAREUR's chief surgeon, drug abuse in the command was not the result of "hardcore addiction." Biochemical testing programs and the opinion survey data supported this claim. In putting together prevalence estimates, Blanchard considered the substances abused, the frequency of their abuse, and the population engaging in that abuse. To arrive at an accurate assessment Blanchard tried to understand the relationship between what surveys and urinalysis testing showed and what soldiers were telling him and other officers.[123]

Blanchard's testimony and the hearings indicate that the drug abuse problem in USAREUR had not been eliminated and that the number of users had not diminished significantly. So had Davison and the USAREUR leadership of the early 1970s failed? Despite the prevailing view that drug abuse was still widespread in USAREUR, the sense of crisis prevalent earlier in the decade was absent. Despite the remaining problems, Blanchard and his subordinates were able to convey the impression that they were retaining control and capable of producing all relevant information. Awareness among officers of the problem was high. Blanchard emphasized openness among his subordinate commanders about drug use in their units.[124] Programs such as the CDAAC provided the army with procedures to deal with the abusers.

This did not shield the army from criticism. The representatives conducting the hearings in 1978 were not always convinced that the numbers and assessments presented to them by the leadership were accurate. However, Blanchard was able to present a coherent picture of the situation in his command supported by subordinates with experience and expertise on the subject. The image of USAREUR presented at these hearings was a far cry from the confused and somewhat helpless image it had presented to the public in 1971. In this Blanchard had profited greatly from the developments his predecessor had set in motion.

Much as had been the case in regard to race relations, Davison's strategy of candid acknowledgment and command responsibility had been successful in robbing the issue of its immediacy. In emphasizing rehabilitation, he reduced the potential for tension and confrontations between commanders and the men serving under them. Again Lawrence Radine's concept of co-optive rational control provides a useful description for Davison strategy. The "rational" in Radine's concept refers to the principle of rationalization: "Rationalization, the other principle within this modern style of control, is based on behavioral science that models itself after physics. This kind of behavioral science sees prediction and careful measurement as key criteria in judging the adequacy of hypotheses and theories."[125] Rationalization was certainly a key principle in USAREUR's efforts to control drug abuse. The programs and facilities created provided an infrastructure to assess and quantify the extent of the abuse and to manage it in a rational manner. This rational management along with the involvement of the individual in the process proved an effective way to eliminate the sense of crisis and alienation within the army in regard to drug abuse.

This understanding of political undercurrents among the enlisted soldiers was one of the strengths of co-optive leadership. It could also be seen in the approach to understanding drug usage, another activity connected with the extent of alienation from army life. Enlisted men's advisory councils and drug advisory councils were useful ways of transmitting these undercurrents to the officers and usually resulted in suggestions for taking the most appropriate actions. While Radine's description of the army's strategy was apt, his assessment that the army's co-optive techniques were merely creating an illusion of unity of officers and men was less so. Again, Radine assumed the motives of army leaders to be sinister or cynical: "Without a true unity of purpose and a diffusion of power, co-optive techniques can only be a smokescreen for class relationships."[126] Radine offered little proof for a lack of sincerity on the part of officers in involving their men in finding solutions. To a certain degree the actual motives of commanders, such as Davison, were moot because they did succeed in restoring at least a perception of being on top of the drug abuse problem. That was sufficient to end the sense of crisis prevalent in 1971.

9

The German Response

The woes of U.S. Army, Europe, did not go unnoticed in its host country. Like their American counterparts, German journalists covered the social problems of U.S. troops in both Vietnam and Germany. Here, too, attention turned increasingly to Germany after 1971. The themes of the German articles mirrored American coverage of three familiar areas. German journalists did not always take advantage of the proximity of U.S. troops. In fact, newsmagazines such as *Der Spiegel* often quoted from articles published by the *New York Times* and the *Washington Post*. Many articles included no interviews of their own. One example of such a story ran in *Der Spiegel* in early 1971 on the armed forces' global drug abuse problems. The articles focused on Vietnam and the United States, providing the account of an arrest of pilots of the Strategic Air Command in California and including a claim that there were more "potheads than airborne soldiers" in the air force.[1] The articles made no reference to the extensive drug abuse among army or air force personnel in Germany. At other times reporters would bring the crisis closer to home.

German press coverage reflected the ambiguity and growing complexity of German attitudes toward U.S. troops. With the exception of the right-leaning Springer Press and other conservative outlets, the major West German news outlets such as *Der Spiegel, Der Stern,* and television networks had displayed skepticism about the U.S. military engagement in Vietnam. Their coverage of the German antiwar movement reflected that skepticism.[2] However, unlike the anti-American attitudes of the antiauthoritarian Left, this skepticism did not necessarily lead the German media to question the German-American alliance or the presence of American troops in West Germany. Looking at the coverage in *Der Spiegel*, few articles published before 1972 reflect on or raise concerns about how the current troubles in USAREUR might affect German-American relations. This changed somewhat in 1972.

In its April 4 issue, the magazine ran a ten-page analysis of what was ailing the Seventh Army. For the first time, a reporter observed changing German attitudes about GIs. In the reporter's opinion, German support for the U.S. troop presence was in decline. GIs stationed in Germany did not exclusively shape these changing attitudes. As a matter of fact, the article emphasized negative attitudes regarding U.S. involvement in Vietnam. However, the problems of USAREUR certainly reinforced negative images. The article starts off by describing the World War II image of victorious soldiers of the Seventh Army landing on the beaches of Sicily and fighting their way north all the way into Bavaria, then contrasting this image with the current conditions in barracks all over southern and southwestern Germany. The author also included references to the atrocities committed at My Lai and My Khe and linked them to domestic racial conflicts in the United States. He described U.S. society as at odds with itself and expressed uncertainty whether the United States could serve as a model of democracy and progress as it had following World War II. These anxieties of U.S. society according to the author were also clearly visible among GIs in Germany. They were becoming evident in the increased violence, crime, drug use, and racial conflicts. Many GIs were expressing doubts about their mission in Germany and were beginning to resent their German hosts. This was partially due to the economic problems enlisted personnel were experiencing due to the devaluation of the dollar. While many soldiers could no longer afford to go off base, their German neighbors were prospering. Their German comrades-in-arms in the Bundeswehr were far better housed and equipped.[3]

Similarly, Germans were increasingly voicing their doubts about the U.S. mission in Germany. The violence and crime surrounding U.S. bases was contributing to a sense that twenty-six years of the U.S. military presence were enough. One local police official in Neu-Ulm, Bavaria, was quoted as saying, "Here like everywhere else in the country we are tired of the Americans." The author concluded that more than two decades of living next to each other had done little to bring Germans and Americans closer. U.S. soldiers remained too isolated in their "Little Americas" to build lasting relationships with German citizens. Accordingly, their presence had contributed little to changing German prejudices. Because of the changing economic fortunes, Germans were no longer eager for access to the closed American societies. Many once scarce consumer products were now readily available to them.

At first glance this article appears to suggest a major shift in German perceptions of the United States and its armed forces stationed in West Germany. As such the article reflects the relative decline of the U.S. government's reputation and that of its armed forces during the second half of the 1960s. The German antiwar movement and the wider student protest movement had called into question the morality of U.S. foreign policy and the western political and economic system in general. Many German students and antiwar activists saw the United States as an exploitive imperialist power, not as a beacon of liberty and democratic values. The German protest movement had strongly shaped political and social debates since at least the mid-1960s. The sentiments expressed in the article seemed to indicate that the activists' criticism of the United States had found its way into the wider German public and that the social crisis within the U.S. Army was reinforcing these increasingly negative views.

However, the article itself also called into question this broad depiction of the West German public turning against an American presence in their country. The author noted some concern over the prospect of an American withdrawal. Major troop withdrawals had become a very real prospect in 1971, less because of any pressure exerted by the German antiwar movement than by the efforts of Senate Majority Leader Mike Mansfield (D-MT). Mansfield had become the proponent of reducing the military presence in Europe as a means of curbing military spending. Additionally, the Nixon administration and the West German government were engaged in tense discussions over cost sharing. These so-called offset negotiations and Mansfield's efforts caused concern among West Germans for two reasons. First, they feared that U.S. withdrawals would make West Germany, the frontline of the Cold War, more vulnerable and would embolden the Soviets. Second, such withdrawals would have severe economic repercussions for the small and midsized communities of southwestern Germany, as pointed out by the mayor of Baumholder. *Der Spiegel* further pointed out that despite the contemporary sense of crisis, many complaints German locals had about the troops in their regions were part and parcel of housing a foreign military community. In regard to the crisis within Seventh Army, the conflicts within the army were much more severe than conflicts between GIs and their German hosts.

While conveying a sense of growing German antipathy toward their American guests, the author of the article offered only anecdotal evidence. He did not cite any opinion polls. Such polls, had he consulted them, would not have borne him out. However, the article does provide evidence that the relationship between GIs and Germans had become more ambiguous. It also names the two major factors contributing to this growing ambiguity: the Vietnam War and the social crisis within USAREUR. This chapter will analyze the extent to which West German attitudes toward the U.S. troops in their country changed between 1968 and 1975. Accordingly, the West German attitudes toward GIs have to be considered from three perspectives: the antiwar and student protest movement, the wider public, and the government.

The 1960s mark a period of convergence in terms of anti-Americanism emanating from the Right and the Left of the political spectrum in West Germany.[4] Traditionally the Right had displayed much greater hostility to American cultural influences, both before and after World

War II. Skepticism and cultural pessimism concerning modernization and technological innovation had a long-standing tradition in German intellectual circles going back to the nineteenth century. By the 1920s and 1930s, many critics of technology and modernity increasingly saw the United States as the embodiment of modernization.[5] Within the New Left, conservative tropes of American cultural dominance now merged with a leftist critique of U.S. foreign and domestic policy as well as its economic system.[6] Criticism of American imperialism and capitalism culminated in marches and protests against the Vietnam War.[7] Within that context the U.S. military presence became another symbol of the American drive for global domination. The anti-Americanism of the German New Left often mirrored the U.S. protest movement's criticisms of conditions in the United States and led to the formation of alliances between the German and American New Left.[8]

In both countries anti-imperialism seemed to offer an answer to the lack of revolutionary fervor among the domestic working class. The New Left drew heavily on the Frankfurt School, particularly Marcuse's concept of repressive tolerance.[9] Their reading of Marcuse also offered them a new definition of which social groups could inspire or take revolutionary action. Marcuse had argued that within advanced industrial societies such as the United States and West Germany, only marginalized social groups, groups on the outside, could initiate a revolutionary transformation.[10] The great affluence of western societies and their emphasis on consumption made workers in West Germany and the United States complicit in the capitalist system that exploited the resources and work of Third World countries. The West German New Left, particularly the increasingly dominant antiauthoritarian faction represented by Rudi Dutschke, saw itself as a marginalized minority that could reawaken the revolutionary fervor in German society.[11] The New Left reinforced this self-perception by emphasizing solidarity with revolutionary struggles in the Third World. These struggles as well as the struggles of African Americans in the United States provided the model and starting point to carry the revolution into the First World.[12]

Opposing the Vietnam War became the focal point of the German student protest movement. The German Socialist Student League (SDS) dominated antiwar protests as early as 1965. Accordingly, political and ideological motives took on much greater importance than pacifist or humanitarian considerations.[13] U.S. engagement and conduct in Vietnam supplied the antiauthoritarian Left with vivid proof of the destructive and exploitive nature and intent of western capitalism. To antiauthoritarian activists, Vietnam revealed the imperialist and fascist nature of the American government and society and that of its ally, West Germany. Demonstrations against the war often targeted U.S. facilities in West Germany and West Berlin. Consulates and *Amerikahäuser* became frequent targets of marches and protest actions.[14] German activists organized two Vietnam conferences, one in Frankfurt am Main, May 1966, and another in West Berlin, February 1968.[15]

Given that three of the major hotbeds of student activism in Germany—West Berlin, Frankfurt am Main, and Heidelberg—also featured major U.S. military installations, it is not surprising that these installations and GIs became a focus of antiwar activism. In 1967 the SDS had proclaimed U.S. military installations in West Germany as legitimate targets for protest activities.[16] Similarly the Verband Deutscher Studentenschaften, another student organization, called on its members to participate in a desertion campaign targeting U.S. soldiers.[17] Activists tried to establish contacts with GIs, discuss the war, and supply them with information on desertion and other means of resistance. West German students and organizations such as the local chapters of the SDS or local student governments were a crucial part of the "underground railway." In 1967 SDS president Karl-Dietrich Wolff claimed that the SDS was channeling 150 GIs out of the country every month. While German students played an important role in helping AWOL soldiers, support for other protest activities was more likely to come from American expatriates or visiting students. American civilians, for example, primarily ran the underground newspaper *Where It's At*.[18]

Both activists and the German press paid considerable attention to the army's racial issues. The visit by Assistant Secretary of Defense

Frank Render in 1971 received extensive coverage. The same issue of *Der Spiegel* reporting on Render's findings also featured an interview with Ronald Bolden and Samuel Robertson. The two black GIs, stationed in West Berlin, had turned themselves in after going AWOL with the stated intention to stand trial and expose racism in the army. Local activists translated the interview and published it in *Forward*. Activists distributed flyers and posters in the barracks, generating major interest in the trial. Ultimately Robertson and Bolden went free.

Radical German activists identified strongly with black nationalism and black power in the late 1960s. The Black Panthers Party became their model. These movements emphasized the connections between the liberation movements of the Third World and the struggles of African Americans in the United States. Bernward Vesper and Gurdrun Ensslin published translations of black power and black nationalism literature. The growing militancy of the movement exemplified by the Black Panthers mirrored the growing militancy within parts of the German movement. The assassination attempt on Rudi Dutschke, which occurred only seven days after Martin Luther King's death, further reinforced this identification.[19]

In November 1969 Frankfurt student leader Karl-Dietrich Wolff launched the Black Panther Solidarity Committee. While support for and solidarity with the exiled Eldridge Cleaver was a major part of the committee's mission, another goal was to provide support for black GIs and their protest activities. Wolff's press, Roter Stern, printed the Black Panther underground paper, *Voice of the Lumpen*. This kind of civilian support was crucial to GI organizing outside of Frankfurt as well. Presses run by civilian activists printed the pamphlets, flyers, and underground newspapers expressing the dissatisfaction of soldiers with the current situation and calling upon fellow soldiers to join in the protest. German students provided crucial logistical support in other areas as well. They secured university facilities for demonstrations and teach-ins, such as the July 4 demonstration at the University of Heidelberg in 1970. German activists participated in the demonstrations in support of the Ramstein 2 or the Darmstadt 53. Activities surrounding the Ramstein 2 marked the high point of collaboration between civilian and military activists. The Black Panther Solidarity Committee, *Voice of the Lumpen*, and the Unsatisfied Black Soldiers of Heidelberg organized fund-raisers. The two defendants had excellent legal counsel thanks to the students.[20]

However, relations between civilian activists, be they Americans or Germans, and the African American GIs were fraught with difficulties. Many black activists were wary of working with white activists. Despite their idealism, German activists used black GIs. Their struggle offered a revolutionary authenticity that the circumstances of the predominantly middle-class German activists lacked. In their fascination with African American culture and political activism, many German activists projected their own desire for escaping the reason and conformity associated with their whiteness onto the black activists and their causes. Ideas of black spontaneity reinforced racial stereotypes as they idealized black experiences and culture. Race-related activism elicited a much more enthusiastic response from GIs and the media than efforts to unionize the army or other efforts to bring down the system. As race-related incidents and protests declined, so did the large-scale collaboration between German civilians and GIs.

The high point of the German protest movement activities in 1968 also saw an attempt to organize GI activism on a national level. The German SDS proclaimed May 8 "International Desertion Day." Activists distributed leaflets and approached soldiers at various posts in Germany. However, turnout for the protests of that day was small compared with other actions of that year. By 1968 the German protest movement focused far more on German issues such as the Springer Press and the "Emergency Laws." GI organizing did not become a major feature of the national protest movement. U.S. State Department officials did not consider German antiwar activists as a threat to U.S. troops. However, for the next few years small groups of local activists would continue to play a role in supporting and organizing GI dissent, as outlined in chapter 3.[21]

German and American civilian activists displayed ambivalence toward GIs. This ambivalence mirrored many activists' attitudes toward workers in their own country. While orthodox Marxist ideas about the centrality of the working class to any revolutionary project remained strong within the New Left, the entire concept of a "New" Left came from the realization that workers in the booming consumer society of 1960s West Germany constituted an unlikely source of social unrest. Many student activists saw themselves as the means to revitalize the revolutionary potential of the working class through education and consciousness raising. German New Left activists did attempt to organize among workers.[22] German unions and the student protest movement sometimes forged temporary alliances, but generally German workers and labor unions displayed little inclination to join the New Left.[23]

The flyers and underground newspapers distributed among GIs made frequent references to working-class solidarity and emphasized social inequality between officers and enlisted men as an indication that the armed forces were another capitalist institution exploiting the proletariat. Articles discussing the racial issues in the army would base their calls for solidarity on claims that ultimately both black and white soldiers were victims of capitalism and imperialism. At the same time many underground publications displayed an impatience and frustration with the lack of revolutionary fervor among most enlisted men that mirrors the ambivalence displayed by the New Left for domestic workers. Many of the GIs, on the other hand, did not necessarily share German activists' political views, even if they were willing to voice their frustrations with the military.

Another source of tension between civilian activists and GIs resulted from the difficult balancing act of condemning the U.S. Army as an oppressive and criminal institution while calling for solidarity with revolutionary causes all over the world among its soldiers. The German New Left, like its American counterparts, frequently drew parallels between U.S. conduct in Vietnam and German atrocities committed during World War II.[24] German antiwar activists used slogans like "USA=SA=SS," "Vietnam is the Auschwitz of America," or "American SS units, known as Green Berets and leathernecks."[25] Many flyers addressed this contradiction attempting to reassure GIs that they were not included in such condemnations. However, distinctions between the individual grunt as a member of the exploited proletariat and the army and the United States in general as imperialist or fascist institutions could easily get lost.

Not all protests against the U.S. military and its installations were nonviolent. The rhetoric of German and American activists at the Vietnam Congress in West Berlin escalated. Student leaders like Dutschke and Wolff were calling for militant action in West Germany and the opening of a second front. Dutschke initially planned to end a march during the congress at McNair Barracks. Observers at the time fully expected violent clashes between demonstrators and the police, possibly even the U.S. military police. Rudi Dutschke ultimately decided to avoid the barracks, and protests remained peaceful. But as the movement radicalized and splintered in the wake of the assassination attempt on Dutschke, debates regarding the need for armed resistance intensified. The development culminated in a small number of activists taking up arms and forming terrorist groups such as Red Army Faction or the Bewegung 2. Juni. U.S. installations and their personnel became targets of attacks.

In May 1972 the RAF staged its "May Offensive." Among the targets were two U.S. military bases. On May 11 a commando bombed the U.S. Fifth Army headquarters in Frankfurt am Main, killing one officer and thirteen enlisted men. Two weeks later, two RAF members drove a car filled with TNT into headquarters in Heidelberg, killing an officer and two enlisted men and wounding five more. The RAF claimed that these attacks represented a response to the United States' recent mining of North Vietnamese harbors and intensified bombing campaign in North Vietnam. The RAF accused the United States of genocide and demanded the withdrawal of U.S. troops from Vietnam. These actions represented the most radical end of the spectrum in terms of opposition to the United States and its institutions. RAF members did not see soldiers as potential allies in their struggles. In their subsequent messages they barely acknowledged the victims of their actions at all.[26]

The members of the RAF and other organizations who committed acts of violence represented a tiny minority within the antiauthoritarian Left. For all its visibility during the late 1960s, the New Left only constituted part of the German antiwar movement. A majority within the German public viewed the more radical student activists with skepticism. Many Germans, influenced no doubt by the negative coverage in parts of the press, blamed the SDS for the violence at demonstrations in 1968.[27] Surveys show that while many in the public were critical of the U.S. engagement in Vietnam, few outside the universities questioned the Cold War consensus. The social crisis in the army did coincide with a rise of anti-Americanism among Germans. U.S. conduct in Vietnam certainly affected West Germans' perceptions of the United States and its soldiers. Skepticism among the German public about U.S. engagement had always been relatively high. In a survey conducted in March 1966, 44 percent of the respondents believed that the United States was defending freedom against communism, while 25 percent believed that U.S. forces had no right to be there and 33 percent were undecided.[28] Most Germans were either ambivalent about or rejected U.S. involvement, and German support would continue to erode. In a survey in March 1968, 60 percent of the respondents disapproved of U.S. troops fighting in Vietnam.[29]

However, opposition or skepticism about the Vietnam War did not necessarily translate into a wholesale rejection of the United States and its role in the world and West Germany. In describing the results of the survey, *Der Spiegel* reporters saw that fewer than half of the respondents, 42 percent, believed that Americans were committing war crimes. At the same time, 61 percent were convinced that the United States' enemies in Vietnam were committing such war crimes. Now, 42 percent is not a low number. It does indicate that German perceptions of the United States had deteriorated. However, the fact that two-thirds of the respondents felt certain that Vietcong and North Vietnamese were committing war crimes does indicate that the anticommunist consensus remained strong in West German society. Throughout most of the 1960s, 50–60 percent supported for the U.S. presence in West

Germany, while only 20 percent favored U.S. withdrawal.[30] German skepticism of the Vietnam War did not translate into support of the strident anti-imperialism and anti-capitalism displayed by the most student protesters. The violence perpetrated by the RAF was highly controversial in leftist circles and found little or no resonance within the general public.

The German press did report on the morale and discipline problems among U.S. troops. Racial issues and drug abuse particularly received frequent coverage.[31] However, the deteriorating physical and social conditions were a minor factor in the changing attitudes among Germans. They mainly came into play in those regions with a strong military presence. The reputation of the army and the bases declined after the 1960s. Germans often viewed them as contributing factors in local crime rates and the illicit drug trade. On the other hand, positive memories of life around the bases in previous decades probably came with a certain degree of misplaced nostalgia. For most of the 1950s and 1960s, Germans and Americans lived as good neighbors. By 1961, 70 percent of the German population believed the Americans viewed them as friends.[32] However, even during this relatively harmonious period, bases caused social and moral concerns.

Stationing so many young men in predominantly rural areas brought some inevitable cultural and economic changes. The new bars and nightclubs emerging around military posts drew not only the soldiers but also the young Germans from around the countryside, particularly women, including prostitutes. This nightlife and the increase in amorous relations between German women and American GIs worried and disturbed German authorities and clergymen during the 1950s. They feared that the new prosperity brought in by the U.S. military was leading to sexual disorder and moral degradation.[33]

Women moving into the area to be with American boyfriends or women frequenting bars and nightclubs popular with U.S. soldiers were frequently harassed by authorities and fellow citizens. Often locals critical of these relations drew few distinctions between actual prostitutes and the soldiers' girlfriends. Racial prejudice increased these tensions further. Biracial relationships between German women and GIs aroused particular scrutiny and public disapproval. Even as acceptance of relationships between white men and German women grew throughout the 1950s, the women dating African Americans continued to face legal and social harassment.[34]

The treatment women associating with black soldiers received demonstrates the ambivalence Germans felt toward African Americans at that time and further compromises the positive image of German-American relations during the 1950s. While the majority of black GIs felt that their stay in Germany gave them a period of relief from the overt racial prejudice and oppression they were accustomed to in the United States, this did not mean that black GIs did not encounter any racism or discrimination during their tours in Germany. Germany had eliminated all forms of legal racism after 1945, but prejudices and discriminatory behavior persisted. Many Germans expressed these prejudices most clearly over sexual relations, but they also found expression in other social and economic relations as well. White GIs introduced some discriminatory practices. By exerting economic pressure, they forced German business owners to segregate their establishments, a problem that persisted through the early 1970s.[35]

Bar fights and criminal activity had always drawn local press attention. What had changed by the 1970s was the economic status of GIs. The devaluation of the dollar paired with rising prices in Germany negatively affected GIs' buying power outside the bases. The bases and their soldiers formed a major part of local economies. GIs who had brought their families over on their own recognizance could no longer afford their upkeep and sent them home. Soldiers and even officers made less use of German stores and restaurants and frequented the PXs in higher numbers.[36] These economic woes would continue throughout the decade.

With sales to GIs declining, local communities were more prone to notice the downside of housing military communities. However, this relative decline in status never led to a major push to eject them. The German response to this economic crisis indicates how invested German communities near bases were in the continued military presence. In 1978 German communities organized food and clothing drives for the soldiers and their families. German mayors asked landlords to lower rents for GIs.[37] So while Germans were wary of the crime and violence around U.S. bases, this did not necessarily translate into a rejection of the GIs' mission and presence in their communities.

A minor controversy in Heidelberg carried out in the local press provides some insights into the different German viewpoints regarding Vietnam and its implications for the soldiers stationed in Germany. In June 1970 the Seventh Army commander in chief, Polk, invited the president of Heidelberg University, Rolf Rendtdorff, and his two vice presidents to an annual summer ball. In an open letter, Rendtdorff declined the invitation. The president argued that he could not in good conscience attend a party with cocktails, dance, entertainment, and a buffet while war was being waged in Indochina against the will of the majority of the Vietnamese people. He referenced the invasion of Cambodia and the Kent State shootings, proclaiming his solidarity with students and faculty in the United States who were opposed to the government's policies.[38] This open letter inspired a flood of letters to the editor and proclamations in denouncing or supporting the president's actions.

Faculty from various departments issued their own statements. The junior faculty of the Theology Department declared their solidarity with the president, who was a theologian himself.[39] On the other hand, the law school initiated a formal meeting to consider whether the president had overstepped the legal boundaries of his office. Student protests disrupted the meeting, and the faculty could not vote on the matter. The law faculty instead distanced themselves from Rendtdorff's actions, arguing that as state employees and representatives of the university, the president and his subordinates had to remain above political controversies.[40] The Heidelberg city council debated the matter. One of the councilmen, a pastor, published an open letter condemning the president's actions, claiming that style and tone of the president's letter resembled an SDS flyer and that Rendtdorff was unworthy of his office.[41] A district chapter of the Social Democratic Party, on the other hand, publicly supported the president.[42]

This controversy shows that relations between the U.S. armed forces and their German hosts had grown more complex in the wake of the Vietnam War. Criticism of U.S. foreign and domestic policy extended beyond the radical student movement to the political and academic establishment. At the same time, even as late as the summer of 1970, when the Vietnam War had become widely unpopular, equally important establishment figures in Heidelberg continued to support the United States and its engagement around the world. Neither side of this debate actually came close to questioning the continued presence of U.S. Army, Europe headquarters in Heidelberg.

If the majority of West Germans supported the American presence in their country despite the well-documented problems, the West German government was even less inclined to make the social crisis a major issue. From Kurt Georg Kiesinger, through Willi Brandt, to Helmut Schmidt, West German leaders' main concern was that the United States could unilaterally decide to withdraw troops from Germany. During the second half of the 1960s and the early 1970s, the governments of the Federal Republic and the United States entered into repeated and tense negotiations over U.S. troop levels in West Germany and the German government's contributions to the maintenance of those troops. During the "offset negotiations," demanding partial or the wholesale withdrawal of USAREUR troops was the furthest from German leaders' minds regardless of the social turmoil.

In 1961 the U.S. government faced a ballooning balance-of-payments deficit vis-à-vis the Federal Republic of Germany. This imbalance was partially due to its military obligations. The two governments agreed that same year that West Germany would offset part of the military costs through annual purchases of U.S. military equipment. These payments remained uncontroversial until the Germans encountered their own budget shortfall during a recession in 1965. Subsequently, the Federal Republic's offset obligations became the object of tense negotiations. These negotiations were made even more complicated by the efforts of Senator Mike Mansfield to reduce the U.S. military presence in Europe as a means to reduce costs. In response to Mansfield's efforts, the Johnson administration reached an agreement with the Federal Republic introducing the concept of dual-basing. Thirty-five thousand troops were removed from Germany and based back in the United States. However, the units remained under European command and returned to Germany once every year for maneuvers. Mansfield was not satisfied with the agreement and continued to introduce resolutions for greater reductions on a yearly basis. The Nixon administration was also determined to reduce the costs of U.S. military obligations and renewed its pressure on the German government to share more of the cost in 1970 and 1971.[43]

In its relations with the European NATO members, the Nixon administration emphasized that its European partners had to start sharing a greater part of the common defense burden. They encouraged Europeans to improve their conventional capabilities so that the United States could reduce its own conventional forces in Europe.[44] In 1969 the Nixon administration prepared for further reductions of troops in Germany. In order not to endanger the readiness of its troops, the reductions mainly would have affected administrative staff. The plan drawn up by General Lemnitzer called for a reduction of administrative personnel of 34,000 by 1973.[45] The West German government viewed the administration's plans and the continued efforts by Mansfield with major concern.[46] The United States used these concerns to exert pressure on the Germans in the offset negotiations, demanding that the Germans increase their own conventional capabilities and contribute more to the maintenance of U.S. forces.[47] Ultimately the threat of troop reductions had the desired effect. In June 1970 the German defense minister, Helmut Schmidt, signaled that his government would consider direct German monetary contributions rather than purchasing U.S. armaments or bonds.[48]

In the course of the negotiations, General Davison convinced the U.S. Treasury and the Department of Defense that the Germans should pay part of their contributions in Deutschmarks and keep the funds in Germany to pay for barracks rehabilitation.[49] From that point on, renovations of U.S. barracks became part of the offset negotiations. In March 1971 German officials conceded that such renovations were important to improve morale among U.S. troops and that the German public would welcome them as well.[50] The two governments concluded the new offset agreement in December 1971. The German government committed 600 million Deutschmarks to "services and deliveries for the modernization, construction, and improvement of barracks, accommodations, housing, and troop facilities."[51] Davison believed that the rehabilitation of U.S. facilities with the help of this money made an important contribution toward resolving the social crisis in his command.[52]

The formal end of the Vietnam War in 1973 improved U.S. Army, Europe's material and spiritual situation. Army strategic and operational planners refocused their attention on Germany. In preparing for a potential confrontation with Warsaw Pact forces, the army put new emphasis on improving mechanized and armored divisions. Training and preparation were also reemphasized. This renewed focus in USAREUR combined with the transition to the all-volunteer force helped boost morale as well as West German confidence in their American partners.[53]

As German government officials realized that improving morale among U.S. troops would reduce the likelihood of further reductions, they also increased their cooperation with USAREUR in drug enforcement. In interdicting the flow of illegal substances onto their bases, U.S. commanders had to work closely with local authorities. Local residents brought many of the drugs into the country and then sold them to soldiers. At first, working relations with the German authorities in the area of drug enforcement were uneasy. When JAG Persons met German law enforcement officials after assuming his position, he encountered skepticism on their part that the drug abuse problem extended beyond the American bases. The officials did not think there was that much German usage of drugs.[54]

The papers of General Davison contain a reference to a back-channel exchange between Davison and Gen. Lyman L. Lemnitzer, who reported on a secret meeting with Defense Minister Helmut Schmidt. According to Lemnitzer, Schmidt accused the army of polluting Germany with drugs. He believed the Americans to be responsible for the spread of illegal drugs among German youth. Lemnitzer responded that in his opinion "the importation of drugs into the FRG and their distribution was accomplished by an organization of FRG civilians, French, Turkish and other foreign nationals who" were "part of a global drug ring organized for that purpose."[55]

USAREUR officials were eventually able to convince German authorities that the problem reached beyond U.S. bases. The CID and the military police started to work more closely with the German police to interdict the drug traffic. Initially the Germans depended heavily on their American counterparts, because they had few resources and little expertise in this area of law enforcement. Persons recalled that the police department in Frankfurt had a narcotics department consisting of two or three civilian policemen.[56] Early on, American CID agents did all the undercover work. The U.S. government was not content to cooperate with the German authorities through its military. It also sent agents from the Drug Enforcement Administration starting in 1970. During the first half of the decade, it had stationed up to thirteen agents in Germany. That number went down to six in 1978. The DEA agents were charged with offering German authorities their "experience in combating illicit drugs, cooperating and exchanging intelligence, and developing intelligence programs." The DEA also sponsored training for German police officials in the United States ranging from "basic enforcement, to special training for instructors to executive observation programs for officers."[57]

In 1972 the U.S. embassy in West Germany established a task force that brought together officers of the embassy and representatives of the armed services to coordinate antidrug efforts. One year later the DEA and the German federal police formed a permanent working group on narcotics, a group consisting of representatives from the German federal and state police, customs agents, the U.S. narcotics and customs attachés, and representatives from the U.S. military. The group became a clearinghouse for the collection and evaluation of relevant information on drug trafficking. The two governments also concluded an agreement in 1973 providing for mutual assistance between the customs services.[58]

The increased cooperation on all levels between the DEA, the CID, and the German police from local to the federal did not quiet all misgivings in the American government about German support for drug suppression efforts. Complaints continued that German authorities did not take the problem seriously enough, even though drug consumption within the German population was rising during the 1970s. The Select Committee on Narcotics Abuse and Control found during its own fact gathering in 1978 that many German political officials did not recognize drug abuse as a major problem to their population and therefore did not share the lawmakers' sense of urgency. The testimony of the USAREUR provost marshal somewhat contradicted those findings when he stated that cooperation between the police and the military was very good.[59] The U.S. ambassador also stated that he believed that awareness of the problem had been growing on the government level as well.[60] The impression conveyed by all of the testimony in 1978 was that U.S. views and interests in protecting its military in Germany played an important role in the development of German law enforcement and interdiction procedures. In interaction with the German authorities, collaboration in law enforcement and interdiction remained a priority, while rehabilitation was not an area of cooperation.

The social crisis in USAREUR showed that the almost thirty-year presence of U.S. forces could at times strain German-American relations. However, it also showed how close the ties between "occupiers" and the "occupied" had become. Within the German public, attitudes toward their American guests became more complex in the late 1960s and the 1970s. The growing anti-Americanism was tied to disillusionment particularly among younger Germans with the United States as a beacon of democracy and liberty. The U.S. engagement in Vietnam and the domestic turmoil associated with the various 1960s protest movements contributed to these more negative views. Racial incidents in USAREUR described in earlier chapters reinforced German perceptions of the United States as a society at war with itself. Accordingly, regard for U.S. troops declined. U.S. barracks became sources of crime and social disturbances. However, even during these crisis years the negative images of GIs did not lead to a widespread rejection of their mission in Germany. The West German government's response to USAREUR's social crisis was primarily determined by a fear of U.S. troop withdrawals. Despite the growing anti-Americanism in parts of the German public, the German government never questioned the need for a substantial U.S. military presence in Germany as a deterrent to the Soviet Union. Accordingly, the government invested in improving morale through the offset payments and supporting U.S. drug interdiction efforts in the 1970s. The formation of the New Left in West Germany had led to the emergence of a vocal and substantial minority that rejected the presence of U.S. troops in Germany. But the activism of the antiauthoritarian Left did not foment a revolution within the German public nor among American troops. The Cold War consensus and the German-American alliance remained intact during this period only to be challenged again with the antimissile protests of the 1980s. The majority of West Germans remained committed to the American presence in Germany even during the social crisis and like their government viewed the prospect of withdrawal with concern.

Conclusion

Toward the end of General Davison's tour in Germany, press reports indicated that the troubles of the Seventh Army were fading. In July 1974 the *New York Times* published an article entitled "Seventh Army Morale Rising in Europe."[1] Less than a year later, the paper published another article, "GIs in Europe Are 'Cooler' than Those of Vietnam Era, but Many Defy Old-Army Rules."[2] Both articles argued that USAREUR had come a long way in resolving the conflicts and difficulties that had beleaguered it since the beginning of the decade. The first article emphasized two factors that had played a decisive role in turning the situation around: the intensified training program implemented by Davison's second in command, Arthur Collins, and the greater stability at the command level due to the army's disengagement from Vietnam. The two factors were connected, of course. As long as experienced officers and other personnel were constantly being withdrawn from Europe and sent to Vietnam, the loss of cohesion and morale in the units in Germany was the inevitable result. Now officers stayed in their posts longer and could become more familiar with problems in their units. Collins's emphasis on intensive small unit training further strengthened cohesion and morale, as well as the amount of responsibility assumed by company and battalion commanders for their units. The positive effects of Collins's efforts were reinforced by the introduction of VOLAR, the precursor to the all-volunteer army. Since this program essentially freed soldiers from unpopular additional duties, they had more time to train and focus on their military specialties and were consequently more highly motivated.[3] The army's renewed focus on USAREUR and its strategic and operational significance also improved morale. USAREUR received new equipment and weapons systems as the army emphasized mobile mechanized warfare over traditional infantry tactics.[4]

The second article's analysis was more complex and somewhat more ambivalent in tone, but still cast a more favorable light on the present status quo in comparison with the situation of four or five years earlier. The reporter opened his article by stating that "the United States Army in Europe is making headway against its Vietnam-era problems of drugs, racism and drift." He came away with the impression that life in the barracks had been "calmed by racial seminars, drug clinics, and a cooler type of GI, who entered the service through a recruiting station, not a draft board." Davison's strategy of opening up channels of communication by means of seminars and clinics was credited with improving the situation. However, the article also pointed to a positive change that was not a result of Davison's policies, the introduction of the All-Volunteer Army. As in the earlier article, the intensified, more specialized training and the reduced rotation of officers were also cited as factors contributing to the positive trend.

The article also contained cautionary notes indicating that the problems that had triggered the breakdown in morale had not simply vanished. The author cited a "recent wave of disciplinary discharges and courts martial" as evidence that some of the new enlisted men were "still reluctant to accept the strict authority and rules of the old Army." Many officers, on the other hand, had not adapted to the changed circumstances: "Many old-line captains and majors who deal with the GIs on a daily basis tend to regard racial and drug issues as disciplinary matters rather than as human problems." The article shows that the social problems of previous years had not ceased to exist, but the article conveyed an impression that morale was up, despite lingering problems. The article observed that Davison, who would be leaving his post in June 1975, felt that he had "achieved his main goal of making the Army in Europe the effective fighting force it was at the height of the cold war."

The *New York Times* depiction of a recovery process in USAREUR under Davison's command was confirmed by other officers, who had served under Davison in Germany. General Persons, Davison's top JAG officer, stated that the most satisfying thing about his four years in Germany under Davison was "that the drug problem, the race problem, the whole discipline/morale/esprit of USAREUR . . . improved dramatically."[5] Many of the officers gave Davison and Collins much credit for the improved situation and concurred with the *New York Times* in asserting the importance of Collins's emphasis on improving training.[6] They also lauded Davison for opening channels of communication and holding his commanders responsible for improving race relations and combating drug abuse. In his oral history interview, Lt. Gen. Robert Haldane credited Davison with turning the racial problem around: "He got the people talking to each other. A lot of people say he made too many concessions to the blacks. I think the main thing to do is just to get the people talking about it, and make overt obvious actions to improve the situation without any loss of discipline."[7]

When Davison took over the command of USAREUR in 1971, racial disturbances and protest activities among African American GIs had reached their peak. His predecessor had been reluctant to publicly admit that the army had a problem regarding racial discrimination. Davison's candid and public assessment that ending discrimination in USAREUR was a top priority contributed greatly to calming down the situation.

Under Davison's command USAREUR implemented structural changes, such as commanders' conferences on race relations and equal opportunity inspection teams, which placed more responsibility on officers for promoting racial harmony within their units. Officers and enlisted men were educated on issues of discrimination and the importance of respecting cultural differences even in an environment that required cohesion and unity. Some measures were part of a wider effort within the army in various parts of the world to reduce instances of discriminatory behavior and racial tension, such as the installment of equal opportunity officers in units all over Germany or the creation of a race relations school in Munich modeled on the DRRI in Florida. Davison also initiated measures for solving problems specific to Germany such as the housing referral system and placing businesses that discriminated against black soldiers off-limits.

Some of the structural changes were initiated to serve a much wider goal, but they also helped to calm race relations and to improve the lot of black soldiers. The reforms of the military justice system in USAREUR undertaken by Davison and his JAG, Wilton Persons, affected black GIs because they were overrepresented as defendants in trials and in the military prison system. Military lawyers also received schooling at race relations seminars, and soldiers in pretrial confinement received better and prompter counseling. Measures such as the 45-day rule prevented commanders from using pretrial confinement as a disciplinary measure. Once again transparency was the cornerstone of a strategy to reduce frustration and inefficiency.

Certainly, Davison deserved the credit given him by journalists and fellow officers for his communication strategy that promoted transparency and candid assessments of the racial situation. Faced with the heightened frustration of black enlisted men, Davison and the army leadership in general demonstrated genuine concern. In reaction to black protests, commanders like Davison created institutions and channels of communication that allowed black GIs to voice their grievances. Rap sessions, race relations seminars, and equal opportunity officers heightened the awareness of officers and enlisted men on issues of racial identity and racial stereotyping.

However, unlike Davison, the GIs who had voiced their grievances and had organized in protest received very little credit for the changes in the treatment of minorities. The absence of any acknowledgment of black dissenters as playing a positive role in bringing about change points to the ambivalence officers felt toward any form of dissent.

While Davison and his subordinate commanders took the issue of racial discrimination seriously, the individuals calling attention to this issue received no recognition. As seen in the example of the Darmstadt 53, soldiers who were categorized as leading voices of dissent were normally dispersed and transferred to other units if they could not be put on trial. Army leaders took advantage of the transitory nature of military service to prevent any permanent activist organization. Accordingly, African American dissent in the army was never really perceived as a movement with identifiable leaders. Nonetheless, despite these obstacles, black GIs collectively managed to force the army to acknowledge the discriminatory treatment of minority soldiers that still permeated the institution despite its official color blindness.

Army leaders' ambivalence toward black activism also became evident in 1973 with the transition to the all-volunteer force. Many army leaders were concerned that the all-volunteer force would draw a disproportionate number of black enlistees.[8] Some even feared that the new army might "become an extension of black militancy."[9] Such fears proved to be unwarranted. As shown above, more radical ideas regarding race relations in the army such as those represented by the Black Panthers gained only very limited influence in Germany. Black GIs were reluctant to be drawn into any larger ideological struggle, be it by the Black Panthers or the RITA organizers. Dissenting black soldiers were successful in confronting army leadership with the very real problems they faced on a daily basis because of the color of their skin, but they had no real interest in a political revolution or solidarity with other revolutionary groups.

To a certain degree black GIs shared the frustrations they encountered in their daily military lives with their white counterparts. Of course, white soldiers did not face discrimination, but their level of frustration was also high. Many faced the prospect of being sent to fight in an unpopular war, but even without that prospect, their situation in Germany was difficult. Because of the decline of the dollar, their economic position weakened. They had little money to spend and so were even more isolated in their barracks, barracks that over the decades had become less and less hospitable. Many expressed their discontent by going AWOL and finding their way to Paris or Sweden. Some GIs became activists. However, a substantial number of GIs expressed their discontent more passively. Drugs became a means of escape. After 1969 the army leadership in Europe was increasingly concerned about the use its service members made of drugs until by 1973 drug abuse had replaced race relations as the number one social problem in USAREUR.

Davison's approach to combating drug abuse among his soldiers was strikingly similar to his approach to race relations. Once again Davison talked candidly about the problem and encouraged his subordinates to do so as well. Educating his men on drug abuse through workshops and seminars became a major priority. Inspection teams were created to hold officers more accountable for implementing drug abuse policies. Drug abuse policy was adjusted. Increasingly the emphasis was placed on treating the abuser instead of punishing the crime.

This shift from drug suppression and interdiction to rehabilitation of the soldier aroused resistance among Davison's officers. Similar to the discomfort they felt when confronted with black GIs expressing their racial pride and demanding changes in the army's racial policies, officers initially showed little inclination to deal with the problem of drug abuse in a reflective manner. The controversy over the Nellingen anti-drug movement showed that many officers had difficulty abandoning a punitive attitude toward suspected drug users. It took a lawsuit filed by the Lawyers Military Defense Committee to curb some of the more excessively punitive measures ensconced in USAREUR drug policies.

Drug use more than any other problem demonstrated the strain that the lengthy presence in Germany had put on USAREUR. By 1975, the measures initiated by Davison were successful in reducing the sense of distress and unrest that had prevailed in the early years of the decade. Another important factor in reducing drug use among soldiers was not only General Collins's renewed emphasis on training but also the extensive program developed for renovating dilapidated barracks. Under an agreement negotiated by Davison and Defense Minister Helmut Schmidt, a portion of Bonn's "offset payments" to help underwrite the costs of stationing U.S. troops in Germany were to be paid in D-Marks and set aside for the renovation of facilities in Germany.[10] Drug abuse as a passive and, more often than not, unintentional form of dissent forced the army to face up to the years of neglect suffered by USAREUR in the wake of the Vietnam War. Ironically, the army was much more responsive to soldiers' eagerness to tune out than to their more active and intentional efforts to protest against army policies.

Expressions of discontent and disagreement with army policy and life had also increased since 1969. A number of soldiers objected to U.S. involvement in Vietnam, some for reasons of personal safety, others out of moral or political conviction. While some soldiers expressed their objection by going AWOL, a small number of soldiers during the early years of the 1970s stayed in the service and expressed their dissent from within. However, this form of protest which was not related to racial issues remained somewhat individualized. The so-called GI movement, which never became a mass movement, was highly dependent on the work of civilian activists who provided the resources and the continuity. Underground newspapers, the most important means of expressing dissent, were a case in point. Papers actually run by GIs were short-lived and mainly appeared around the years 1970 and 1971. The two longest running papers, however, *Forward* and *Fight Back*, were run by civilians. Moreover, the most important organization, RITA, was basically run by a single civilian activist, Max Watts, also known as Thomas Schwaetzer. Because a mass movement never emerged, the most viable form of protest was expressed by means of trials in which soldiers' constitutional freedoms were at issue, as in the case of the GI Committee or Private Olais. These trials were successful in marking the boundaries beyond which the army could not go in interfering with a soldier's right to privacy and free expression.

Although a more conciliatory approach was adopted toward drug abuse and race relations, the USAREUR leaders' reactions to political protest were more negative and defensive. Davison never publicly addressed the problem. The only discernible reactions, the covert surveillance program and the counterintelligence program, constituted an overreaction completely out of proportion to the threat posed by a movement of such limited scope. Radine called this kind of response "coercive control." Instead of showing concern or at least meeting some marginal demands, the army leadership was mainly engaged in suppressing dissent. Demands such as the unionization of the enlisted men were never seriously considered. The army as a whole did adjust its hair length policy somewhat. The protest inspired and supported by RITA elicited primarily irritated and defensive reactions, whereas army leaders were more willing to reconsider their own attitudes and policies when confronted with racial dissent or drug abuse.

While army leaders never specifically addressed the grievances brought up by RITA, they inadvertently managed to undermine RITA's efforts by developing strategies for improving low morale. The new training programs and the renovated barracks, for example, deprived RITA of the necessary pool of discontent from which protest movements could be fueled. After losing Victnam as an issue, RITA activists had tried to focus on grievances associated with army life, such as harassment by officers or inhuman living conditions. Once these conditions had been improved, civilian activists had no means of reaching GIs, particularly because most soldiers had no interest in becoming part of a wider class struggle or critiques of U.S. capitalism.

The strategies adapted by Davison and Collins to deal with the social disturbances in USAREUR fit Lawrence Radine's definition of co-optive control: "The co-optive principle takes no ideology seriously; it is a form of cooperation for any end. The view on dissent is that dissidence appears because there are "irritants" that alienate GIs from the military. The very word irritant connotes a trivial response to the military and to national policy generally. The expectation is that if the Army gets rid of the irritant, the anger will disappear." Radine makes a value judgment in claiming that the military prefers to focus on the trivial and ignores the political implications. As mentioned earlier, Radine believed that co-optation was a cynical strategy employed by the army leadership to control the underclass. Radine shares RITA activists' view of enlisted men as representatives of the underclass, and he interprets the army's leadership policies as cynical attempts to exploit and manipulate this underclass.

While Radine and the RITA activists were certainly correct in maintaining that the majority of enlisted men during the Vietnam era came from the working class, their view of these soldiers as badly exploited victims of the capitalist ruling class represented by the officer corps was somewhat exaggerated and dogmatic. As evidenced by the difficulties experienced by RITA in recruiting them, GIs resisted such crude categorizations. While individual soldiers certainly often felt helpless and powerless, collectively they were not. Soldiers were capable of giving voice to their frustrations either directly by demonstrating or writing articles in underground newspapers or indirectly by tuning out with the help of drugs.

Army leadership could ill afford to ignore the social problems in USAREUR. Although the need to promote efficiency, readiness, and discipline in the troops was the major driving force in initiating social reform in the army, the emphasis placed on creating racial harmony or the rehabilitation of addicted soldiers was more than cynical tokenism. Army leaders could not prevent the social conflicts of the 1960s from entering the military. Nor were they responsible for the wear and tear of three decades in West Germany. The Vietnam conflict had seriously weakened their ability to do so and in itself led to serious morale problems within the ranks. However, the pragmatism of officers such as Davison prevented these social conflicts and the communication gap between officers and soldiers from escalating into the type of class warfare that RITA activists implicitly were hoping for. The majority of GIs did not become politically radicalized. Although social problems such as racial discrimination or drug abuse could not be completely eliminated from USAREUR troops, Davison and his subordinates as well as the army leadership back in the United States had been able to create institutions and channels of communication to deal with these problems with some degree of success. They could also rest assured that even in a time of heightened social and cultural unrest, their hosts remained committed to keeping U.S. forces in West Germany.

INTRODUCTION

1. Haynes Johnson and George C. Wilson, "The U.S. Army: A Battle for Survival," *Washington Post,* September 12, 1972.

2. Heinl, "The Collapse of the Armed Forces."

3. Hauser, *America's Army in Crisis,* 3–4.

4. Westmoreland, "Facing Up to the External and Internal Challenges," 23–25, 42.

5. See Edelstein, *Occupational Hazards*; Dobbins, *America's Role in Nation-Building.*

6. Downs, *After Appomattox.*

7. Baker, *American Soldiers Overseas.*

8. See Wiggers, "From Supreme Authority to Reserved Rights and Responsibilities," 107.

9. Sweringen, "Variable Architectures of War and Peace," 217; Leuerer, *Die Stationierung amerikanischer Streitkräfte in Deutschland,* 94.

10. Goedde, "Gender, Race, and Power," 515–21; Goedde, *GIs and Germans*; Willoughby, *Remaking the Conquering Heroes.*

11. To Goedde this development represented a feminization of the German population that found its most obvious expression in the countless sexual relationships between GIs and German women. See Goedde, "From Villains to Victims."

12. Nelson, *A History,* 35, 45, 55; Sweringen, "Variable Architectures," 218, 219.

13. Leuerer, *Stationierung amerikanischer Streitkräfte,* 171–73, 331. In 1969, for example, the army alone had 169,180 soldiers. See Annual Historical Summary Headquarters U.S. Army, Europe and Seventh Army, 1 January to December 1969, U.S. Army Military History Center.

14. Trauschweizer, *The Cold War U.S. Army,* 81–113.

15. There are two major regional studies that deal with the American presence in Germany during the 1950s: Scharnholz, *Heidelberg und die Besatzungsmacht,* and Höhn, *GIs and Fräuleins.*

16. Leuerer, *Stationierung amerikanischer Streitkräfte,* 174–77.

17. Nelson devotes a chapter titled "Deterioration" to the period between 1967 and 1973. However, his analysis is based on clippings from German

newspapers and therefore only scratches the surface. Other works that make any mention of this period rely on Nelson's account, offering no primary research of their own. See Nelson, *A History*, 87–130. Also see Goedde, "Gender, Race, and Power," 520–21, and Leuerer, *Stationierung amerikanischer Streitkräfte,* 196.

18. Trauschweizer, *The Cold War U.S. Army,* 114–46, 162–94.

19. Interview with Arthur S. Collins, Senior Officers' Oral History Program, U.S. Army Military History Institute, Carlisle Barracks PA (1981), 397–400.

20. Radine, *The Taming of the Troops.*

21. MacGregor and Nalty, *Blacks in the Military,* 239.

22. For example, in his oral history interview, Reynaldo Puente describes various instances in which officers and fellow soldiers would use prejudicial language toward him. He recalled that for ten months in 1974 he was the only Hispanic in his company. See interview with Reynaldo Puente in Reynaldo Puente Collection (AFC/2001/001/85195), Veterans History Project, American Folklife Center, Library of Congress.

23. Beverly Jean Brown, the final commander of the last Women's Army Corps company in Germany in 1973, recalls the frequent belief among her superiors that female soldiers were all closet lesbians whose behavior needed to be closely monitored, revealing the widespread prejudice against women and LGBTQ soldiers. See interview with Beverly Jean Brown in Beverly Jean Brown Collection (AFC/2001/001/30895), Veterans History Project, American Folklife Center, Library of Congress.

24. De Nike, *Inter-Theater Transfer,* 1, 30.

25. Musto and Korsmeyer, *The Quest for Drug Control,* 48–53.

26. "Gen. Davison: 'Toughest Period . . . Ever,'" *Washington Post,* September 12, 1971.

1. BLACK GIS IN GERMANY

1. MacGregor, *Integration,* 450–53.

2. Höhn, *GIs and Fräuleins,* 89–90; Höhn, "Heimat in Turmoil," 149–50. See also Goedde, *GIs and Germans*: 63; Willoughby, *Remaking,* 60.

3. Höhn, *GIs and Fräuleins,* 91.

4. In Europe, African Americans constituted 7.73 percent (67,372) of the U.S. force in April 1946. This number rose to 10.33 percent in December of the same year and dropped to 9.96 percent in June 1947. MacGregor, *Integration,* 152, 182. Also see Willoughby, *Remaking,* 56.

5. MacGregor, *Integration,* 182.

6. MacGregor, *Integration,* 211; Nalty and MacGregor, *Blacks in the Military,* 209–11.

7. Willoughby, *Remaking*, 16–28, 35–39. Willoughby points out that these numbers do not necessarily mean that a fourth of the army was afflicted with venereal disease, since the method of calculation used by the army did not differentiate between repeat "offenders" and newly afflicted.

8. MacGregor, *Integration*, 208.

9. MacGregor, *Integration*, 210–11; Nalty and MacGregor, *Blacks in the Military*, 209–12.

10. This had been the recommendation of a review board chaired by Lt. Gen. Alvan C. Gillem. The board charged with reviewing the military's racial policies from October 1945 to April 1946 did not fundamentally challenge segregation, but it did recommend that the black soldier "should be given every opportunity and aid to prepare himself for effective military service in company with every other citizen who is called." Nalty and MacGregor, *Blacks in the Military*, 192.

11. Nalty and MacGregor, *Blacks in the Military*, 217.

12. MacGregor, *Integration*, 213–14; Willoughby, *Remaking*, 60.

13. Nalty and MacGregor, *Blacks in the Military*, 217.

14. Nalty and MacGregor, *Blacks in the Military*, 211, 217.

15. MacGregor, *Integration*, 214–15; Willoughby, *Remaking*, 62.

16. Nalty and MacGregor, *Blacks in the Military*, 211.

17. Willoughby, *Remaking*, 63. On treatment of women associating with GIs and the treatment of "mixed-race" children from these early postwar liaisons, see Lee, "A Forgotten Legacy of the Second World War," 171–79.

18. MacGregor, *Integration*, 309. See also Donaldson, *Truman Defeats Dewey*, 97–101.

19. MacGregor, *Integration*, 302–9; Moskos and Butler, *All That We Can Be*, 30; Donaldson, *Truman Defeats Dewey*, 187–91.

20. Nalty and MacGregor, *Blacks in the Military*, 239.

21. MacGregor, *Integration*, 313.

22. The newly appointed chief of staff, Gen. Omar N. Bradley, who was unaware of Truman's order being issued, declared the army had to maintain segregation as long as it remained the national pattern. On this and on the position of the army secretary, see MacGregor, *Integration*, 317, 322.

23. MacGregor, *Integration*, 431, 434, 442, 443–47; Bogart, *Social Research and the Desegregation of the U.S. Army*, 51, 53–56, 104–52; Nalty and MacGregor, *Blacks in the Military*, 309.

24. MacGregor, *Integration*, 450–54; Nalty and MacGregor, *Blacks in the Military*, 311–13.

25. MacGregor, *Integration*, 455; Nalty, "The Black Servicemen and the Constitution," 152.

26. MacGregor, *Integration*, 450–53; Nalty and MacGregor, *Blacks in the Military*, 311–14.

27. Höhn, *GIs and Fräuleins*, 92, 103.

28. Höhn, *GIs and Fräuleins*, 96–97. See also "Army Denies Bias at German Bases," *New York Times*, December 29, 1964.

29. Höhn, *GIs and Fräuleins*, 99.

30. Grundgesetz für die Bundesrepublik Deutschland, Artikel 3.

31. Höhn, *GIs and Fräuleins*, 101.

32. Moskos and Butler, *All That We Can Be*, 31.

33. MacGregor, *Integration*, 456–59.

34. See particularly "When Jim Crow Came to the German Heimat," in Höhn, *GIs and Fräuleins*, 85–108.

35. Shapely, *Promise and Power*, 388–89.

36. MacGregor, *Integration*, 511–13, 517; Nalty and MacGregor, *Blacks in the Military*, 316, 322–23.

37. White House press release, June 24, 1962. Printed in MacGregor and Nalty, *Blacks in the United States Armed Forces*, 3.

38. Gesell Committee Initial Report. Printed in MacGregor and Nalty, *Blacks in the United States Armed Forces*, 21–119.

39. DOD Directive 5120.36, *Equal Opportunity in the Armed Forces*, July 26, 1963.

40. MacGregor, *Integration*, 549; Nalty and MacGregor, *Blacks in the Military*, 333.

41. *Congressional Record: The Gesell Report and Preservation of the Mission of the Military*, July 31, 1963; Nalty and MacGregor, *Blacks in the Military*, 180.

42. The President's Committee on Equal Opportunity in the Armed Forces, "Final Report," 137. See also "U.S. Bases Abroad Scored on Rights," *New York Times*, December 28, 1964.

43. President's Committee, "Final Report," 132–33. Also see "U.S. Bases Abroad Scored on Rights."

44. President's Committee, "Final Report," 129–30.

45. "Less Bonn Racial Bias Seen for GIs," *Washington Post*, December 29, 1964; "Army Denies Bias at German Bases."

2. GROWING RACIAL TENSIONS

1. "Organized Servicemen Abroad Intensify Drive against Racism," *New York Times*, November 19, 1971.

2. MacGregor, *Integration*, 501–2. MacGregor puts this more mildly, arguing that the black serviceman "was beginning to perceive from the vantage of his improved position that other and perhaps more subtle barriers stood in his way."

3. Cortright, *Soldiers in Revolt*, 39.

4. See Moskos, *American Enlisted Man*, 114–17; Appy, *Working-Class War*, 19–21.

5. Graham, *The Brothers' Vietnam War*, 112. See also Terry, *Bloods*, xvi–xvii.

6. Graham, *The Brothers' Vietnam War*, 113.

7. Appy, *Working-Class War*, 223.

8. Graham, *The Brothers' Vietnam War*, 113.

9. SP4 Charles Strong in Terry, *Bloods*, 71–72.

10. White, *An Assessment of Racial Tension in the Army*, 1.

11. White, *An Assessment of Racial Tensions in the Army*, 2–5.

12. Joseph, "The Black Power Movement," 756.

13. Cha-Jua and Lang, "The 'Long Movement' as Vampire," 270.

14. Both Joseph's "Black Power State of the Field" and Cha-Jua and Lang's "'Long Movement' as Vampire" provide excellent overviews of "new black power studies" up to 2009 and 2007, respectively. For monographs on the history of black power, see Joseph, *Waiting 'til the Midnight Hour* and Ogbar, *Black Power*.

15. Student Nonviolent Coordinating Committee (SNCC), "Position Paper on Black Power," *New York Times*, August 5, 1966. Also see Joseph, *Waiting 'til the Midnight Hour*, 142, and Van Deburg, *Modern Black Nationalism*, 120–26.

16. Carmichael, "Toward Black Liberation" and "Black Power."

17. "Give Us Afros or Give Us None!" *Overseas Weekly*, February 8, 1970.

18. "Racial Problems at Finthen," *Overseas Weekly*, February 8, 1970. See also White Briefing, 3.

19. Thomas A. Johnson, "GIs in Germany: Black Is Bitter," *New York Times*, November 23, 1970.

20. "Racial Unrest Leads to Jail for Black GI," *Overseas Weekly*, December 7, 1969.

21. "The EM Club Race Riot," *Overseas Weekly*, February 15, 1970.

22. "GI Racial Conflict Flares Up," *Overseas Weekly*, April 12, 1970.

23. "Prisoners Riot in Stockade," *Overseas Weekly*, March 22, 1970.

24. Barry Irvin, "Mystery GI Poisons Juice," *Overseas Weekly*, April 12, 1970.

25. "Schlägerei zwischen Schwarzen und Weißen," *Rhein-Neckar-Zeitung*, August 6, 1970.

26. Barry Irvin, "Mannheim Guards Expose Brutality, Discrimination," *Overseas Weekly*, July 26, 1970.

27. "Another Rumble in Mannheim Stockade," *Overseas Weekly*, October 25, 1970.

28. "The Hohenfels Grenade Blast," *Overseas Weekly*, May 31, 1970.

29. "Bomb Blast Ends Silence in Augsburg," *Overseas Weekly*, June 21, 1970.

30. James E. Hobson to James H. Polk, September 14, 1970, James H. Polk Papers, USAMHI. Hobson also pleaded his innocence before the court; see "Black Sergeant Denies Guilt in Stuttgart Court-Martial," *New York Times*, November 4, 1970.

31. "Inside the Hobson Trial," *Overseas Weekly*, November 15, 1970.

32. "Black GI in Germany Is Freed on 6 Charges, Convicted on 7th," *New York Times*, November 7, 1970.

33. Interview with Wilton B. Persons, conducted by Herbert J. Green and Thomas M. Crean, Senior Officer Oral History Program (1985), 348–49.

34. "Is the KKK Threat a Hoax?" *Overseas Weekly*, June 7, 1970; "KKK Cross Burners Still Free," *Overseas Weekly*, April 19, 1970; Horst Switalski, "Ku Klux Klan in Deutschland," *Der Stern*, no. 42 (October 1970).

35. "Officer in Germany Denies U.S. Base Has Klan Unit," *New York Times*, June 3, 1970.

36. "KKK Cross Burners Still Free."

37. Craig Davidson, "Karlsruhe GIs Set Up Black Defense Group," *Overseas Weekly*, May 24, 1970.

38. "Black GI Activists in Germany Will Boycott Pentagon Inquiry," *New York Times*, September 28, 1970.

39. Thomas A. Johnson, "GIs in Germany: Black Is Bitter," *New York Times*, November 23, 1970.

40. "Black Soldiers Attend Huge Rally," *Overseas Weekly*, July 12, 1970.

41. "I'll Bleed for Myself, Says Black Soldier in Europe," *New York Times*, October 11, 1970, and Johnson, "GIs in Germany: Black Is Bitter."

42. Aside from White's report, see also Reed and Whitmire, "Soldiers Look at Race Relations," 4–13.

43. James H. Polk, "Information Sheet-USAREUR & 7 A Commanders' Conference: Meetings on Installations," Polk Papers.

44. C. E. Hutchinson, "Racial Equality and the V Corps," memorandum, Polk Papers. The memo was inspired by comments Polk made on the issue during a meeting with CENTAG commanders as Hutchinson indicated in a letter to Polk. See Hutchinson to Polk, April 10, 1970, Polk Papers.

45. See Polk to John S. Barge, May 11, 1970, Polk Papers.

46. Hutchinson, "Racial Equality and the V Corps."

47. James H. Polk, "Suggested Speech before the Interservice Legal Committee," June 1, 1970, Polk Papers.

48. Trauschweizer, *The Cold War U.S. Army*, 162.

49. John Robert Bauer Collection (AFC/2001/001/50191), Veterans History Project, American Folklife Center, Library of Congress.

50. In his autobiographic sketch and oral history interview, Col. Raymond R. Battreall refers to the lack of preparedness of his assigned unit during his tour of duty in Germany from 1966 to 1968. See Battreall Collection (AFC/2001/001/02447), Veterans History Project, American Folklife Center, Library of Congress.

51. Trauschweizer, *The Cold War U.S. Army*, 180.

52. "Watch for These Men," *Overseas Weekly*, September 13, 1970; "The President's Fact-Finders: After the Fact?" *Overseas Weekly*, September 13, 1970; "Civil Rights Team In Europe to Assess Equal Opportunity Programs," *Commanders Digest* 8, no. 25 (September1970).

53. Paul Delaney, "U.S. to Study Race Issues among Troops in Europe," *New York Times*, August 31, 1970. Polk's papers at the Military History Institute include a flyer printed by SDS Heidelberg that invites GIs to hear two members of the Black Panther Party speak at the new University Building in Heidelberg on December 13, 1969. FTA, "Black Panther Party Speakers," December 1969, Polk Papers.

54. FTA, "Black Panther Party Speakers." Also see Frank W. Render, *U.S. Military Race Relations in Europe—September 1970*, Memorandum for the Secretary of Defense, Assistant Secretary of Defense, November 2, 1970, 1.

55. Delaney, "U.S. to Study Race Issues among Troops in Europe."

56. Render, *U.S. Military Race Relations*, 7–8

57. "Doubters Challenge Nixon Group," *Overseas Weekly*, October 11, 1970.

58. "Black GI Activists in Germany Will Boycott Pentagon Inquiry," *New York Times*, September 28, 1970; "Black GI Activists Boycott a Meeting," *New York Times*, September 30, 1970.

59. White Briefing, 3.

60. Render, *U.S. Military Race Relations* 11.

61. See Butler, "Inequality in the Military," 811–16; Butler, *Inequality in the Military*, 102–3.

62. Moskos, "The American Dilemma in Uniform," 99; Nordlie et al., *Improving Race Relations*, 4.

63. Butler, "Inequality in the Military," 807.

64. Butler, "Assessing Black Enlisted Participation in the Army," 562–63; Moskos, "Minority Groups in Military Organization," 194.

65. For a similar argument, see Moskos, "The American Dilemma," 101; Moskos, "Minority Groups," 195; and Persons interview, appendix H, 2.

66. Butler, "Inequality in the Military," 811–17.

67. Render, *U.S. Military Race Relations*, 14.

68. NAACP, *The Search for Military Justice*, 3.

69. NAACP, *The Search for Military Justice*, 4.

70. "Dapping" was the term used to describe the ritualized slapping of each other's hands.

71. Schexnider, "The Development of Racial Solidarity," 428.

72. For an explanation of these symbols from an African American officer, see Bailey, "The Trouble with . . . ," 4–8. In his Library of Congress oral history interview, Nathan Timothy Walker recalls the importance of the dap to declare solidarity among black soldiers in Vietnam. Even though Walker did not identify strongly with black activism, he still maintains that racism was prevalent in the army at the time. See interview with Walker, Walker Collection (AFC/2001/001/97525), Veterans History Project, American Folklife Center, Library of Congress.

73. Schexnider, "The Development of Racial Solidarity," 425–27.

74. Thomas A. Johnson, "Black GI Activists in Germany Will Boycott Pentagon Inquiry," *New York Times*, September 28, 1970; Johnson, "'I'll Bleed for Myself' Says Black Soldier."

75. See Nordlie et al., *Improving Race Relations*, 55–64.

76. William C. Westmoreland to Arthur S. Collins, June 3, 1971, Collins Papers, USAMHI.

77. "Racial Problems at Finthen," *Overseas Weekly*, February 8, 1970.

78. "General Okays Afro Haircuts," *Overseas Weekly*, December 14, 1969.

79. "General Vaughan's Race Memo," *Overseas Weekly*, December 14, 1969.

80. "Trooper Fights Haircut Order," *Overseas Weekly*, December 14, 1969.

81. "Afro Haircuts: Should Troops Wear Them?" *Overseas Weekly*, January 4, 1970.

82. NAACP, *The Search for Military Justice*, 6.

83. NAACP, *The Search for Military Justice*, i.

84. "The Drawings Which Shook Up the Army," *Overseas Weekly*, December 14, 1969.

85. White Briefing, 6–7.

86. Render, *U.S. Military Race Relations*, 10.

87. See Johnson, "GIs in Germany: Black Is Bitter."

88. Transcript of Armed Forces Network interview between James H. Polk and Dan Allen, 3. Broadcast on July 31 and August 2, 1970, Polk Papers.

89. Nalty and MacGregor, *Blacks in the Military*, 347.

90. NAACP, *The Search for Military Justice*, 6.

91. U.S. Task Force on the Administration of Military Justice in the Armed Forces. *Report* (November 30, 1972), 27–28.

92. See NAACP, *The Search for Military Justice*, 6. In 1972 the task force also found that black soldiers were more likely to receive punishments for confrontation-type offenses. See Task Force, *Report*, 28.

93. The statistics presented in the report showed that 50–60 percent of all military prisoners were in pretrial confinement. NAACP, *The Search for Military Justice*, 8–11.

94. Task Force, *Report*, 28–29.

95. NAACP, *The Search for Military Justice*, 10.

96. Task Force, *Report*, 32.

97. NAACP, *The Search for Military Justice*, 12–14.

98. Thomas A. Johnson, "Black Legal Help for GIs Is Urged," *New York Times*, February 15, 1971.

99. Disposition in interview with Persons, appendix H, 2.

100. Disposition in interview with Persons, appendix H, 2.

101. "Their point of view was that because they were black they really didn't have a chance. The first time they did anything wrong, they got an Article 15, and then they got another Article 15, then they were on their way out of the army with a bad discharge." Persons interview, 380.

102. "Military Discrimination Fight," *Christian Science Monitor*, January 12, 1971; "Military Justice Task Force Report," *Commanders Digest*, March 1973.

103. Task Force, *Report*, 26–32.

104. Render, *U.S. Military Race Relations*, 11–13.

105. NAACP, *The Search for Military Justice*, 18.

106. Render, *U.S. Military Race Relations*, 13.

107. Moskos, "The American Dilemma," 104.

108. *Frederic E. Davison, Major General, Retired*, conducted by James E. Brayboy, Senior Officer Oral History Program (1981), 82–85.

109. Render, *U.S. Military Race Relations*, 2–13.

110. NAACP, *The Search for Military Justice*, 19.

111. AR 600-18, Equal Opportunity in Off-Post Housing (73).

112. "New Directive Outlines Actions to End Discriminatory Practices," *Commanders Digest* 9, no. 11 (December 1970).

113. NAACP, *The Search for Military Justice*, 16–17.

114. Washington C. Hill, Curtis S. Smothers, and Edwin Dorn to Stanley R. Resor, "Application for a Court of Inquiry," December 25, 1970, Polk Papers.

115. See also Thomas A. Johnson, "Monitors Urged for Army Reform," *New York Times*, March 21, 1971.

116. "Letters to the Editor," *New York Times*, December 27, 1970.

117. John G. Kester to Washington C. Hill, January 9, 1971, Polk Papers. Also see "Army Denies Judge's Plea for Inquiry into Race Bias," *New York Times*, April 1, 1970.

118. It is possible that the people the NAACP team interviewed were the petitioners asking for a court of inquiry. NAACP, *The Search for Military Justice*, 17. On NAACP's demands to USAREUR, see also Robert D. McFadden, "GI Housing Bias in Germany Cited," *New York Times*, April 23, 1971.

119. NAACP, *The Search for Military Justice*, 18.

3. FAILED LEADERSHIP RESPONSES

1. Render, *U.S. Military Race Relations*, 9.

2. Render, *U.S. Military Race Relations*, 10. See also "Doubters Challenge Nixon Group," *Overseas Weekly,* October 11, 1970.

3. Render, *U.S. Military Race Relations*, 9.

4. NAACP, *In Search of Military Justice*, i.

5. Render, *U.S. Military Race Relations*, 10.

6. "Doubters Challenge Nixon Group."

7. Render, *U.S. Military Race Relations*, 15.

8. John J. Flynt to James H. Polk, September 4, 1970, Polk Papers.

9. Polk to William C. Westmoreland, January 5, 1971, Polk Papers.

10. Transcript of Armed Forces Network interview between James H. Polk and Dan Allen, 3. Broadcast on July 31 and August 2, 1970, Polk Papers.

11. Polk to Westmoreland, July 17, 1970, Polk Papers.

12. Jim Morgan, "Blacks Unite in USAREUR," *Overseas Weekly*, July 19, 1970.

13. David Binder, "Overseas Weekly's Editor Forced Out," *New York Times*, September 1, 1970.

14. Polk to David C. Burchinal, August 4, 1970, Polk Papers.

15. Westmoreland to Polk, August 5, 1970, Polk Papers.

16. Burchinal to Polk, August 12, 1970, Polk Papers.

17. Polk to Westmoreland, January 5, 1971, Polk Papers.

18. Thomas A. Johnson, "Pentagon Aide Calls for Fight on Racism," *New York Times*, November 24, 1970.

19. The issue was discussed during a press conference held by a Pentagon speaker. See Transcript: Morning Briefing, July 29, 1971, Polk Papers. Two days earlier, Render had claimed at a press conference that ten to twelve

high-ranking officers had been relieved because they had not followed the new civil rights regulations. Render would not comment when asked whether Polk had been one of them. See wire services news release, July 27, 1971, Polk Papers.

20. Polk to Westmoreland, January 5, 1971, Polk Papers; "Army to Spot-Check in Europe for Bias," *New York Times*, October 14, 1970.

21. Polk to Westmoreland, January 5, 1971, Polk Papers.

22. NAACP, *In Search of Military Justice*, i.

23. NAACP, *In Search of Military Justice*, 19.

24. Radine, *The Taming of the Troops*, 125.

25. Radine, *The Taming of the Troops*, 126.

26. "Wir müssen den Berg sprengen," *Rhein-Neckar-Zeitung*, April 1971.

27. Cleaver was hardly the first to make connections between African Americans as an "internal colony" and Third World struggles. However, he became one of the more prominent advocates of Third World solidarity after 1968. See Malloy, "Uptight in Babylon," 544–46.

28. "Kathleen Cleaver rief zum Kampf auf," *Rhein-Neckar-Zeitung*, July 5, 1971; "Kathleen Cleaver in Heidelberg," *Heidelberger Tageblatt*, July 5, 1971.

29. "Wir müssen den großen Berg sprengen."

30. "The Ramstein Incident Continued," *Voice of the Lumpen*, no. 2, January or February 1971. The latest incidents reported in the paper took place in January.

31. "The Trial of the Ramstein 2," *Voice of the Lumpen*, no. 6, between May 18 and June 16, 1971.

32. Smith, *An International History of the Black Panther Party*, 35–36.

33. "Bobby, Panthers, and Political Prisoners," "The Angela Davis Story," and "On the Trial of Bobby Seale and Ericka Huggins," *Voice of the Lumpen*, no. 2.

34. "Who the 'Voice of the Lumpen' Are," *Voice of the Lumpen*, no. 2.

35. Jones, "Black Power"; Bloom and Martin, *Black against the Empire*, 36–44, 310–12; Smith, *An International History*, 49–60.

36. Cleaver, "The Land Question and Black Liberation"; Cleaver, "After Brother Malcolm," *Voice of the Lumpen*, no. 6.

37. Malloy, "Uptight in Babylon," 550.

38. Smith, *An International History*, 54–60, 65–86.

39. Bloom and Martin, *Black against the Empire*, 318–19.

40. Malloy, "Uptight in Babylon," 559, 562.

41. Bloom and Martin, *Black against the Empire*, 341–71.

42. The three *K*s are a reference to the Ku Klux Klan. In "Augsburg," *Voice of the Lumpen*, no. 6.
43. "Kirch-Göns: Rebellion," "Schwetzingen: Off the Pigs," and "Pressure Program," *Voice of the Lumpen*, no. 6.
44. "What Is a Pig?" *Voice of the Lumpen*, no. 6.
45. "What Is Meant by Freedom for Everybody or Freedom for Nobody," *Voice of the Lumpen*, no. 6.
46. "The Ramstein Incident Continued," *Voice of the Lumpen*, no. 2.
47. "Black Bars in Germany," *Voice of the Lumpen*, no. 6.
48. "Mannheim Express" and "Pentagon Missing 8,000 GIs," *Voice of the Lumpen*, no. 2.
49. "Struggle of Black GI's (West Germany)," *Voice of the Lumpen*, no. 6.
50. "CSM Evans—A Tool?" and "CSM Evans—A Trap?" *Voice of the Lumpen*, no. 6.
51. Michael S. Davison, "Remarks at the International Institute for Strategic Studies, London, England, March 16, 1972," in A Collection of Speeches, 69. USAMHI, Carlisle PA.
52. "Use What You Got to Get What You Need!" *Voice of the Lumpen*, no. 2.
53. "Black Bars in Germany," *Voice of the Lumpen*, no. 6.
54. See Library of Congress interview with Nathan Timothy Walker.
55. See Memorandum for Correspondents (April 9, 1971), Polk Papers.
56. Wire services news item, July 28, 1971, Polk Papers. See also Thomas A. Johnson, "Pentagon Said to Penalize Officers on Racial Policy," *New York Times*, July 28, 1971.
57. See transcripts of the morning briefing by DASD/PA Friedman of July 28 and July 29, 1971, Polk Papers.
58. See 1976 interview with Bruce Palmer Jr., Senior Officer Oral History Program, 443, USAMHI.

4. NEW RACE RELATIONS POLICIES

1. James E. Brayboy, 1981 interview with Maj. Gen. Frederic E. Davison, Senior Officer Debriefing/Oral History Program, USAMHI.
2. During the interim period from April 1971 to September 1971, Davison's chief of staff, Lt. Gen. Michael Collins, was in charge of USAREUR.
3. "Gen. Davison: 'Toughest Period . . . Ever,'" *Washington Post*, September 12, 1971.
4. Michael S. Davison to Filmore K. (Ken) Mearns, September 22, 1971, Davison Papers, USAMHI. According to a note on the letter, similar letters were sent to LTG Pearson, LTG Eifler, MG Cobb, BG LeTellier, BG Hayward,

MG McAlister, and MG LeVan. The letter actually does not give a year, but considering its content it is reasonable to assume it was written when Davison had assumed command.

5. Persons interview, 351.

6. Text of the afternoon session of the Commanders' Conference, September 14, 1971, 12. The text is attached to a letter from Davison to his subordinate commanders, September 27, 1971, Davison Papers.

7. Persons interview, 350.

8. Text of the Commanders Conference, 12.

9. Persons interview, 350.

10. "U.S. Army in Germany: Vexing Racial Picture," *Los Angeles Times*, November 21, 1971; "Trial Set for 6 of 25 GIs Charged in Racial Fracas," *Stars and Stripes*, October 3, 1971; "Rassenterror in der US-Armee," *Die Tat*, October 2, 1971.

11. "U.S. Army in Germany: Vexing Racial Picture," *Los Angeles Times*, November 21, 1971.

12. Persons interview, 353.

13. "U.S. Army in Germany: Vexing Racial Picture," *Los Angeles Times*, November 21, 1971.

14. Hearings before the Special Subcommittee on Recruiting and Retention of Military Personnel (Washington DC 1972): 8740.

15. "Militärprozeß platzte nach Beginn: Staranwälte wollen Schwarze verteidigen," *Heidelberger Tageblatt*, October 5, 1971; "Musterprozeß gegen Rassendiskriminierung," *Rhein-Neckar-Zeitung*, October 5, 1971.

16. "Rassismus in der US-Army unter Beschuß: Eine Frau kämpft für ihre Brüder in Darmstadt," *Heidelberger Tageblatt*, October 27, 1971.

17. Persons interview, 354–55. See Hearings before the Special Subcommittee for exact date of dismissal, 8741.

18. Hearings before the Special Subcommittee, 8748.

19. Persons interview, 356; Congress, Hearings before the Special Subcommittee, 8739; DPA Meldung 23.10.71, filed as RITA Note 144, Archiv für Soldatenrechte e.V. Weichselstr. 37, 12045 Berlin.

20. See "U.S. Army in Germany: Vexing Racial Picture," *Los Angeles Times*, November 21, 1971. Also see Persons interview, 353–66, and Frederic Davison interview, vii, 214.

21. Persons interview, 355, 365; Hearings before the Special Subcommittee, 8749.

22. Persons interview, 366.

23. AStA Sozialistischer Deutscher Studentenbund, *Rassismus in Darmstadt*, flyer, October 1, 1971, filed under RITA Note 144, Archiv für Soldatenrechte

e.V. Weichselstr. 37, 12045 Berlin; RITA/ACT, Darmstadt-K'Town-Vietnam, flyer, early October 1971, filed under RITA Note 144, Archiv für Soldaten-rechte e.V. Weichselstr. 37, 12045 Berlin; "Darmstadt 53 vs. United Pigs," flyer, between October 4 and 26, 1971, filed under RITA Note 144, Archiv für Soldatenrechte e.V. Weichselstr. 37, 12045 Berlin; "Prozess gegen Schwarze GI's in Mannheim," *Was tun,* Sondernummer, early October 1971, filed under RITA Note 144, Archiv für Soldatenrechte e.V. Weichselstr. 37, 12045 Berlin.

24. Transcript of report for the *CBS Morning News* with John Hart (Benton substituting), August 31, 1971. Filed under RITA Note 144, Archiv für Soldatenrechte e.V. Weichselstr. 37, 12045 Berlin.

25. "Army Orders Transfer of 35 Darmstadt GIs Involved in July Protest," *Stars and Stripes,* October 26, 1971.

26. "Strafversetzung statt Gerichtsverfahren," *Mannheimer Morgen,* October 25, 1971; "Militärverfahren in Heidelberg geplatzt," *Heidelberger Tageblatt,* October 25, 1971; "Als Strafe droht Versetzung," *Rhein-Neckar-Zeitung,* October 26, 1971; "Rassismus in der US-Army unter Beschuß," *Heidelberger Tageblatt,* October 27, 1971; "Die kranke Armee," *Der Stern,* November 14, 1971.

27. "U.S. Army in Germany: Vexing Racial Picture," *Los Angeles Times,* November 21, 1971.

28. Joseph, "The Black Power Movement," 756.

29. Persons interview, 356; Hearings before the Special Subcommittee, 8737–8807.

30. Persons interview, 366.

31. James H. Polk, "New Weapons, Realistic Training Mark NATO Vigil," *Army* 20, no. 10 (October 1970): 47–51.

32. Michael S. Davison, "In Europe, the Focus Is on People," *Army* 21, no. 10 (October 1971): 49–53.

33. See Davison, A Collection of Speeches, 69.

34. Persons interview, 322; Frederic E. Davison interview, 213, 219–20.

35. Michael S. Davison, "Opening Remarks at Equal Opportunity Conference, Berchtesgaden, Germany, November 10, 1971," in A Collection of Speeches, 15. USAMHI.

36. Persons interview, 352.

37. Michael S. Davison, "Lecture, Woodrow Wilson International Center for Scholars, Washington DC, March 25, 1972," in A Collection of Speeches, 88, USAMHI.

38. See also L. James Binder, "New Iron for NATO's Backbone," *Army* 22, no. 7 (July 1972): 12–13.

39. Binder, "New Iron for NATO's Backbone," *Army* 22, no. 7 (July 1972): 97.

40. Michael S. Davison, "Remarks for the Commander' Equal Opportunity/ Human Relations Conference, Garmisch, Germany, June 6, 1972," in A Collection of Speeches, 159, USAMHI.

41. Persons interview, 321–22.

42. See Drew Middleton, "First Black U.S. Division Chief," *New York Times*, May 19, 1972.

43. "Coping with People Problems," *Soldiers* 27, no. 5 (May 1972).

44. Harry B. Ellis, "Ending Army Racism: Strategy for Europe," *Christian Science Monitor*, November 18, 1971.

45. Backchannel from Davison to Kerwin, DCSPER DA, Washington DC, November 8, 1971.

46. Backchannel from Davison to Kerwin, November 12, 1971.

47. Hearings before the Special Subcommittee, 8804.

48. Davison to Subordinate Commanders, "Community Human Relations Discussion Groups," November 16, 1972.

49. Davison to Pearson, September 12, 1972.

50. Davison to Subordinate Commanders, "National Brotherhood Week," February 14, 1972, and February 5, 1973.

51. Davison, "Woodrow Wilson Lecture," 96–97.

52. Michael S. Davison, "Remarks at the Annual Meeting, European Department, AUSA, Garmisch, Germany, June 1, 1972," in A Collection of Speeches, 141, USAMHI, Carlisle PA.

53. Interview Frederic Davison, 217–18, 220; interview Michael Davison, 6–8.

54. Davison, "Woodrow Wilson Lecture," 96. Also see Davison, "Remarks at the Annual Meeting, AUSA," 145.

55. Davison to Mearns, November 6, 1972.

56. Davison to Willard Pearson, September 20, 1972, October 3, 1972, and November 6, 1972; Davison to Fillmore K. Mearns, September 20, 1972.

57. Davison to Pearson, September 20, 1972, October 3, 1972; Davison to Mearns, October 17, 1972, and November 7, 1972.

58. Davison to Pearson, September 20, October 3, 1972, November 6, 1972; Davison to Mearns, October 17, 1972.

59. Davison to Pearson, September 20, 1972. A similar complaint was made against the Forty-Second Artillery Group and the Giessen Military Community. See Davison to Pearson, November 6, 1972.

60. Davison to Mearns, September 20, 1972; Davison to Pearson, October 3, 1972. In this case the Third Armored Division Support Command did have an EO staff officer, but he was part-time and also burdened with the task of being

the drug and alcohol abuse control officer. See also Davison to Mearns, October 17, 1972. In this case the officer had not been officially appointed on orders and was not on the personal staff of the commander. In the case of the Second Battalion, Thirteenth Infantry, the team had found that most soldiers did not know their EO staff officer. See Davison to Pearson, "Racial Complaint–2d Battalion, 13th Infantry," August 23, 1972.

61. Davison to Mearns, September 20, 1972, October 17, 1972, and November 7, 1972; Davison to Pearson, October 3, 1972

62. Davison to Mearns, September 20, 1972; Davison to Pearson, October 3, 1972.

63. Davison to Pearson, October 20, 1972.

64. Davison to Paul Saunders, October 20, 1972.

65. Davison to Mearns, October 6, 1972.

66. Davison to Robert Lercy Coger, October 6, 1972.

67. A third example of Davison following up on complaints by individual enlisted men can be seen in his letter to Pearson where he called attention to the allegations of Pvt. James Stansberry. See Davison to Pearson, "Racial Complaint–2d Battalion, 13th Infantry," August 23, 1972.

68. Michael S. Davison, "Remarks for the Commander' Equal Opportunity/ Human Relations Conference, Garmisch, Germany, June 6, 1972," in A Collection of Speeches, 160, USAMHI.

69. Davison, "Remarks for the Commander' Equal Opportunity/Human Relations Conference, 162.

70. Davison to Pearson, September 12, 1972.

71. Gilbert and Nordlie, *An Analysis of Race Relations/Equal Opportunity Training in USAREUR,* 70.

72. Davison to Pearson, September 12, 1972, Davison Papers.

73. Gilbert and Nordlie, *RR/EO in USAREUR,* 70–72.

74. Memorandum from Davison to Commanders of USAREUR Major Commands and Assigned Units and Activities, Heads of Staff Offices, February 14, 1972, Davison Papers.

75. George C. Wilson and Haynes Johnson, "GI Crime, Violence Climb Overseas," *Washington Post,* September 13, 1971.

76. Persons interview, 315.

77. Persons interview, appendix C.

78. Davison to USAREUR Major Commands and Assigned Units, Heads of Staff, September 27, 1971, Davison Papers.

79. Persons interview, 369. See also appendix H of the interview for the report.

80. *Report of the Task Force on the Administration of Military Justice in the Armed Forces*, vol. 1 (Washington DC, November 23, 1972), 1.

81. Persons interview, 389.

82. Persons interview, appendix H, 3, and appendix I, 6.

83. Persons interview, appendix I, 1–2.

84. Persons interview, 3.

85. Persons interview, 324–25.

86. Persons interview, 328.

87. Persons interview, 330. Michael Davison made a similar observation in his own oral history interview: "I think we were on the road to a real scandal. Because the commanders were using the, they were using their authority to place a man in pretrial confinement, as a punitive measure. And more often than not, they put a man in there when they had no intention of preferring any charges." *Senior Officer Debriefing Program: Conversations between General Michael S. Davison and Colonel Douglas H. Farmer and Lieutenant Colonel Dale K. Brudvig.* U.S. Army Military History Collection, 1976, Davison Papers, Section 5, 11.

88. U.S. Task Force on the Administration of Military Justice in the Armed Forces. *Report of the Task Force on the Administration of Military Justice in the Armed Forces*, November 30, 1972, 78–79.

89. Persons interview, appendix 1, 4.

90. Persons interview, 338.

91. U.S. Task Force, *Report of the Task Force on the Administration of Military Justice in the Armed Forces*, 77.

92. Persons interview, 383.

93. Gilbert and Nordlie, *RR/EO in USAREUR*, ii, iv.

94. Gilbert and Nordlie, *RR/EO in USAREUR*, v, vi.

95. Persons interview, 350.

96. Gilbert and Nordlie, *RR/EO in USAREUR*, 22–23.

97. Radine, *The Taming of the Troops*, 89.

98. Frederic Davison interview, 214.

5. RESISTANCE AND DISSENT

1. Maslowski and Winslow, *Looking for a Hero*, 357, 359; Appy, *Working-Class War*, 241, 245–47.

2. Klimke, *The Other Alliance*, 81–86.

3. Cortright, *Soldiers in Revolt*, 50–51.

4. Cortright, *Soldiers in Revolt*, 52; John Rechy, "Lieutenant on the Peace Line," *Nation*, February 21, 1966, 204–8; Lynd, *We Won't Go*.

5. Lynd, *We Won't Go*. See also Stapp, *Up against the Brass*, 41–43; Ira Glasse, "Justice and Captain Levy," Columbia Forum, Spring 1969, 46–49.

6. Stapp, *Up against the Brass*, 9–17, 20–24.

7. Stapp, *Up against the Brass*, 43–48, 53–57.

8. See "Order Violates Free Speech, Soldier Says," *Los Angeles Times*, May 31, 1967, and "Soldier Faces Trial over Leftist Material," *Washington Post*, May 31, 1967.

9. First quote taken from "GI Sentenced for Refusal to Open His Footlocker," *Washington Post*, June 2, 1967. Second quote taken from "GI Who Refused to Open Locker Convicted," *Los Angeles Times*, June 2, 1967.

10. "2 in Antiwar Case Sentenced," *New York Times*, August 26, 1967.

11. "Critic of Vietnam Cleared by Army: Lack of Evidence Found—Two Demonstrators Held," *New York Times*, August 1, 1967.

12. "War Protesters in Oklahoma Jail: Trespass Charged to Pair Who Gave GIs Books," *New York Times*, July 27, 1967, and "General Bars Protesters from GI's Court-Martial," *New York Times*, July 30, 1967.

13. "2 in Antiwar Case Sentenced," and "Hearing Denied in Ft. Sill Entry," *Washington Post*, August 2, 1967.

14. Heinl, "The Collapse of the Armed Forces," 32.

15. Cortright, *Soldiers in Revolt*, 53–54; "Summer of Support," *New York Times*, August 12, 1968; *New York Times*, November 8, 1969; *New York Times*, February 15, 1970.

16. Cortright, *Soldiers in Revolt*, 53, 61; Heinl, "The Collapse of the Armed Forces," 32.

17. Donald Janson, "Antiwar Coffeehouses Delight GIs but Not Army," *New York Times*, August 12, 1968.

18. Janson, "Antiwar Coffeehouses Delight GIs."

19. "Students and Soldiers Protest Closing of Antiwar Coffeehouse," *New York Times*, April 18, 1970.

20. Army officials put the number at half a dozen. See Carroll Maurice, "Petition by GIs Raises War Issue," *New York Times*, March 16, 1969.

21. Maurice, "Petition by GIs Raises War Issue." See also "Coffeehouse Is Center of GI Dissent in S.C. Army Town," *Washington Post*, April 3, 1969.

22. Robert Sherrill, "Must the Citizen Give Up His Civil Liberties When He Joins the Army? *New York Times*, May 18, 1968.

23. "March Inspired by Coffeehouse," *Washington Post*, January 19, 1970.

24. Bruce Galphin, "GI Coffeehouse Owners Sue, Charge Harassment," *Washington Post*, February 7, 1970; "Operators of Antiwar Coffeehouse Tried on Rare Charge in S.C.," *Washington Post,* April 17, 1970.

25. "S.C. Jury Convicts 3 Operators of GI Coffeehouse," *Washington Post,* April 17, 1970; "Six-Year Sentence Given to 3 Owners of GI Coffeehouse," *New York Times,* April 29, 1970; "'Public Nuisance'—Six Years," *New York Times,* May 3, 1970.

26. Douglas E. Kneeland, "War Stirs More Dissent among GIs," *New York Times,* June 21, 1970.

27. Heinl, "The Collapse of the Armed Forces" 31.

28. Cortright, *Soldiers in Revolt,* 55.

29. Cortright, *Soldiers in Revolt,* 56.

30. Cortright, *Soldiers in Revolt,* 57. The *Christian Science Monitor* puts the number at three hundred. David Holmstrom, "Antiwar Marches Draw More GIs," *Christian Science Monitor*, April 4, 1969.

31. "9 GI Foes of War Arrested in Church," *New York Times*, July 18, 1968.

32. Cortright, *Soldiers in Revolt,* 53, 56.

33. "Protest Riot Duty," *Chicago Tribune,* August 25, 1968.

34. Stapp, *Up against the Brass,* 145. See also Cortright, *Soldiers in Revolt,* 56. The *Chicago Tribune* ran an article on August 21 in which it reported that 7,500 men at Ft. Hood had undergone special training to control civil disturbances. In April of that same year, 3,000 troops from Ft. Hood had bivouacked in Jackson Park. At this point army officials denied that there had been any requests to send the troops, but logistics posts were established in Chicago in case the president called on the Ft. Hood units. See "Army Asks CTA for 100 Riot Buses" and "Guard Is Called Up to Protect Chicago during Convention," *Chicago Tribune*, August 21, 1968; "Arrange Jail in Hall Near Meeting Site," *Chicago Tribune*, August 23, 1968. One thousand Ft. Hood soldiers were transported to Bergstrom Air Force base on stand-by to be sent to Chicago on August 24. See "Protest Riot Duty." Eventually troops from Ft. Hood and other bases were flown to Chicago, but they were not used. See Steven V. Roberts, "5000 Troops Flown to Convention Duty," *New York Times*, August 26, 1968, and "Guard Is Awaiting Release from Duty," *Chicago Tribune*, August 31, 1968.

35. "Protest Riot Duty." See also John Kifner, "Politics: Thousands of U.S. Troops Mobilized for Guard Duty at Democratic National Convention," *Chicago Tribune*, August 25, 1968.

36. "Free Negro GI in Refusal of Chicago Duty," *Chicago Tribune,* September 8, 1968; "Negro GI Cleared of Having Refused Chicago Riot Duty," *New York Times*, September 8, 1968.

37. Stapp brought in Michael Kennedy. Stapp, *Up against the Brass,* 147. See also "Courts-Martial of 41 End; Protested Chicago Duty," *New York Times,* December 19, 1968; "5 Foes of Riot Duty Convicted by Army," *New York Times*, September 22, 1968; AP-Item, *New York Times,* September 28, 1968; "3 More Convicted in Protest at Fort," *New York Times*, September 29, 1968; "Army Court Finds 4 Negroes Guilty," *New York Times*, October 26, 1968.

38. J. Anthony Lukas, "War Critics Liken Chicago to Prague," *New York Times,* August 25, 1968.

39. Cortright, *Soldiers in Revolt,* 57.

40. Stapp, *Up against the Brass,* 155. See also "Head of Servicemen's Union Seized on Vagrancy Charge," *New York Times,* September 12, 1968, and "3 Aiding Soldiers in Texas Are Convicted of Vagrancy," *New York Times*, September 13, 1968.

41. For clips from the CBS documentary, see *Sir! No Sir! The Suppressed Story of the GI Movement to End the Vietnam War.*

42. Cortright, *Soldiers in Revolt,* 84.

43. "10 Held for Picketing Store," *New York Times,* June 3, 1971.

44. "GIs and Veterans, Seized in Picketing, Sue Texas Officials," *New York Times,* June 27, 1971.

45. Cortright, *Soldiers in Revolt,* 84.

46. Robert M. Smith, "Army Sets Rules on Troop Dissent," *New York Times*, September 12, 1969; "Army Issues Guidelines on Servicemen Dissent," *Los Angeles Times,* September 13, 1969.

47. Peter Osnos, "Army Moves to Curb Antiwar Center," *Washington Post*, January 4, 1970.

48. Melvin Goo, "Army Seeks to Bar GI Coffeehouse," *Washington Post,* February 22, 1970.

49. Douglas E. Kneeland, "War Stirs More Dissent among GIs," *New York Times*, June 21, 1970.

50. The activists involved with the coffeehouse were not convinced that the army's "hands-off" policy was genuine and maintained that the army was behind the civilian activities against the coffeehouse. See "The Coffeehouse Story," *FTA*, Fort Knox KY, October 1969, reprinted in Waterhouse and Wizard, *Turning the Guns Around,* 95–96.

51. Ben A. Franklin, "Antiwar Coffeehouse Vexes Town near Fort Knox," *New York Times,* November 8, 1969; "Post Town Upset by Antiwar GIs," *New York Times,* November 9, 1969.

52. Tom Zito, "Coffeehouse Seeks GIs outside DMZ," *Washington Post,* July 29, 1970; Sanford J. Ungar, "Codes Block GI Coffeehouse," *Washington Post,* August 1, 1970.

53. Adrienne Cook and Tom O'Brien, "The GI Movement and the 'DMZ,'" *Washington Post,* July 29, 1970. See also "GI Movement Office Firebombed," AFB, July 1970, reprinted in Waterhouse and Wizard, *Turning the Guns Around.*

54. Ben A. Franklin, "Army Plan to Spy on Civilians Was Sent to 319 U.S. Officials," *New York Times,* February 18, 1971.

55. "The Guilt of Silence," *New York Times,* February 21, 1971.

56. Cortright, *Soldiers in Revolt,* 58.

57. On cooperation between Stapp and YAWF, see Stapp, *Up against the Brass,* 46–49, 53–54, 56–59, 65–66, 83, 93.

58. Cortright gives the number of one hundred. Cortright, *Soldiers in Revolt,* 159. *New York Times* put the number at two hundred, but also reported that the majority were onlookers and estimated that only about forty really took part in the events. See Sherrill, "Must the Citizen Give Up His Civil Liberties When He Joins the Army?"

59. Cortright, *Soldiers in Revolt,* 61, 78, 79.

60. Nicosia, *Home to War,* 41.

61. Jan Barry quoted according to Nicosia, *Home to War,* 42.

62. To his colleague Major General Persons, the JAG commented that he believed the case should never have been handled as a mutiny and had been blown out of proportion. Persons interview 367.

63. Michels, "Interview mit Andy Stapp," 66–76.

64. Harris, "Forderungen," 77.

65. See Appy, *Working-Class War,* 17–43.

66. Harris, "Forderungen," 77; Michels, "Interview mit Stapp," 68, 70.

67. Harris, "Forderungen," 78.

68. Michels, "Interview mit Andy Stapp," 67.

69. Harris, "Forderungen," 78.

70. Stapp had an extremely apologetic view of soldiers killing their officers, interpreting such actions as a sign of growing discontent within the ranks. See Michels, "Interview mit Any Stapp," 70–71.

71. Harris, "Forderungen," 78–79.

72. Stapp, *Up against the Brass,* 21; Michels, "Interview mit Andy Stapp," 60, 70–71, 73–74.

73. Harris, "Forderungen," 79–80.

74. Michels, "Interview mit Andy Stapp," 72.

75. "What We're for and Why We're for It," in *Up against the Bulkhead,* June 15, 1970, reprinted in Waterhouse and Wizard, *Turning the Guns Around.*

76. Waterhouse and Wizard, *Turning the Guns Around,* 138–39.

77. Waterhouse and Wizard, *Turning the Guns Around,* 139.

6. THE SITUATION IN USAREUR

1. Watts, "US-Army-Europe," 8–10, 17, 18, 26.

2. Radio transcript, "This Week: The Deserters," reported by John Williams, produced by Philip Whitehead, directed by Randal Beattie, transmitted August 17, 1967. RITA Notes 7, 1–2, Archiv Soldatenrechte e.V. Weichselstr. 37, 12045 Berlin.

3. Watts, "US-Army-Europe," 41–44. In a rare Library of Congress interview, Frank Garcia describes going AWOL while stationed in Germany. Garcia did not go to France or Sweden. Instead he quickly found his way back to the United States and then Canada where he maintained a low profile. Interview with Frank Garcia, Garcia Collection (AFC/2001/001/18420), Veterans History Project, American Folklife Center, Library of Congress.

4. Watts, "US-Army-Europe," 44–45.

5. "Paris Underground Is Starting to Crumble," *Overseas Weekly,* July 13, 1969.

6. Watts, "US-Army-Europe," 61–66.

7. Department of the Army, Office of the JAG, DAJA, LTS, File on Thomas Schwaetzer: Agent Report Filed on December 15, 1969, Archiv Soldaten-rechte e.V., Weichselstr. 37, 12045 Berlin.

8. Rita Note 3205.1.12, "Abstract: The Development of Resistance inside the Armies (RITA) as a Function of Capital Accumulation," April 2000, Archiv Soldatenrechte e.V. Weichselstr. 37, 12045 Berlin.

9. File on Thomas Schwaetzer. The deportation to Corsica was also reported in "Paris Underground Is Starting to Crumble."

10. The bookstore, Politische Buchhandlung, was located in Marstallstr. 11a in Heidelberg. See *Fight Back,* issues February 16–19 to May 1974, Archiv Soldatenrechte e.V. Weichselstr. 37, 12045 Berlin.

11. De Nike, *Inter-Theater Transfer,* 2.

12. De Nike, *Inter-Theater Transfer,* 2.

13. Cortright, *Soldiers in Revolt,* 94.

14. Cortright and Grossman, "Die GI-Bewegung in Deutschland." See also Cortright, *Soldiers in Revolt*, 93.
15. "Protester Punished with Article 15," *Overseas Weekly*, April 19, 1970.
16. "How GIs Feel about Protest," *Overseas Weekly*, February 15, 1970.
17. Cortright, *Soldiers in Revolt*, 99.
18. *Supplemental Manpower Hearing before the Committee on Armed Services*, U.S. Senate, 92nd Cong., 1st sess. On HR 6531, 107. Also see *Hearings before the Special Subcommittee on Recruiting and Retention of Military Personnel of the Committee on Armed Services*, U.S. House, 92nd Cong., 1st and 2nd sess., 8352.
19. RITA Note 110, May 31, 1971, Archiv für Soldatenrechte e.V. Weichselstr. 37, 12045 Berlin.
20. RITA Note 115, approximately June 20, 1971, Archiv Soldatenrechte e.V. Weichselstr. 37, 12045 Berlin.
21. Initiative Internationale Vietnam Solidarität, "Deutsch-amerikanische Völkerfreundschaft-Ja, Kriegspropaganda-Nein," RITA Note 111, May 1971, Archiv Soldatenrechte e.V. Weichselstr. 37, 12045 Berlin.
22. "Notes of Court-Martial Case of Private O'Brien," August 15, 1971, RITA Note 132, Archiv Soldatenrechte e.V. Weichselstr. 37, 12045 Berlin.
23. RITA Note 113, June 6, 1971, Archiv Soldatenrechte e.V. Weichselstr. 37, 12045 Berlin.
24. "To all GIs in Western Germany," RITA Note 123, Archiv Soldatenrechte e.V. Weichselstr. 37, 12045 Berlin.
25. AstA Sozialistischer Heidelberger Studentenbund, "Rassismus in Darmstadt," RITA Note 138, Archiv Soldatenrechte e.V. Weichselstr. 37, 12045 Berlin.
26. "Prozess gegen schwarze GI's in Mannheim," *was tun*, Sondernummer (October 1, 1971).
27. Klimke, *The Other Alliance*, 121.
28. Höhn and Klimke, *A Breath of Freedom*, 152–54.
29. RITA Note 237, 1.
30. RITA Note 235, *RITA F. Act to Gil Merkx*, August 7, 1972, 1, Archiv Soldatenrechte e.V. Weichselstr. 37, 12045 Berlin.
31. RITA Note 235, 6–7.
32. "A Message from German Demonstrators," *Where It's At*, ca. fall 1970, Archiv Soldatenrechte e.V. Weichselstr. 37, 12045 Berlin.
33. RITA Note 3205.1.12.
34. Craig Davidson, "Army Hunts Phantom Editor," *Overseas Weekly*, February 22, 1970.

35. Craig Davidson, "Army Suspects Troop of Editing GI Paper," *Overseas Weekly*, April 19, 1970.

36. Davidson, "Army Hunts Phantom Editor."

37. "If It Doesn't Move Salute It: GI Paper Holds Protest Week," *Overseas Weekly*, March 22, 1970.

38. Davidson, "Army Suspects Troop of Editing GI Paper."

39. "If It Doesn't Move Salute It."

40. "Mess Hall Boycott Slated for Easter," *Overseas Weekly*, March 29, 1970.

41. Davidson, "Army Suspects Troop of Editing GI Paper"; "Army Drops Charge against Suspected GI Paper Editor," *Overseas Weekly*, May 31, 1970; "Underground Newspaper Buys Brass," *Overseas Weekly,* April 5, 1970.

42. Department of Defense Directive No. 5230.9 (December 24, 1966), paragraph 23, USAREUR Regulation 632–10. For a discussion on the restrictions on GIs' freedom of speech from this period, see Brown, "Must the Soldier Be a Silent Member of Our Society?" 94–97.

43. "GI Supporter to Be Deported from West Germany," *LIBERATION* News Service, no 554 (September 19, 1973).

44. De Nike, *Inter-Theater Transfer*, 35.

45. Harris, *Forward*, 131–32, Archiv für Soldatenrechte.

46. Harris, *Forward*, 132–34.

47. "Troop Withdrawal," *Where It's At,* special M-Day issue [no date provided; most likely published between mid-October and mid-November 1969], Archiv Soldatenrechte e.V. Weichselstr. 37, 12045 Berlin.

48. "Mass Strike on M-Day," *Where It's At*, November 1969.

49. "14th Moratorium Day November 15," *Where It's At*, November 1969.

50. "Grafenwoer" and "Kaiserslautern," *Where It's At*, November 1969.

51. "14th Moratorium Day November 15," *Where It's At*, November 1969

52. "GI Struggles," *Where It's At*, November 1969.

53. Harris, *Forward*, 136–39.

54. Harris, *Forward*, 140.

55. "Justice on Trial," *Forward*, special edition (July 1971); "Military Justice," *Forward*, no. 6 (December 1971); Harris, "Forderungen," 141–42.

56. *Graffiti*, no. 2 (November 1969): 1, Archiv Soldatenrechte e.V. Weichselstr. 37, 12045 Berlin.

57. "Help," *Graffiti*, no. 2 (November 1969): 8.

58. *Fight Back*, no. 5 (1973).

59. Stadt Heidelberg, Amt für öffentliche Ordnung to Karen Seelye Bixler, "Ausweisung und Abschiebung aus dem Bundesgebiet Deutschland incl. West-Berlin," Az. 32/2-VIII/73 (August 31, 1973).

60. Paul Kemezis, "GIs in Europe Are 'Cooler' than Those of Vietnam Era, but Many Defy Old-Army Rules," *New York Times*, April 21, 1975.

61. "Darmstadt-K'Town-Vietnam: Black+White+Yellow=Red??? " RITA Note 139, Archiv Soldatenrechte e.V. Weichselstr. 37, 12045 Berlin.

62. Cortright and Grossman, "Die GI-Bewegung in Deutschland," 162–65.

63. "Black Baptist Gives Up Gun," *Overseas Weekly*, April 26, 1970.

64. Barry Irvin, "The Trial of Lunnie Smith," *Overseas Weekly*, May 10, 1970.

65. "Army Chains, Shaves Black Baptist GIs," *Overseas Weekly*, August 30, 1970.

66. On this issue see Griffith, *The U.S. Army's Transition to the All-Volunteer Force*, 73–74.

67. "Darmstadt-K'Town-Vietnam."

68. "Free the Ramstein 2," RITA Note 118, Archiv Soldatenrechte e.V. Weichselstr. 37, 12045 Berlin.

69. "The KTtown 14," RITA Note 127, September 10, 1971, Archiv Soldatenrechte e.V. Weichselstr. 37, 12045 Berlin.

70. "Freedom for Marshall," *Forward* 1, no. 3 (August 1971): 6–8, Archiv Soldatenrechte e.V. Weichselstr. 37, 12045 Berlin.

71. "Freedom for Marshall."

72. "Freedom for Marshall," 2, 7.

73. "Freedom for Marshall," 2, 10–11.

74. Editorial, *Forward* 1, no. 6 (December 1971): 2.

75. RITA Note 135, RITA F. Act to Gil Merkx, August 7, 1972, 4.

76. RITA Note 237, 1.

77. RITA Note 237, 1.

78. *New Testament*, no. 2 (June 5, 1972), Archiv Soldatenrechte e.V. Weichselstr. 37, 12045 Berlin.

79. RITA Note 237, 2.

80. *New Testament*, no. 4 (July 31, 1972): 2–3, Archiv Soldatenrechte e.V. Weichselstr. 37, 12045 Berlin.

81. *New Testament*, no. 2 (June 5, 1972), Archiv Soldatenrechte e.V. Weichselstr. 37, 12045 Berlin.

82. RITA Note 237, 2–3.

83. RITA Note 237, 5.

84. See also "GIs Pelt Firemen, Officers with Rocks at Neu Ulm," *Stars & Stripes*, August 17, 1972; "Aufruhr in US-Kasernen," *Filderzeitung,* August 16, 1972.

85. "Aufruhr in US-Kasernen," *Filderzeitung,* August 16, 1972.

86. "At War with the Army," *Time*, February 8, 1971. "Counsel for the GI Defense," *Time*, October 19, 1970; "Lawyers Military Defense," *New York Review of Books* 18, no. 10 (June 1, 1972).

87. De Nike, *Inter-Theater Transfer*, 1, 30, 13.

88. De Nike, *Inter-Theater Transfer*, 37, 43–46.

89. De Nike, *Inter-Theater Transfer*, 65, 72–75.

90. De Nike, *Inter-Theater Transfer*, 68–70.

91. Department of the Army, Headquarters, Kaiserslautern Army Depot Complex, "Special Court Martial Order no. 10," September 19, 1973, RITA Note 366, Archiv Soldatenrechte e.V. Weichselstr. 37, 12045 Berlin.

92. De Nike, *Inter-Theater Transfer*, 70–71, 78–79.

93. "Troop Withdrawal."

94. AETL-AG-PA, Elimination for Unfitness UP Chap 13, AR 635–200" (July 18, 1973), RITA note 366, Archiv Soldatenrechte e.V. Weichselstr. 37, 12045 Berlin.

95. Cal Posner, "Blitz Tactic Helps Spot Drug Users," *Stars & Stripes*, February 2, 1973.

96. AMEX, no. 34 (February 1973).

97. De Nike, *Inter-Theater Transfer*, 64.

98. Committee for GI Rights v. Foehlke, ACLU news release, PR #15-73 (April 30, 1973).

99. "U.S. Military Cracks Down on 'Drug Abuse' on Army Bases in W. Germany," *Liberation News Service*, no. 496 (January 24, 1973), 10.

100. "Army Brass in Germany Move to Break GI Resistance," *Bond* 71 (February 12, 1973), 4, 7.

101. De Nike, *Inter-Theater Transfer*, 83, 89

102. "Liebesgrüße von BR-262," *Stern* 33 (July 1973): 76.

103. De Nike, *Inter-Theater Transfer*, 82.

104. De Nike, *Inter-Theater Transfer*, 77. See also letter from Robert S. Rivkin to Col. Lawrence P. Hansen, "United States v. Larry Johnson" (October 2, 1973), RITA note 366, Archiv Soldatenrechte e.V. Weichselstr. 37, 12045 Berlin.

105. "USAREUR: Vorläufig kein Kommentar," *Heidelberger Tageblatt*, July 28, 1973.

106. Craig R. Whitney, "U.S. Army Is Said to Spy on Its Critics in Germany," *New York Times*, July 28, 1973; Dan Morgan, "Army Admits West German Spy Activity," *Washington Post*, July 31, 1973.

107. "Bugs on the Rhine," *Time*, August 13, 1973; "Weicker Provides Evidence: Army Spying Charges Turned In," *Los Angeles Times*, August 4, 1973.

108. Dan Morgan, "Senators Rap Army Snooping," *Washington Post*, August 1, 1973.

109. Craig R. Whitney, "Some of the Spooks Have Had It," *New York Times*, August 12, 1973.

110. "Weicker Provides Evidence: Army Spying Charges Turned In," *Los Angeles Times*, August 4, 1973.

111. "Judge Curbs Army on Overseas Taps," *New York Times*, March 18, 1975.

112. John M. Crewdson, "Military Flouted Civilians' Rights, Senate Unit Says," *New York Times*, May 17, 1976.

113. Rivkin to Hansen: Letter from Robert S. Rivkin to Major General George Prugh (August 21, 1973) and Howard De Nike to Convening Authority Kaiserslautern Army Depot Complex, Re: United States v. Larry V. Johnson (August 2, 1973), RITA note 366, Archiv Soldatenrechte e.V. Weichselstr. 37, 12045 Berlin.

114. Letter from Howard De Nike to Captain Elvis Lewis, re: United States v. Larry Johnson, PFC, Archiv Soldatenrechte e.V. Weichselstr. 37, 12045 Berlin.

115. Nicholas Horrock, "Data Show Army Used Informant," *New York Times*, October 4, 1975.

116. Howard De Nike knew *New York Times* correspondent Craig R. Whitney because they had lived next door to each other in Saigon a year earlier. See De Nike, *Inter-Theater Transfer*, 91.

117. "Surveillance: USAREUR Rescinds 8th Inf Div's Drive on Dissidence— Termed 'Inappropriate,'" *Stars & Stripes*, August 11, 1973.

118. Craig R. Whitney, "U.S. Army's Plan in Germany Fights Dissenters in Ranks," *New York Times*, August 7, 1973. See also Whitney, "Some of the Spooks Have Had It."

119. "Surveillance: USAREUR Rescinds 8th Inf Div's Drive on Dissidence— Termed 'Inappropriate.'" See also "Army Halts Surveillance of GI Dissidents in Germany," *Chicago Tribune*, August 11, 1973.

120. Eighth Infantry Division Regulation 381-25, "Military Intelligence Counter-dissidence Program," July 23, 1973, 1.

121. Eighth Infantry Division Regulation 381-25, Annex A.

122. Eighth Infantry Division Regulation 381-25, Annex B.

123. Eighth Infantry Division Regulation 381-25, Annex D.

124. Despite RITA's claims to the contrary, Karen Bixler's crucial involvement is corroborated by fellow activist Howard De Nike. See De Nike, *Inter-Theater Transfer*, 5–6.

125. §103 and §104 of the German Code of Criminal Law (Strafgesetzbuch).

126. Stadt Heidelberg, Amt für öffentliche Ordnung to Karen Seelye Bixler, "Ausweisung und Abschiebung aus dem Bundesgebiet Deutschland incl. West-Berlin," Az. 32/2–VIII/73 (August 31, 1973).

127. "Solidarität mit Karen Bixler," flyer put out by the Zentrales Aktions-Komitee der Baden-Württembergischen Studentenschaften, September 13, 1973, Collegium Academicum der Universität Heidelberg, "Presseerklärung des Collegium Academicum zur Ausweisungsverfügung gegen Karen Bixler," September 12, 1973, and "Erklärung von *Fight Back* zur Ausweisungsverfügung gegen Karen Bixler," September 12, 1973. All three flyers were collected in RITA note 372, Archiv Soldatenrechte e.V. Weichselstr. 37, 12045 Berlin.

128. Craig R. Whitney, "Germans Expelling U.S. Student for Work on Anti-Army Paper," *New York Times,* September 14, 1973.

129. "US-Studentin soll ausgewiesen werden," *Rhein-Neckar-Zeitung,* September 11, 1973; "Zersetzung der Schlagkraft," *Heidelberger Tageblatt,* September 11, 1973; "Materialien von dritter Seite," *Heidelberger Tageblatt,* September 12, 1973; "Protest gegen Ausweisung von US-Studentin," *Stuttgarter Zeitung,* September 12, 1973.

130. De Nike, *Inter-Theater Transfer,* 104.

131. "Karen Will Stay! Deportation Stopped," *Fight Back,* no. 16 (February 1974): 1, Archiv Soldatenrechte e.V. Weichselstr. 37, 12045 Berlin.

132. De Nike, *Inter-Theater Transfer,* 51–52.

133. Persons interview, 440.

134. Even Persons acknowledged that military intelligence had been heavily involved in the wiretapping of dissident groups. See Persons interview, 453.

135. "Energy Crisis? Crisis or Rip-Off," *Fight Back,* no. 16 (February 1974): 4–5, Archiv Soldatenrechte e.V. Weichselstr. 37, 12045 Berlin.

136. "Phony Shortage: Real Crisis," *Fight Back,* no. 19 (May 1974): 8–9, Archiv Soldatenrechte e.V. Weichselstr. 37, 12045 Berlin.

137. Cover, *Fight Back,* no. 17 (March 1974), Archiv Soldatenrechte e.V. Weichselstr. 37, 12045 Berlin.

138. "March 8: International Women's Day," *Fight Back,* no. 17 (March 1974), Archiv Soldatenrechte e.V. Weichselstr. 37, 12045 Berlin.

139. "Women and the Military," *Fight Back,* no. 17 (March 1974), Archiv Soldatenrechte e.V. Weichselstr. 37, 12045 Berlin.

140. Interview with Beverly Jean Brown, Brown Collection (AFC/2001/001/30895), Veterans History Project, American Folklife Center, Library of Congress.

141. "Army Dependent Speaks Out," *Fight Back*, no. 17 (March 1974), Archiv Soldatenrechte e.V. Weichselstr. 37, 12045 Berlin.

142. "Women Fight Back in Heidelberg," *Fight Back*, no. 17 (March 1974): 8, Archiv Soldatenrechte e.V. Weichselstr. 37, 12045 Berlin.

143. "Women in Struggle," *Fight Back*, no. 19 (May 1974): 5, Archiv Soldatenrechte e.V. Weichselstr. 37, 12045 Berlin.

144. "The Militarization of Women," *Fight Back*, no. 23 (September 1974): 3, Archiv Soldatenrechte e.V. Weichselstr. 37, 12045 Berlin.

145. Rivkin, *GI Rights and Army Justice*, 183–84.

146. De Nike, *Inter-Theater Transfer*, 51.

147. Rivkin, *GI Rights*, 185.

148. De Nike, *Inter-Theater Transfer*, 70–71.

149. "Filing Charges under the UCMJ," *Fight Back*, no. 17 (March 1974): 8, Archiv Soldatenrechte e.V. Weichselstr. 37, 12045 Berlin.

150. See, for example, "Redress of Grievance & Article 138," *Fight Back*, no. 23 (September 1974): 6, Archiv Soldatenrechte e.V. Weichselstr. 37, 12045 Berlin.

151. "Injuries to Property & Article 139," *Fight Back*, no. 19 (May 1974): 7, Archiv Soldatenrechte e.V. Weichselstr. 37, 12045 Berlin.

152. "Braided Hair: Our Heritage" and "Haircut Hassles in Gelnhausen," *Fight Back*, no. 16 (February 1974): 6, Archiv Soldatenrechte e.V. Weichselstr. 37, 12045 Berlin.

153. "Haircuts: Airman Challenges Regs," *Fight Back*, no. 17 (March 1974): 2–3.

154. "The Hair Struggle," *Fight Back*, no. 23 (September 1974): 2, Archiv Soldatenrechte e.V. Weichselstr. 37, 12045 Berlin.

155. Persons interview, 443–45.

156. Persons interview, 443–45.

157. See "Pig of the Month," *Fight Back*, no. 16 (February 1974): 4; no. 19 (May 1974): 4; no. 23 (September 1974): 9.

158. Griffith, *The U.S. Army's Transition*, 81. See also George I. Forsythe, "The Impact of VOLAR," *Army* 21, no. 10 (October 1971): 29–32.

159. Griffith, *The U.S. Army Transition*, 103, 106–7.

7. DRUG ABUSE PREVENTION

1. Joseph R. L. Sterne, "GI Drug in Europe Is Hashish, Not Heroin," *Baltimore Sun*, July 4, 1971.

2. Barbara Campbell, "Extent of Drug Use and Addiction in Armed Forces Appears Wider than Pentagon's Statistics Show," *New York Times*, June 8, 1970; Warren Rogers, "Military Drug Abuse Rising at Alarming Rate,

Pentagon Says," *Los Angeles Times*, August 21, 1970; "3 Out of 10 GIs Said to Try Drugs," *New York Times*, August 21, 1970; George W. Ashworth, "Military vs. Drugs: Task Force Urges Detection and Rehabilitation," *Christian Science Monitor*, August 22, 1970; "Army Reports 89 Drug Deaths in Viet," *Chicago Tribune*, October 31, 1970.

3. Musto, *American Disease*, 1–7.
4. Bertram et al., *Drug War Politics*, 62–63.
5. Musto, *Drugs in America*, 253.
6. Bertram et al., *Drug War Politics*, 66–69.
7. Musto, *American Disease*, 3, 5–8, 65. See also Musto, *Drugs in America*, 361–67.
8. Bertram et al., *Drug War Politics*, 69–75.
9. Musto, *American Disease*, 190; Inciardi, *The War on Drugs*, 98.
10. Hoff, "Drug Abuse," 171.
11. Bertram et al., *Drug War Politics*, 79; Musto, *American Disease*, 210–11; McWilliams, "Through the Past Darkly," 365.
12. Kinder, "Shutting Out the Evil," 479, and McWilliams, "Through the Past Darkly," 368.
13. United States vs. Ellington, 32 BR 391 (ABR 1944); United States vs. Bareto, 3 BR (ETO) 137 (ABR 1948); cited according to Hoff, "Drug Abuse," 171.
14. Hoff, "Drug Abuse," 171–72.
15. Bertram et al., *Drug War Politics*, 84–85.
16. Musto and Korsmeyer, *The Quest for Drug Control*, 1.
17. Bertram et al., *Drug War Politics*, 86–87.
18. Musto, *American Disease*, 235.
19. Musto, *American Disease*, 3, 12, 13.
20. Musto, *American Disease*, 17–19.
21. Bertram et al., *Drug War Politics*, 90–93.
22. Nixon had discovered the value of this issue in his 1962 gubernatorial campaign when he had accused California governor Edmund "Pat" Brown of being "soft on Dope." See McCoy, *The Politics of Heroin*, 391.
23. Statement by Richard M. Nixon, Republican presidential nominee, Anaheim, California, September 16, 1968, folder Len-13-3, box 29, Presidents' Advisory Council on Executive Organization, WHCF, Nixon Presidential Material Staff, National Archives. A copy of the statement can be found on the compact disc containing "Searchable Drug Policy Documents" attached to Musto and Korsmeyer, *Quest for Drug Control*.
24. Draft, Message to Congress on Narcotics and Dangerous Drugs, April 14, 1969, folder OA 5256 Narcotics and Dangerous Drugs, box 67, Emil Krogh

files, WHCF, Nixon Presidential Material Staff, National Archives, in David F. Musto and Pamela Korsmeyer, "Searchable Drug Policy Documents," CD-Rom attached to *The Quest for Drug Control*.

25. The government mainly based its numbers on an estimate based on the number of arrested users. Arrested users represented the known number of narcotics abusers. Officials made the reasonable assumption that many abusers would remain unknown to officials and that an estimate had to be made based on the known number. However, such estimates could vary even among different branches of the government.

26. McCoy, *The Politics of Heroin*, 393.

27. Musto, *American Disease*, 39, 74. See, for example, "Gallup Finds War Declines as Issue," *New York Times*, December 19, 1971.

28. The Senate bill had three main goals. The act would (1) "provide more meaningful regulation over legitimate sources of drugs," (2) "strengthen law enforcement against illicit drug traffic," and (3) "eliminate some of the inconsistencies in the present regulation of drugs." See *Congressional Quarterly Almanac* (Washington DC Congressional Quarterly New Features, 1969), 707.

29. Musto, *American Disease*, 56–62, 68–69.

30. Musto, *American Disease*, 62, 66–71.

31. Musto, *American Disease*, 50, 52, 74. See also interview with Jerome H. Jaffe, October 6, 1994, quoted in Musto, *American Disease*, 91. "Sammy Davis Jr. Says Drug Program 'Is Positively Working,'" *Commanders Digest* 11, no. 25 (April 20, 1972): 1–2.

32. Concern for the treatment of addicted GIs became a frequent feature in the major newspapers in 1970 and 1971. See, for example, "Extent of Drug Use and Addiction in Armed Forces Appears Wider than Pentagon's Statistics Show," *New York Times*, June 8, 1970; George W. Ashworth, "Military vs. Drugs," *Christian Science Monitor*, August 20, 1970; "Bill Would Allow Discharge of Addicts," *New York Times*, May 16, 1971; "A Few GI Addicts Aided in U.S.," *New York Times*, May 17, 1971; "U.S. Aid to Addicts in Military Called Farcical and Inept," *New York Times*, October 29, 1971; "Hughes Scores the Military on Drug Testing Program," *New York Times*, October 10, 1972.

33. Two of the groups charged with reviewing policy were the Ad Hoc Committee on Drug Abuse and the President's Advisory Council on Executive Organization. The White House also created a Special Action Office for Drug Abuse Prevention, which was to oversee all federal demand-related programs from the Executive Office of the President. See Musto, *American Disease*, 74–75, 90.

34. Richard M. Nixon, "Statement on Establishing the Office for Drug Abuse Law Enforcement," January 28, 1972, *Public Papers of the Presidents of the United States: Richard Nixon, 1972*, 115–18.

35. Richard M. Nixon, "Remarks to Athletes Attending a White House Sponsored Conference on Drug Abuse," February 3, 1972, and "Remarks about a Heroin Seizure by Miami Customs Patrol Officers," April 8, 1972, both in *Public Papers of the Presidents of the United States: Richard Nixon, 1972*, 144–47, 524.

36. Musto, *American Disease*, 116–17. Also see McCoy, *The Politics of Heroin*, 392; Richard M. Nixon, "Remarks to the Washington Conference on International Narcotics Control," September 18, 1972, and Nixon, "Radio Address on Crime and Drug Abuse," October 15, 1972, both in *Public Papers of the Presidents of the United States: Richard Nixon, 1972*, 873–76, 982–85.

37. McCoy, *The Politics of Heroin*, 393–94.

38. The claims by the government did not go unchallenged. Democratic candidate George McGovern argued that Nixon's claims that heroin was drying up was based on bogus street price statistics. See McCoy, *The Politics of Heroin*, 392–93. Also see *New York Times*, October 14, 1972.

39. Cabinet Committee on International Narcotics Control, *World Opium Survey, 1972* (Washington DC: Department of State, 1972), 13. Also see Musto, *American Disease*, 118. While there was some justification in the government's claim that it was slowing smuggling into the United States, it did little to attack the production capacity of Southeast Asian syndicates. Ultimately this led to a diversion of the heroin trade to the European and Australian markets, thereby contributing to a growing complexity of the worldwide trade. See McCoy, *The Politics of Heroin*, 395–97.

40. "Nixon Optimistic on Drug Abuses," *New York Times*, September 12, 1973.

41. Musto, *American Disease*, 115, 130–32.

42. "33 U.S. Servicemen Seized in German Narcotics Raid," *New York Times*, November 5, 1964.

43. "Service Addiction Study Urged," *New York Times*, May 26, 1966.

44. "Wide Narcotics Use by Military Forces Denied by Pentagon," *New York Times*, June 19, 1966.

45. "Pentagon Steps Up Fight on Drug Use in Vietnam," *New York Times*, February 26, 1968. See also Department of Defense Directive No, 1300.1.

46. Hoff, "Drug Abuse," 194, 180.

47. Presentation, Department of Defense, folder Len-12-7, box 48 PACEO, in Musto and Korsmeyer, "Searchable Drug Policy Documents." Also see

"Reviews 'Amnesty Program': Drug Abuse in Armed Forces Outlined to Special Subcommittee," *Commanders Digest* 8, no. 28 (October 10, 1970): 13; Hoff, "Drug Abuse," 196–97.

48. In 1968 it had been 8.92 per 1,000 in Vietnam and 5.17 worldwide. Presentation, Department of Defense, folder Len-12-7, box 48 PACEO, in Musto Document Disk.

49. Barbara Campbell, "Extend of Drug Use and Addiction in Armed Forces Appears Wider than Pentagon's Statistics Show," *New York Times,* June 8, 1970.

50. Warren Rogers, "Military Drug Abuse Rising at Alarming Rate, Pentagon Says," *Los Angeles Times*, August 21, 1970; "3 Out of 10 GIs Said to Try Drugs," *New York Times*, August 21, 1970; George W. Ashworth, "Military vs. Drugs: Task Force Urges Detection and Rehabilitation," *Christian Science Monitor*, August 22, 1970.

51. "Army Reports 89 Drug Deaths in Viet," *Chicago Tribune*, October 31, 1970.

52. "Group of GIs Polled in Viet Nam: Wide Use of Marijuana Found," *Chicago Tribune*, December 3, 1970; "Survey Shows Rise in Drug Use in War," *New York Times*, December 3, 1970.

53. *After-Action Report: Drug Abuse Program, Vietnam*, submitted by Maj. Gen. M. G. Roseborough to Deputy Chief of Staff for Personnel, Department of the Army, Washington DC, March 1, 1973, foreword.

54. House Military Appropriations Hearings, 164.

55. McCoy, *The Politics of Heroin*, 222–23.

56. See "GI Heroin Addiction Epidemic in Vietnam," *New York Times*, May 16, 1971.

57. Warren Rogers, "Military Drug Abuse Rising at Alarming Rate, Pentagon Official Says," *Los Angeles Times*, August 21, 1970; "3 Out of 10 Said to Try Drugs," *New York Times,* August 21, 1970. See also "Reviews Amnesty Program," 1, 13–15; House Subcommittee of the Committee on Appropriations, *Department of Defense Appropriations for 1972*, 92d Cong., 1st sess., 1971, 163; U.S. District Court for the District of Columbia, Committee for GI Rights vs. Robert F. Froehlke, Civ. A. No. 835-73, v. II *Memorandum of Points and Authorities in Support of Defendants' Motion to Dismiss or in Alternative for Summary Judgment and Opposition to Motion for Preliminary Injunction*, filed July 23, 1973, 3. See also George W. Ashworth, "Military vs. Drugs," *Christian Science Monitor,* August 20, 1970.

58. *Memorandum of Points and Authorities*, 41–51. See also "New DoD Directive Encourages Medical Evaluation of Drug Users, Authorizes Services to Establish Rehabilitation-Amnesty Programs," *Commanders Digest* 9, no. 4 (November 7, 1970): 1, 8, and "Reviews Amnesty Program," 1, 13–15,

presentation, Department of Defense, folder Len-12-7, box 48 PACEO, in Musto Document Disk.

59. *Memorandum of Points and Authorities,* 1–2; "New DoD Directive,"

60. Department of Defense Directive 1300.11, 4–6.

61. Department of Defense Directive 1300.11, 7–8.

62. Department of Defense Directive 1300.11, 9–10.

63. Senate Armed Services Committee, *Staff Report on Drug Abuse in the Military,* 19–20; Robert G. Gard Jr., "The 'Other War' on Drugs, Alcohol," *Army* 22, no. 7 (October 1972): 107–8. For a summary of the varying approaches of different branches of the armed forces in Vietnam, see Allison, *Military Justice in Vietnam,* 125–32.

64. *Staff Report on Drug Abuse,* 29.

65. *Staff Report on Drug Abuse,* 30.

66. *Staff Report on Drug Abuse,* 31.

67. Department of Defense Directive 1300.11, 4. Also see Gard, "The 'Other War' on Drugs, Alcohol," 108.

68. Department of Defense Directive 1300.11, 4. See also Gard, "The 'Other War' on Drugs, Alcohol," 107, 108.

69. Gard, "The 'Other War' on Drugs, Alcohol," 107.

70. AR 600-32, September 23, 1970, 2–3.

71. *Memorandum of Points and Authorities,* 5.

72. AR 600-32. The USAREUR supplement was published on March 9, 1971.

73. AR 600-32, 1-1, 1-2, 2-2.

74. James H. Polk, "U.S. Army Europe: New Weapons, Realistic Training Mark NATO Vigil," *Army* 20, no. 10 (October 1970): 51.

75. The engineer interviewed for the article was Maj. John R. Franklin, who was in charge of the Post-Engineer-Command. "Schmutziges-düsteres amerikanisches Heidelberg," *Tageblatt,* August 30, 1968. The translation of the headline is the author's.

76. On the situation in the Heilbronn barracks, see "GIs Blast Freezing Barracks," *Overseas Weekly,* December 21–28, 1969. The electrocution of Pvt. Robert Wilkerson was reported in "Space Heater Kills Trooper," *Overseas Weekly,* February 15, 1970.

77. "The Forgotten GI," *Overseas Weekly,* February 15, 1970.

78. "Welcome to the 'Snakepit,'" *Overseas Weekly,* January 4, 1970.

79. "Ticked-Off Sarges Blast Worst Army Mess Hall," *Overseas Weekly,* June 28, 1970. On the German contractor, see "Troops Get Dirty End of Labor

Dispute," *Overseas Weekly*, September 27, 1970. See also Johanna Prym, "German Blames Army for His Bankruptcy," *Overseas Weekly*, November 1, 1970.

80. House Committee on Appropriations, Subcommittee on Department of Defense, *Department of Defense Appropriations for 1972*, 92nd Cong., 1st sess., 1971, 561.

81. Polk, "U.S. Army Europe: New Weapons, Realistic Training Mark NATO Vigil."

82. Appropriations Subcommittee 1971, 561, 563.

83. Polk to David A. Burchinal, June 29, 1967. Polk stressed his commitment to fiscal responsibility in his 1969 Green Book Report. He wrote that one of the goals of his command was "to find ways to give the American citizen the most for his tax dollar without compromising effectiveness and capabilities while reducing the gold flow." See James H. Polk, "Improvements in Readiness Posture Highlight 1969 Watch in Europe," *Army* 19, no. 10 (October 1969): 45.

84. Interview with Lt. Gen. Arthur S. Collins Jr., conducted by Chandler Robbins III, Senior Officer Oral History Program (1981), 397–99. Also see Library of Congress interview with John Robert Bauer.

85. In the second case, the GI had apparently intended to drive the tank to New York City. See "The Beak and I," *Overseas Weekly*, November 23, 1969. On the raid in October, see "German Judge Releases Potheads in Greatest Dope Scandal," *Overseas Weekly*, October 12, 1969.

86. "Stoolie Says Trooper Is a One Man Mafia," *Overseas Weekly*, May 10, 1970; CID LSD Fink Land Spec 5 in Stockade," *Overseas Weekly*, June 7, 1970; "Weirdo Fink Leads El CID to Hash," *Overseas Weekly*, June 21, 1970; "El Cid Out for Blood," *Overseas Weekly*, October 4, 1970.

87. "Stay Off the Acid," *Overseas Weekly*, May 24, 1970; Kathy Russeth, "The Speed Freak," *Overseas Weekly*, July 12, 1970; Kathy Russeth, "Daily Use of Hash Is Not Good for You," *Overseas Weekly*, October 18, 1970.

88. Allan Rick, "Trouble Surfaces in Nuclear Unit," *Overseas Weekly*, September 13, 1970; "Undercurrent Simmers in Super-Secret Unit," *Overseas Weekly*, September 27, 1970.

89. Transcript of opening speech at the 29th session of the Interservice Legal Committee, Polk Papers.

90. David A. Burchinal to James H. Polk, August 12, 1970, Polk Papers.

91. Anonymous to Polk, December 31, 1970, Polk Papers.

92. Polk to Patrick W. Powers, January 25, 1971, Polk Papers.

93. U.S. General Accounting Office, Comptroller General, *Drug Abuse Control Program Activities in Europe: Department of Defense*, August 11, 1972, 31–33.

94. U.S. General Accounting Office, Comptroller General, *Drug Abuse Control Program Activities in Europe*, 34–35.

95. U.S. General Accounting Office, Comptroller General, *Drug Abuse Control Program Activities in Europe*, 32–34, 36.

8. DRUG ABUSE IN USAREUR

1. Davison's own estimate was that between 10 and 15 percent of his soldiers in the junior enlisted ranks (E5 and lower) had been using heroin. "Gen. Davison: 'Toughest Period . . . Ever,'" *Washington Post*, September 12, 1971.

2. Davison to Willard Pearson, December 9, 1971, Davison Papers.

3. Davison to Pearson, December 9, 1971.

4. Davison, "Lecture at the Woodrow Wilson International Center for Scholars," Washington DC, March 25, 1972, in A Collection of Speeches, 92.

5. U.S. General Accounting Office, Comptroller General, *Drug Abuse Control Program Activities in Europe, Department of Defense*, August 11, 1972, 14.

6. Davison to Pearson, December 9, 1971, Davison Papers.

7. General Accounting Office, *Drug Abuse Control Program Activities in Europe*, 14–15.

8. General Accounting Office, *Drug Abuse Control Program Activities in Europe*, 17.

9. Davison, "In Europe, the Focus Is on the People," 51.

10. Davison, "In Europe, the Focus Is on the People," 51–52.

11. Davison to Pearson, December 20, 1971, Davison Papers.

12. Davison, "Address at the Command and General Staff College, Fort Leavenworth, Kansas, April 10, 1972," in A Collection of Speeches, 109.

13. Davison, "Remarks at the Annual Meeting, European Department, AUSA Garmisch, Germany, June 1, 1972," 144.

14. Davison interview, section 5, 12.

15. Affidavit Persons, GI Committee vs. Froehlke, 1.

16. Affidavit Persons, GI Committee vs. Froehlke, 1.

17. Memorandum of Points and Authorities in Support of Defendants' Motion to Dismiss or in Alternative for Summary Judgement and Opposition to Motion for Preliminary Injunction, filed July 23, 1973, GI Committee vs. . . .

18. U.S. General Accounting Office, *Drug Abuse Control Program Activities in Europe, Department of Defense*, by the Comptroller General of the United States, August 11, 1972, 1–2.

19. Affidavit Hayward, 6.

20. Staff Report on Drug and Alcohol Abuse among U.S. Military Personnel and Dependents in Germany. For the Information of the Subcommittee on Drug Abuse in the Military of the Committee on Armed Services, United

States Senate, 96th Cong., 2nd sess. (Washington DC: Government Printing Office, 1972), iii.

21. Affidavit, deposition of Maj. Christopher R. Robbins, Defendants' Exhibit 3, GI committee vs. . . . 2.

22. Deposition Robbins, 4.23 percent out of 19,478 admitted to using amphetamines, 16.

23. U.S. General Accounting Office, Comptroller General, *Drug Abuse Control Program Activities in Europe: Department of Defense*, August 11, 1972, 25–26.

24. Draft circular 600-84, September 7, 1972, Defense Exhibit, GI Committee.

25. Affidavit Hayward, 4.

26. Morgan and Steele, *World Narcotics Problem*, 51–52.

27. Affidavit Robbins, 16.

28. Willard Pearson to Commanders, Major Subordinate Commands and Assigned Units (to company level) and Community and Subcommunity Leaders Appointed by V Corps Headquarters, and Chiefs of General and Special Staff Sections V Corps Headquarters, GI Committee vs. . . . See also Frank Pettengill, "Pearson Addresses NCO Academy," *Stars and Stripes*.

29. Willard Pearson to Commanders, Major Subordinate Commands and Assigned Units (to company level) and Community and Subcommunity Leaders Appointed by V Corps Headquarters, and Chiefs of General and Special Staff Sections V Corps Headquarters, GI Committee vs. . . .

30. "V Corps Drug Control Counter-Offensive," Phase 1, 1. See also Donald R. Bansler, "Battalion Commander's Policy Letter #20 (Room Safety, Security, and Décor)," GI Committee vs. . . . Plaintiffs' Exhibit X.

31. "V Corps Drug Control Counter-Offensive." See also Daniel W. Freach to S. A. Hoefling, "Drug and Alcohol Control Program-Ray Barracks." The community leader of Friedberg ordered officers to conduct inspections while a unit underwent urinalysis testing.

32. V Corps used this term for the CDAAC.

33. V Corps Counter-Offensive, Phase II, 3.

34. V Corps Counter-Offensive, Phase III, 1.

35. "Nellingen Anti-Drug Movement: Put Pressure on Drug Abusers," Plaintiff's Exhibit P, GI Committee vs. . . .

36. Affidavit Daskevich, 3. Daskevich admitted that he had not been able to verify those numbers, but that even so they had been cause for alarm.

37. Affidavit Daskevich, 4, 7–8.

38. "Nellingen Anti-Drug Movement," 1–3.

39. Anthony F. Daskevich, "Brief Your Troops ASAP," GI Committee vs . . . , Plaintiff's Exhibit P: 2.
40. Affidavit Daskevich, 8–9.
41. Davison, "Remarks, Afternoon Session Commanders' Conference," Heidelberg, Germany, January 16, 1973, in A Collection of Speeches, U.S. Army Military History Institute, Carlisle PA, 279.
42. Davison, "Remarks, Afternoon Session Commanders' Conference, 281–84. Davison reiterated his theme that compassion did not mean softness during a speech four days later. See Michael S. Davison, "Remarks for the V Corps Alcohol and Drug Abuse Prevention and Control Seminar, Dorfweil, Germany, January 19, 1973," in A Collection of Speeches.
43. Davison, "Remarks for the V Corps Alcohol and Drug Abuse Prevention and Control Seminar," January 19, 1973, Dorfweil, Germany, Speeches, 2, 7.
44. VII Corps Circular 600-3, February 9, 1973, 1.
45. VII Corps Circular 600-3, A-1-3.
46. VII Corps Circular 600-3, A-3-6.
47. VII Corps Circular 600-3, A-3-6.
48. VII Corps Circular 600-3, A-7.
49. VII Corps Circular 600-3, B-11.
50. VII Corps Circular 600-3, B-2.
51. VII Corps Circular 600-3, B-3.
52. VII Corps Circular 600-3 C-1.
53. VII Corps Circular 600-3 C-2.
54. During the trial the committee brought before the U.S. District Court in Washington DC defined itself as "an unofficial, unincorporated association of American military personnel, formed in Butzbach, West Germany, in February 1973 in order to protest policies and practices which give rise to this suit." Action for Declamatory Judgement, GI Committee v. Robert F. Froehlke.
55. Ted Strickland, "The Challenge Is Now before Us!" Flyer, Butzbach, Germany, February 10, 1973, Plaintiffs' Exhibit AA, GI Committee vs . . .
56. The Committee for GI Rights vs. Robert F. Froehlke.
57. Plaintiffs' Allegations, GI Committee v. Froehlke, 2.
58. Plaintiffs' Memorandum of Law in Support of Motion for a Preliminary Injunction, GI Committee . . . , 5–6.
59. Plaintiffs' Memorandum, 7.
60. Affidavit Ron G. Borolov, GI Committee v. Froehlke.
61. Affidavit Vernon L. Lyght.
62. Affidavit Dennis C. K. Puccia.

63. Affidavit Ramon L. Alvero-Cruz.

64. Affidavit Daniel R. Zenk.

65. Affidavit Gary D. Henderson.

66. Affidavit Oliver J. Ozment Jr.

67. Persons interview, 416, 422, and 419.

68. Persons interview, 422; "Court Overrules Army Drug Drive," *New York Times*, January 15, 1974. See also Craig R. Whitney, "Army Drug Plan in Germany Hinges on Court Suit," *New York Times*, January 31, 1974.

69. Persons interview, 422.

70. Senior Officer Oral History Program, Lt. Gen. Arthur S. Collins, interview by Chandler Robbins III, Colonel, 1981, USAMHI, 415.

71. Wilton B. Persons, memorandum for General Davison, Davison Papers, 2–3.

72. Persons, memorandum for Davison, 3.

73. Persons, memorandum for Davison, 6. This was also consistent with DA Circular 600-85, which stated that "command policies should encourage soldiers to volunteer for treatment and should avoid actions that would discourage soldiers from seeking help. DA CIR 600-85: 46 (1).

74. Persons interview, 410.

75. Memorandum from Peck to Persons, February 26, 1973, GI Committee v. Froehlke, 2.

76. Memorandum from John R. Thornock to Persons, n.d., GI Committee v. Froehlke, 3. The memo was presumably written in February or March 1973. The memo reports on events taking place between October 1972 and January 1973, but must have been written before the trial.

77. See above. See also memo from Peck, 2.

78. Backchannel Davison to Subordinate Commanders, March 23, 1973, 2, 3.

79. Backchannel Davison, March 23, 5.

80. Backchannel Davison, March 23, 6–8.

81. Backchannel Davison, March 23, 8–9.

82. Backchannel Davison, March 23, 10.

83. Persons interview, 287–88.

84. Persons interview, 297.

85. Persons interview, 415–16.

86. Message from Pearson to Subordinate Commanders, "V Corps Drug Control Counter-Offensive," March 9, 1973, Pearson Papers, USMHI.

87. Davison to George S. Blanchard, June 25, 1973, 1, Davison Papers.

88. General Accounting Office, Comptroller General, *Drug Abuse Control Program Activities in Europe: Department of Defense*, August 11, 1972, 2–3.

89. Senate Committee on Armed Services, Subcommittee on Drug Abuse in the Military, Staff Report on Drug Abuse among U.S. Military Personnel and Dependents in Germany, 92nd Cong., 2nd sess., Washington DC: Government Printing Office, 1972, 2.

90. Alan Strachan, Summary of Developments and Current Status of the Frankfurt Youth Health Center, June 23, 1973: 1, 3–4, Davison Papers; William R. Desobry to Davison, Youth Health Center, June 27, 1973.

91. Memorandum for the Record, Drug and Alcohol Abuse Division Program Assessment Branch Team Visit to Ludwigsburg, August 3, 1973, Davison Papers; Memorandum for the Record, Drug and Alcohol Abuse Division Program Assessment Branch Team Visit to Panzer Kaserne, Boeblingen, August 13, 1973, Davison Papers; Memorandum for Major General Hayward, Drug and Alcohol Abuse Division Program Assessment Branch Team Visit to Mainz Community, August 29, 1973, Davison Papers.

92. Assessment Team Visit to Ludwigsburg, August 3, 1973: 5–6.

93. Assessment Team Visit to Mainz, August 29, 1973: 1.

94. Backchannel to Davison, Subject: PFC David C. Coffey, August 3, 1973, Davison Papers.

95. See, for example, interview with Barry A. Burnett, Burnett Collection (AFC/2001/001/09833), or interview with Reynaldo Puente, Puente Collection (AFC/2001/001/85195), Veterans History Project, American Folklife Center, Library of Congress.

96. Backchannel Davison, PFC Coffey, Background Investigation of PFC David C. Coffey by SP6 Ronald D. Neal, Investigation of Coffey and His Unit by SGM James W. Hardin, Davison Papers.

97. Backchannel Davison, PFC Coffey.

98. Backchannel Davison, PFC Coffey; Panzer Kaserne CDAAC Assessment.

99. VII Corps Circular 600-3, February 9, 1973.

100. "Army in Germany Drops Drug Drive," *New York Times,* September 17, 1973.

101. Lee Barracks, Wackernheim, and the Finthen Army Air Field.

102. Drug Assessment Branch Report, Mainz, August 29, 1973, Summary, 1–3.

103. Drug Assessment Branch Report, Report Lloyd R. Burton, Drug Trafficking in Mainz, and Report R. D. Neal, Source of Drugs in Mainz.

104. Drug Assessment Branch Report, Summary, 3.

105. Drug Assessment Branch Report, Report James W. Hardin.

106. Michael S. Davison to William R. Desobry, October 4, 1973, Davison Papers.

107. Backchannel DA to Davison, "Congressional Inquiry," Davison Papers.

108. Memorandum for General Harold I. Hayward: Drug and Alcohol Abuse Assessment Team Visit to Aschaffenburg Community, 1, Davison Papers.

109. Memorandum Hayward, "Additional Observations of 3d Medical Battalion," 1–2.

110. House, Committee on Armed Services, Subcommittee No. 2 (Military Personnel), *Hearings on Military Posture and the H.R. 12564 Department of Defense Authorization for Appropriations for Fiscal Year 1975*, 93rd Cong., 2nd sess., Washington , 1974, 1603–4. *New York Times* had reported on the rise of hepatitis cases as an indicator of increased drug use on several occasions in 1973 and 1974. See "Army in Germany Drops Drug Drive," *New York Times*, September 17, 1973; Craig R. Whitney, "Army Drug Plan in Germany Hinges on Drug Suit," *New York Times*, January 31, 1974; John W. Finney, "Gains Reported against GI Drug Use in Europe," *New York Times*, February 26, 1974.

111. Memorandum for General Harold I. Hayward: Drug and Alcohol Abuse Division/Program Assessment Branch Team Visit to Neu Ulm Community, 1, Davison Papers; Memorandum to General Harold I. Hayward: Drug and Alcohol Abuse Division/Program Assessment Branch Team Visit to Schwäbisch Gmünd Community, 1. Other communities receiving favorable assessments were Nuremberg, Nellingen, and Böblingen. See Michael S. Davison to Willard Blanchard, April 8, 1974, July 3, 1974, and August 5, 1974.

112. Davison to Blanchard, April 8, 1974, 2–3. The assessment team was particularly complimentary in regard to the Schwäbisch Gmünd CDAAC: "The CDAAC has an excellent operation and is staffed with competent, motivated and dedicated personnel. The administrative procedures . . . are precise and efficient. Case histories from counselling sessions are developed with sufficient comments to base an effective opinion of an individual's progress or lack of progress." See also Memorandum to Hayward, Drug and Alcohol Abuse Division/Program Assessment Branch Team Visit to the Crailsheim Sub-community, 1.

113. Memorandum for General Gannon, Drug and Alcohol Abuse Division/ Program Assessment Branch Team Visit to Nellingen Community, June 6–7, 1974, Davison Papers; memorandum to General Gannon, Drug and Alcohol Abuse Division/Program Assessment Branch Team Visit to Böblingen Subcommunity, July 18–19, 1974, Davison Papers.

114. Davison to Desobry, June 20 and July 3, 1974.

115. Memorandum for the Record: Debrief by Secretary of the Army Calloway, May 3, 1974, 1, Davison Papers.

116. Persons interview, 424–26.

117. Persons interview, 425–26.

118. House, Select Committee on Narcotics Abuse and Control, *Hearings on Drug Abuse among U.S. Armed Forces in the Federal Republic of Germany and West Berlin November 20 and 22, 1978,* 95 Cong., 2d sess. (Washington DC: Government Printing Office, 1979), 2.

119. Select Committee Hearings on Drug Abuse in Germany, 1.

120. Select Committee Hearings on Drug Abuse in Germany, 5–6.

121. Select Committee Hearings on Drug Abuse in Germany, 6. The concern over young soldiers' isolation and boredom would be repeated by several of the officers testifying before the committee.

122. Select Committee Hearings on Drug Abuse in Germany, 18, 27.

123. Select Committee Hearings on Drug Abuse in Germany, 18, 20.

124. Select Committee Hearings on Drug Abuse in Germany, 28.

125. Radine, *The Taming of the Troops,* 89.

126. Radine, *The Taming of the Troops,* 127.

9. THE GERMAN RESPONSE

1. On global drug abuse problems, see "Vietnam: Rauschgift, Kruecke zum Leben," *Der Spiegel,* no. 36 (August 31, 1970): 100. The quote came from "Mehr Kiffer als Fallschirmjäger: Die moralische Krise der amerikanischen Streitkraefte," *Der Spiegel,* no. 16 (April 12, 1971): 104.

2. Hodenberg, "Mass Media and the Generation of Conflict," 387.

3. "Wir mußten die 7. Armee ruinieren," *Der Spiegel,* no. 17 (April 4, 1972): 64–81.

4. U.S. diplomatic missions in Germany were keenly aware of this: Ambassador to Germany (McGhee) to Secretary of State Rusk, in Patterson, *Foreign Relations of the United States,* 1964–1968, vol. 15, *Germany and Berlin,* document 258; paper prepared in the Department of State, Patterson, *FRUS, 1964–1968,* vol. 15, *Germany and Berlin,* document 262. Egbert Klautke provides an excellent overview of the historiography on anti-Americanism. See Klautke, "Anti-Americanism in Twentieth-Century Europe," 1125–39.

5. Mausbach, "'Burn, Ware-House, Burn!'" 176–79.

6. Gassert, "With America against America," 502.

7. For a concise English-language history of 1960s protest movements in the Federal Republic, see Thomas, *Protest Movements in 1960s West Germany.*

8. For a groundbreaking study on the ties between the German and American protest movements, see Klimke, *Other Alliance.*

9. Klimke, *Other Alliance,* 89–90.

10. Marcuse, "Repressive Tolerance," 55.

11. See Dirke, *"All Power to the Imagination,"* 47. Also see Varon, *Bringing the War Home,* 43.

12. Klimke, *Other Alliance,* 91–93. On a detailed analysis of the influence guest students from Third World countries exerted on the German activists, see Slobodian, *Foreign Front.*

13. For an excellent recent analysis of the German student protest movement, particularly the antiauthoritarian faction, see Brown, *West Germany and the Global Sixties.*

14. Thomas, *Protest Movements,* 69–73; Klimke, *Other Alliance,* 62, 170, 177, 181, 187–93; Brown, *West Germany and the Global Sixties,* 72.

15. Thomas, *Protest Movements,* 76, 155.

16. See, for example, Thomas, *Protest Movements,* 147

17. "Nichts geht uns nichts an," *Der Spiegel,* no. 12 (March 18, 1968): 85–86.

18. Klimke, *Other Alliance,* 85, 87.

19. Höhn and Klimke, *Breath of Freedom,* 112–14.

20. Höhn and Klimke, *Breath of Freedom,* 113, 149.

21. Höhn and Klimke, *Breath of Freedom,* 183–87.

22. Dirke, *"All Power to the Imagination,"* 46–48.

23. Varon, *Bringing the War Home,* 67; Brown, *West Germany and the Global Sixties,* 242.

24. For a study on the significance of the Holocaust for antiwar protesters in West Germany and the United States, see Mausbach, "America's Vietnam in Germany—Germany in America's Vietnam," 41–64.

25. See Schmidtke, "The German New Left and National Socialism," 182. Also see Thomas, *Protest Movements,* 82.

26. Varon, *Bringing the War Home,* 209–12.

27. Brown, *West Germany and the Global Sixties,* 238.

28. Thomas, *Protest Movements,* 69.

29. "Diesen Krieg kann niemand gewinnen," *Der Spiegel* 10 (March 4, 1971): 30.

30. Gassert, "With America against America," 505.

31. For *Der Spiegel*'s coverage of Davison's antidrug measures, see "Auf Verdacht," *Der Spiegel,* no. 10 (May 5, 1973): 44–46; "Für die Katz," *Der Spiegel,* no. 38 (September 17, 1973): 196–97; "US-Armee verlor Prozeß," *Der Spiegel,* no. 4 (January 21, 1974): 17.

32. Höhn, *GIs and Fräuleins,* 52, 84. See also Nelson, *A History,* 58.

33. Höhn, *GIs and Fräuleins,* 107–8.

34. Höhn, *GIs and Fräuleins,* 126–54, 190–92.

35. Höhn, *GIs and Fräuleins,* 94–97.

36. "Weniger Watt," in *Der Spiegel*, no. 30 (July 23, 1973): 32–33.

37. "Ernste Bedränis," in *Der Spiegel*, no. 12 (March 27, 1978): 90.

38. "Absage des Rektors and die Amerikaner," *Rhein-Neckar-Zeitung*, June 10, 1970.

39. "Volle Zustimmung," *Heidelberger Tageblatt*, June 18, 1970.

40. "Amt pflichtwidrig mißbraucht?" *Rhein-Neckar-Zeitung*, June 18, 1970.

41. "Mit größter Sorge," *Heidelberger Tageblatt*, June 18, 1970.

42. "SPD Neuenheim begrüßt Ball Absage," *Heidelberger Tageblatt*, June 22, 1970.

43. For a succinct summary of this issue, see Ruddy, "A Limit to Solidarity," 129.

44. Memorandum from Assistant Secretary of Defense for International Security Affairs (Warnke) to Secretary of Defense Laird, June 28, 1969, Patterson, *FRUS, 1969–1972*, vol. 41, *Western Europe and NATO*.

45. Memorandum from Secretary of Defense Laird to President Nixon, February 20, 1969, Patterson, *FRUS, 1969–1972*, vol. 41: *Western Europe and NATO*, 40.

46. See, for example, translation of a Mansfield speech from June 30, 1971, by Leitungsstab 2, Bonn, 4 August 1971, "Eilige Rohübersetzung unter Vorbehalt," 26 April 1971, VI B/3-FA2810-14/71, Bundesarchiv.

47. Memorandum from Assistant Secretary of State European Affairs (Hillenbrand) to Secretary of State Rogers, April 7, 1969, Patterson, *FRUS 1969–1972*, vol. 41, *Western Europe and NATO*, 48–49. Also see National Security Decision Memorandum 12, April 14, 1969, Patterson, *FRUS, 1969–1972*, vol. 41, *Western Europe and NATO*, 57.

48. Telegram from the embassy in Germany to the Department of State, June 12, 1970, Patterson, *FRUS 1969–1972*, vol. 41, *Western Europe and NATO*, 157–58.

49. Interview with Michael S. Davison, 7–8.

50. Bundesminister der Finanzen, 6 April 1971, "Vermerk über die Sitzung der deutsch-amerikanischen Arbeitsgruppe vom 31 März 1971," VI B/3-FA2810-US 12/71, Bundesarchiv.

51. Telegram from Secretary of State Rogers to the Department of State, December 10, 1971, Patterson, *FRUS, 1969–1972*, vol. 41, *Western Europe and NATO*, 333.

52. Davison interview, 6.

53. Trauschweizer, *Cold War U.S. Army*, 195–205.

54. Persons interview, 400. On German resentment, see also *New York Times*, February 26, 1973.

55. Backchannel communication, Lemnitzer to Davison, October 22, 1971, USAMHI, Carlisle PA.

56. Persons interview, 401.

57. House, Select Committee on Narcotics Abuse and Control, Hearings, "Drug Abuse among U.S. Armed Forces in the Federal Republic of Germany and West Berlin," 95th Cong., 2nd sess., November 20 and 22, 1978, 194, 199, 219.
58. Select Committee Hearings on Drug Abuse, 194.
59. Select Committee Hearings on Drug Abuse, 54.
60. Select Committee Hearings on Drug Abuse, 203.

CONCLUSION

1. Drew Middleton, "Seventh Army Morale Rising in Europe," *New York Times*, July 16, 1974.
2. Paul Kemezis, "GIs in Europe Are 'Cooler' than Those of Vietnam Era, but Many Defy Old-Army Rules," *New York Times*, April 21, 1975.
3. Griffith, *The U.S. Army's Transition*, 107.
4. Trauschweizer, *The Cold War U.S. Army*, 195–229.
5. Persons interview, 481.
6. See, for example, Palmer interview, 443.
7. Haldane interview, 78.
8. Griffith, *The U.S. Army's Transition*, 235–36.
9. Maj. Don Gordon, "Volunteer Army and the Black Soldier," *New York Times*, March 30, 1973.
10. Interview with Michael Davison, section 5, 7–8.

BIBLIOGRAPHY

ARCHIVAL MATERIALS

Annual Historical Summary, Headquarters U.S. Army, Europe and Seventh
    Army, January 1–December 31, 1969. RCS CSHIS–6 (R2).

Archiv für Soldatenrechte e.V. Weichselstr. 37, 12045 Berlin:
    Flyers, correspondence, and underground newspapers relating to the
        activities of resistance inside the army (RITA) filed and numbered as
        RITA Notes.
    Long-running underground newspapers: *Where It's At, Up Against the Wall,
        Forward,* and *Fight Back.*

Library of the Army War College, Carlisle PA
    Forney, Leslie R. Chief, Alcohol and Drug Policy Division, Office of the
        Deputy Chief of Staff for Personnel, Department of the Army. State-
        ment before the Senate Subcommittee on Drug Abuse in the Armed
        Services Committee on Armed Services. 93rd Cong., 1st sess., Drug
        Abuse Problems in the Armed Forces, September 18, 1973.

U.S. Army Military History Center, Fort McNair, Washington DC
    After-Action Report: Drug Abuse Program, Vietnam. Submitted by Maj. Gen.
        M. G. Roseborough to Deputy Chief of Staff for Personnel, Depart-
        ment of the Army, Washington DC, March 1, 1973.
    White, James S. *An Assessment of Racial Tension in the Army: Text of ODC-
        SPER, DA Briefing for CINCUSAREUR,* October 27, 1969.

U.S. Army Military History Institute (USAMHI), Carlisle PA
    Personal Papers of George S. Blanchard, Arthur S. Collins, Michael S.
        Davison, James H. Polk, Willard Pearson
    Senior Officer Debriefing/Oral History Program
        Arthur S. Collins, interviewed by Chandler Robbins III, 1981
        Frederic E. Davison, interviewed by James E. Brayboy, 1981
        Michael S. Davison, interviewed by Douglas H. Farmer and Dale K.
            Brudvig, 1976
        William R. Desobry, interviewed by Ted S. Chesney, 1978
        Andrew J. Goodpaster, interviewed by William D. Johnson and James
            C. Ferguson, 1976

Robert Haldane, interviewed by Ralph L. Hagler Jr., 1985

Bruce Palmer Jr., interviewed by James E. Shelton and Edward P. Smith, 1976

Wilton B. Persons, interviewed by Herbert J. Green and Thomas M. Crean, 1985

Other Documents

A Collection of Speeches and Remarks Delivered by General Michael S. Davison during His Service as Commander in Chief, United States Army, Europe, and Seventh Army. Bound collection at the U.S. Army Military History Institute, Carlisle PA.

Render, Frank W. *U.S. Military Race Relations in Europe—September 1970.* Memorandum for the Secretary of Defense, Assistant Secretary of Defense, November 2, 1970.

U.S. General Accounting Office. Comptroller General. *Drug Abuse Control Program Activities in Europe: Department of Defense,* August 11, 1972.

U.S. National Archives, Washington DC

U.S. District Court for the District of Columbia, The Committee for GI Rights vs. Robert F. Froehlke, Civ. A. No. 835-73, v. 2, *Memorandum of Points and Authorities in Support of Defendants' Motion to Dismiss or in Alternative for Summary Judgment and Opposition to Motion for Preliminary Injunction,* filed July 23, 1973.

PUBLISHED WORKS

Allison, William Thomas. *Military Justice in Vietnam: The Rule of Law in an American War.* Lawrence: University Press of Kansas, 2007.

Ambrose, Stephen A. "Blacks in the Army in Two World Wars." In *The Military and American Society,* edited by Stephen E. Ambrose and James A. Barber Jr., 170–89. New York: Free Press, 1972.

Appy, Christian C. *Patriots: The Vietnam War Remembered from All Sides.* New York: Viking, 2003.

———. *Working-Class War: American Combat Soldiers and Vietnam.* Chapel Hill: University of North Carolina Press, 1993.

Army Regulation 600-18, *Equal Opportunity for Military Personnel in Off-Post Housing.* Washington DC: Headquarters Department of the Army, December 17, 1970.

Army Regulation 600-18, *Equal Opportunity in Off-Post Housing.* Washington DC: Headquarters Department of the Army, November 19, 1973.

Army Regulation 600-21, *Equal Opportunity and Treatment of Military Personnel.* Washington DC: Headquarters Department of the Army, May 18, 1965.

Army Regulation 600-21, *Race Relations and Equal Opportunity.* Washington DC: Headquarters Department of the Army, September 1, 1973.

Army Regulation 600-21, *Equal Opportunity Program in the Army.* Washington DC: Headquarters Department of the Army, March 15, 1984.

Army Regulation 600-32, *Drug Abuse Prevention and Control.* Washington DC: Headquarters Department of the Army, September 23, 1970.

Army Regulation 600-42, *Race Relations Education for the Army.* Washington DC: Headquarters Department of the Army, December 11, 1973.

Bailey, Tom. "The Trouble with . . . ," *Soldiers* 26, no. 10 (October 1971): 4–8.

Baker, Anni P. *American Soldiers Overseas: The Global Military Presence.* Westport CT: Praeger, 2004.

Bertram, Eva, Morris Blachman, Kenneth Sharpe, and Peter Andreas. *Drug War Politics: The Price of Denial.* Berkeley: University of California Press, 1996.

Bloom, Joshua, and Waldo E. Martin. *Black against the Empire: The History and Politics of the Black Panther Party.* Berkeley: University of California Press, 2013.

Bogart, Leo, ed. *Social Research and the Desegregation of the U.S. Army: Two Original 1951 Field Reports by Leo Bogart, John Morsell, Robert Bower, Ira Cisin, Leila Sussmann, and Elmo C. Wilson.* Chicago: Markham, 1969.

Bradford, Zeb B., Jr., and Frederic J. Brown. *The United States Army in Transition.* Beverly Hills: Sage, 1973.

Brown, Michael A. "Must the Soldier Be a Silent Member of Our Society?" *Military Law Review* 43 (January 1, 1969): 94–97.

Brown, Timothy Scott. *West Germany and the Global Sixties: The Antiauthoritarian Revolt, 1962–1978.* Cambridge: Cambridge University Press, 2013.

Butler, John S. "Assessing Black Enlisted Participation in the Army." *Social Problems* 23, no. 5 (1976): 558–66.

———. "Inequality in the Military: An Examination of Promotion Time for Black and White Enlisted Men." *American Sociological Review* 41 (1976): 811–16.

———. *Inequality in the Military: The Black Experience.* Saratoga CA: Century Twenty-One, 1980.

Carmichael, Stokely. "Black Power." In *African American Political Thought.* Vol. 6, *Integration vs. Separatism, 1945 to the Present,* edited by Marcus D. Pohlmann, 161–68. New York: Routledge, 2003.

———. "Toward Black Liberation." In *African American Political Thought.* Vol. 6, *Integration vs. Separatism, 1945 to the Present,* edited by Marcus D. Pohlmann, 177–89. New York: Routledge, 2003.

Cha-Jua, Sundiata Keita, and Clarence Lang. "The 'Long Movement' as Vampire: Temporal and Spatial Fallacies in Recent Black Freedom Studies." *Journal of African American History* 92, no. 2 (2007): 265–88.

Cincinnatus. *Self-Destruction: The Disintegration and Decay of the United States Army during the Vietnam Era.* New York: W. W. Norton, 1981.

Circular 600-70, *Equal Opportunity and Treatment in the Armed Forces.* Statement by the Secretary of Defense. Washington DC: Headquarters Department of the Army, January 30, 1970.

Circular 600-84, *Drug Abuse Testing Program.* Washington DC: Headquarters Department of the Army, May 1, 1972.

Circular 600-85, *Alcohol and Drug Abuse Prevention and Control Program.* Washington DC: Headquarters Department of the Army, June 30, 1972.

Cleaver, Eldridge. "The Land Question and Black Liberation," April/May 1968. In *African American Political Thought*, vol. 2, *Confrontation vs. Compromise: 1945 to the Present*, edited by Marcus D. Pohlmann. New York: Routledge, 2003.

Conant, Ralph W. *Prospects for Revolution: A Study of Riots, Civil Disobedience, and Insurrection in Contemporary America.* New York: Harper's Magazine, 1971.

Cortright, David. *Soldiers in Revolt: GI Resistance during the War.* New ed. Chicago: Haymarket, 2005. Originally published by Anchor/Doubleday, 1975.

Cortright, David, and Zoltan Grossman. "Die GI-Bewegung in Deutschland." In *Widerstand in der US-Armee: Vom Krieg in Vietnam bis zum Golf.* Berlin: Harald Kater, 2003. Originally published in *Dollars und Träume* 10 (October 1984).

Davis, Belinda, Wilfried Mausbach, Martin Klimke, and Carla MacDougall, eds. *Changing the World, Changing Oneself: Political Protest and Collective Identities in West Germany and the U.S. in the 1960s and 1970s.* New York: Berghahn, 2010.

De Nike, Howard J. *Inter-Theater Transfer: Contemplations of a Civilian Lawyer in Military Court, West Germany, 1972–1973.* Berlin: Harald Kater, 2001.

Dirke, Sabine von. *"All Power to the Imagination": The West German Counterculture from the Student Movement to the Greens.* Lincoln: University of Nebraska Press, 1997.

Dobbins, James, ed. *America's Role in Nation-Building: From Germany to Iraq.* Santa Monica CA: RAND, 2003.

Donaldson, Gary A. *Truman Defeats Dewey.* Lexington: University of Kentucky Press, 1999.

Downs, Gregory P. *After Appomattox: Military Occupation and the Ends of War.* Cambridge: Harvard University Press, 2015.

Edelstein, David M. *Occupational Hazards: Success and Failure in Military Occupa-tion*. Cornell Studies in Security Affairs. Ithaca: Cornell University Press, 2008.

Fantina, Robert. *Desertion and the American Soldiers, 1776–2006*. New York: Algora, 2006.

Feenberg, Andrew, and William Leiss, eds. *The Essential Marcuse: Selected Writings of Philosopher and Social Critic Herbert Marcuse*. Boston: Beacon, 2007

Fletcher, Marvin. *The Black Soldier and Officer in the United States Army, 1891–1917*. Colombia: University of Missouri Press, 1974.

Foner, Jack D. *Blacks and the Military in American History: A New Perspective*. New York: Praeger, 1974.

Foreign Relations of the United States, 1964–1968. Vol. 15, *Germany and Berlin*, ed. James E. Miller. Washington: Government Printing Office, 1999.

Foreign Relations of the United States, 1969–1976. Vol. 41, *Western Europe and NATO*, ed. James E. Miller and Laurie Van Hook. Washington: Government Printing Office, 2012.

Fortas, Abe. *Concerning Dissent and Civil Disobedience*. New York: Signet, New American Library, 1968.

Gabriel, Richard A., and Paul L. Savage. *Crisis in Command: Mismanagement in the Army*. New York: Hill and Wang, 1978.

Gassert, Philipp. "With America against America: Anti-Americanism in West Germany." In *The United States and Germany in the Era of the Cold War, 1968–1990: A Handbook,* edited by Detlef Junker, 2:502–9. Cambridge: Cambridge University Press, 2004.

Gassert, Philipp, and Alan E. Steinweis, eds. *Coping with the Nazi Past: West German Debates on Nazism and Generational Conflict, 1955–1975*. New York: Berghahn, 2006.

Gilbert, Marcia A., and Peter G. Nordlie. *An Analysis of Race Relations/Equal Opportunity Training in USAREUR*. U.S. Army Research Institute for the Behavioral and Social Sciences. McLean VA: Human Sciences Research, 1978.

Goedde, Petra. "From Villains to Victims: Fraternization and the Feminization of Germany, 1945–1947." *Diplomatic History* 23 (1999): 1–20.

———. "Gender, Race, and Power: American Soldiers and the German Population." In *The United States and Germany in the Era of the Cold War, 1945–1968: A Handbook*, edited by Detlef Junker, 1:515–21. Cambridge: Cambridge University Press, 2004.

———. *GIs and Germans: Culture, Gender, and Foreign Relations, 1945–1949*. New Haven: Yale University Press, 2003.

Graham, Herman, III. *The Brothers' Vietnam War: Black Power, Manhood, and the Military Experience.* Gainesville: University Press of Florida, 2003.

Griffith, Robert K., Jr. *The U.S. Army's Transition to the All-Volunteer Force.* Washington DC: Center of Military History, 1997.

Harris, David. "Die Forderungen der American Servicemen's Union." In *Widerstand in der US-Armee: Vom Krieg in Vietnam bis zum Golf*, 76–82. Berlin: Harald Kater, 2003.

Hauser, William L. *America's Army in Crisis: A Study in Civil Military Relations.* Baltimore: Johns Hopkins University Press, 1973.

Heinl, Robert D., Jr. "The Collapse of the Armed Forces." *Armed Forces Journal* 108, no. 19 (June 7, 1971).

Hodenberg, Christina von. "Mass Media and the Generation of Conflict: West Germany's Long Sixties and the Formation of a Critical Public Sphere." *Contemporary European History* 15 (August 2006): 367– 95.

Hoff, Charles G., Jr. "Drug Abuse." *Military Law Review* 51 (January 1971): 147–209.

Höhn, Maria. GIs *and Fräuleins: The German-American Encounter in 1950s West Germany.* Chapel Hill: University of North Carolina Press, 2002.

———. "Heimat in Turmoil: African-American GIs in 1950s West Germany." In *The Miracle Years: A Cultural History of West Germany, 1949–1968*, edited by Hanna Schissler, 146–63. Princeton NJ: Princeton University Press, 2001.

Höhn, Maria, and Martin Klimke. *A Breath of Freedom: The Civil Rights Struggle, African American GIs, and Germany.* New York: Palgrave Macmillan, 2010.

Hope, Richard. *Racial Strife in the U.S. Military: Toward the Elimination of Discrimination.* New York: Praeger, 1979.

Inciardi, James A. *The War on Drugs: Heroin, Cocaine, Crime, and Public Policy.* Mountain View CA: Mayfield, 1986.

Janowitz, Morris, and Charles C. Moskos. "Racial Composition in the All-Volunteer Force. *Armed Forces and Society* 1, no. 1 (November 1974): 109–23.

Jenkins, Philip. *Decade of Nightmares: The End of the Sixties and the Making of Eighties America.* Oxford: Oxford University Press, 2006.

Jones, Clinton B. "Black Power: An Analysis of Select Strategies for the Implementation of Concept." PhD diss., Claremont Graduate School and University Center, 1971. Ann Arbor: University Microfilms.

Joseph, Peniel E. "The Black Power Movement: A State of the Field." *Journal of American History* 96, no. 3 (2009): 751–76.

———. *Waiting 'til the Midnight Hour: A Narrative History of Black Power in America.* New York: Henry Holt, 2006.

Junker, Detlef, ed. *The United States and Germany in the Era of the Cold War, 1945–1968: A Handbook,* 2 vols. Cambridge: Cambridge University Press, 2004.

Kinder, Douglas Clark. "Shutting Out the Evil: Nativism and Narcotics Control in the United States." *Journal of Policy History* 3, no. 4 (1991): 479.

Klautke, Egbert. "Anti-Americanism in Twentieth-Century Europe." *Historical Journal* 54, no. 4 (December 2011): 1125–39.

Klimke, Martin. *The Other Alliance: Student Protest in West Germany and the United States in the Global Sixties.* Princeton: Princeton University Press, 2010.

Lee, Sabine. "A Forgotten Legacy of the Second World War: GI Children in Post-War Britain and Germany." *Contemporary European History* 20, no. 2 (2011): 157–81.

Lee, Ulysses. "The Draft and the Negro." *Current History* 55 (1968): 28–33.

Leuerer, Thomas. *Die Stationierung amerikanischer Streitkräfte in Deutschland: Militärgemeinden der U.S. Army in Deutschland seit 1945 als ziviles Element der Stationierungspolitik der Vereinigten Staaten.* Würzburg: Ergon, 1997.

Liston, Robert A. *Dissent in America.* New York: McGraw-Hill, 1971.

Lynd, Alice. *We Won't Go: Personal Accounts of War Objectors.* Boston: Beacon Press, 1968.

MacGregor, Morris J., Jr. *Integration of the Armed Forces 1940–1965.* Washington DC: Center of Military History, 1981.

MacGregor, Morris J., Jr., and Bernard C. Nalty, eds. *Blacks in the United States Armed Forces: Basic Documents.* Vol. 13, *Equal Treatment and Opportunity: The McNamara Doctrine.* Wilmington DE: Scholarly Resources, 1977.

Malloy, Sean L. "Uptight in Babylon: Eldridge Cleaver's Cold War." *Diplomatic History* 37, no. 3 (2013): 538–71.

Marcuse, Herbert. "Repressive Tolerance." In *The Essential Marcuse: Selected Writings of Philosopher and Social Critic Herbert Marcuse,* edited by Andrew Feenberg and William Leiss, 32–59. Boston: Beacon, 2007.

Marmion, Harry A. "Historical Background of Selective Service in the United States." In *Selective Service and American Society,* ed. Roger W. Little, 37. New York: Russell Sage Foundation, 1969.

Maslowski, Peter, and Don Winslow. *Looking for a Hero: Staff Sergeant Joe Ronnie Hooper and the Vietnam War.* Lincoln: University of Nebraska Press, 2004.

Mausbach, Wilfried. "America's Vietnam in Germany—Germany in America's Vietnam: On the Relocation of Spaces and the Appropriation of History." In *Changing the World, Changing Oneself: Political Protest and Collective Identities in West Germany and the U.S. in the 1960s and 1970s,* edited by

Belinda Davis, Wilfried Mausbach, Martin Klimke, and Carla MacDougall, 41–64. New York: Berghahn, 2010.

———. "'Burn, Ware-House, Burn!' Modernity, Counterculture, and the Vietnam War in West Germany." In *Between Marx and Coca-Cola: Youth Cultures in Changing European Societies, 1960–1980*, edited by Axel Schildt and Detlef Siegfried, 175–202. New York: Berghahn, 2006.

McCoy, Alfred W. *The Politics of Heroin: CIA Complicity in the Global Drug Trade: Afghanistan, Southeast Asia, Central America, Colombia.* Chicago: Lawrence Hill, 2003.

McPherson, James M. *Für die Freiheit Sterben.* Translated by Holger Fließbach und Christa Seibicke. München: List, 1992.

McWilliams, John C. "Through the Past Darkly: The Politics and Policies of America's Drug War." *Journal of Policy History* 3, no. 4 (1991): 365.

Michels, Peter M. "Die American Servicemen's Union: Interview mit Andy Stapp." Reprinted in *Widerstand in der US-Armee: Vom Krieg in Vietnam bis zum Golf,* 66–76. Berlin: Harald Kater, 2003.

Moser, Richard R. *The New Winter Soldiers: GI and Veteran Dissent during the Vietnam Era.* New Brunswick: Rutgers University Press, 1996.

Moskos, Charles C. "The American Dilemma in Uniform: Race in the Armed Forces." *Annals of the American Academy of Political and Social Science* 406 (1973): 94–106.

———. *The American Enlisted Man: The Rank and File in Today's Military.* New York: Russell Sage Foundation, 1970.

———. "The Military." *Annual Review of Sociology* 2 (1976): 55–77.

———. "Minority Groups in Military Organization." In *The Military and American Society: Essays and Readings,* edited by Stephen E. Ambrose and James A. Barber Jr., 192–201. New York: Free Press, 1972.

Moskos, Charles C., and John S. Butler. *All That We Can Be: Black Leadership and Racial Integration the Army Way.* New York: Twentieth Century Fund, 1996.

Murphy, Morgan F., and Robert H. Steele. *The World Heroin Problem.* Report of the Special Study Mission. U.S. Congress. House. Committee on Foreign Affairs. Washington DC: Government Printing Office, 1971.

———. *The World Narcotics Problem: The Latin American Perspective.* Report of the Special Study Mission to Latin America and the Federal Republic of Germany. U.S. Congress. House. Committee on Foreign Affairs. Washington DC: Government Printing Office, 1973.

Musto, David F, ed. *The American Disease: Origins of Narcotic Control.* 3rd ed. New York: Oxford University Press, 1999.

————. *Drugs in America: A Documentary History*. New York: New York University Press, 2002.

Musto, David C., and Pamela Korsmeyer. *The Quest for Drug Control: Politics and Federal Policy in a Period of Increasing Substance Abuse, 1963–1981*. New Haven: Yale University Press, 2002.

NAACP. *The Search for Military Justice: Report of an NAACP Inquiry into the Problems of the Negro Servicemen in West Germany*. New York: NAACP, 1971.

————. "The Search for Military Justice: Report of an NAACP Inquiry into the Problems of the Negro Serviceman in West Germany." In *Blacks in the United States Armed Forces: Basic Documents*, edited by Morris J. MacGregor and Bernard C. Nalty, 13:407–39. Equal Treatment and Opportunity: The McNamara Doctrine. Wilmington DE: Scholarly Resources, 1977.

Nalty, Bernard C. "The Black Servicemen and the Constitution." In *The United States Military under the Constitution of the United States, 1789–1989*, edited by Richard H. Kohn, 152. New York: New York University Press, 1991.

Nalty, Bernard C., and Morris J. MacGregor. *Blacks in the Military: Essential Documents* Wilmington DE: Scholarly Resources, 1981.

Nelson, Daniel J. *Defenders or Intruders? The Dilemmas of U.S. Forces in Germany*. Boulder: Westview, 1987.

————. *A History of U.S. Military Forces in Germany*. Boulder: Westview, 1987.

Nichols, Lee. *Breakthrough on the Color Front*. New York: Random House, 1954.

Nicosia, Gerald. *Home to War: A History of the Vietnam Veterans' Movement*. New York: Carroll and Graf, 2001.

Nordlie, Peter G., Bruce C. Allnutt, C. Gail Rasmussen, and Guy R. Marbury. *Improving Race Relations in the Army: Handbook for Leaders*. McLean VA: Human Sciences Research, 1972.

Ogbar, Jeffrey O. G. *Black Power: Radical Politics and African American Identity*. Baltimore: Johns Hopkins University Press, 2004.

Pohlmann, Marcus D., ed. *African American Political Thought*. Vol. 2, *Confrontation vs. Compromise: 1945 to the Present*. New York: Routledge, 2003.

Porter, Eric. "Affirming and Disaffirming: Remaking Race in the 1970s." In *America in the Seventies,* edited by Beth L. Bailey and Dave Farber, 50–74. Lawrence: University Press of Kansas, 2004.

Public Papers of the Presidents of the United States: Richard Nixon, 1972. Washington DC: Government Printing Office, 1974.

Quarles, Benjamin. *The Negro in the American Revolution*. Chapel Hill: University of North Carolina Press, 1961.

Radine, Lawrence B. *The Taming of the Troops: Social Control in the United States Army.* Westport CT: Greenwood, 1977.

Reed, Horace A., and Charles W. Whitmire. "Soldiers Look at Race Relations." *Army Digest* 25, no. 4 (April 1970): 4–13.

"Report of the Gesell Committee." In *Blacks in the United States Armed Forces: Basic Documents*, vol. 13, edited by Morris J. MacGregor and Bernard C. Nalty. Equal Treatment and Opportunity: The McNamara Doctrine. Wilmington DE: Scholarly Resources, 1977.

Rivkin, Robert S. *GI Rights and Army Justice: The Draftee's Guide to Military Life and Law.* New York: Grove, 1970.

Ruddy, T. Michael. "A Limit to Solidarity: Germany, the United States, and the Vietnam War." In *The United States and Germany in the Era of the Cold War, 1945–1968: A Handbook,* edited by Detlef Junker, 1:126–32. Cambridge: Cambridge University Press, 2004.

Sandler, Stanley. *Segregated Skies: All-Black Combat Squadrons of WWII.* Washington DC: Smithsonian Institution Press, 1992.

Saunders, Robert M. *In Search of Woodrow Wilson: Beliefs and Behavior.* Westport CT: Greenwood Press, 1998.

Scharnholz, Theodor. *Heidelberg und die Besatzungsmacht: Zur Entwicklung der Beziehungen zwischen einer deutschen Kommune und ihrer amerikanischen Garnison (1948/49–1955).* Heidelberg: Regionalkultur, 2002.

Schexnider, Alvin J. "The Development of Racial Solidarity in the Armed Forces." *Journal of Black Studies* 5, no. 4 (1975): 415–35.

Schildt, Axel, and Detlef Siegfried, eds. *Between Marx and Coca-Cola: Youth Cultures in Changing European Societies, 1960–1980.* New York: Berghahn, 2006.

Schmidtke, Michael. "The German New Left and National Socialism." In *Coping with the Nazi Past: West German Debates on Nazism and Generational Conflict, 1955–1975,* edited by Philipp Gassert and Alan E. Steinweis, 176–93. New York: Berghahn, 2006.

Shapely, Deborah. *Promise and Power: The Life and Times of Robert McNamara.* Boston: Little, Brown, 1993.

Slobodian, Quinn. *Foreign Front: Third World Politics in Sixties West Germany.* Durham NC: Duke University Press, 2012.

Smith, Jennifer B. *An International History of the Black Panther Party.* Studies in African American History and Culture. New York: Garland, 1999.

Stapp, Andy. *Up against the Brass: The Amazing Story of the Fight to Unionize the United States Army.* New York: Simon and Schuster, 1970.

Sweringen, Bryan T. van. "Variable Architectures of War and Peace." In *The United States and Germany in the Era of the Cold War, 1945–1968: A Handbook*, edited by Detlef Junker, 1:217–24. Cambridge: Cambridge University Press, 2004.

Takaki, Ronald. *Double Victory: A Multicultural History of America in World War II*. Boston: Little, Brown, 2000.

Taylor, Arnold H. *American Diplomacy and the Narcotics Traffic, 1900–1939: A Study in International Humanitarian Reform*. Durham NC: Duke University Press, 1969.

Terry, Wallace. *Bloods: An Oral History of the Vietnam War by Black Veterans*. New York: Ballantine, 1984.

Thomas, Nick. *Protest Movements in 1960s West Germany: A Social History of Dissent and Democracy*. Oxford: Berg, 2003.

Thompson, John A. *Woodrow Wilson*. London: Pearson Education, 2002.

Trauschweizer, Ingo. *The Cold War U.S. Army: Building Deterrence for Limited War*. Lawrence: University Press of Kansas, 2008.

Turse, Nick. *Kill Anything That Moves: The Real American War in Vietnam*. New York: Picador, 2014.

U.S. Congress. House. Committee on Appropriations. *Department of Defense Appropriations for 1972*. Hearings before the Subcommittee on the Department of Defense. 92nd Cong., 1st sess. Washington DC: Government Printing Office, 1971.

U.S. Congress. House. Committee on Armed Services. Hearings on Military Posture and HR 12564 Department of Defense Authorization for Appropriations for Fiscal Year 1975. 93rd Cong., 2nd sess. Washington DC: Government Printing Office, 1974.

———. Hearings before the Special Subcommittee on Recruiting and Retention of Military Personnel. 92nd Cong., 1st and 2nd sess. Washington DC: Government Printing Office, 1972.

———. Report of Special Subcommittee on Recruiting and Retention of Military Personnel. 92nd Cong., 2nd sess. Washington DC: Government Printing Office, 1972.

U.S. Congress. Senate. Hearing before the Subcommittee on Drug Abuse in the Military. 92nd Cong., 2nd sess. Washington DC: Government Printing Office, 1972.

———. *Staff Report on Drug Abuse among U.S. Military Personnel and Dependents in Germany for the Subcommittee on Drug Abuse in the Military*. 92nd Cong., 2nd sess. Washington DC: Government Printing Office, 1972.

———. *U.S. Forces in Europe: Hearings before the Subcommittee of Arms Control, International Law and Organization*. 93rd Cong., 1st sess. Washington DC: Government Printing Office, 1973.

U.S. President's Committee on Equal Opportunity in the Armed Forces. "Final Report: Military Personnel Stationed Overseas and Membership and Participation in the National Guard." In *Blacks in the United States Armed Forces: Basic Documents*, vol. 13, edited by Morris MacGregor and Bernard C. Nalty. Equal Treatment and Opportunity: The McNamara Doctrine. Wilmington DE: Scholarly Resources, 1977.

U.S. Task Force on the Administration of Military Justice in the Armed Forces. *Report of the Task Force on the Administration of Military Justice in the Armed Forces*. Washington DC: Government Printing Office, 1972.

Van Deburg, William L., ed. *Modern Black Nationalism: From Marcus Garvey to Louis Farrakhan*. New York: New York University Press, 1997.

Varon, Jeremy. *Bringing the War Home: The Weather Underground, the Red Army Faction, and Revolutionary Violence in the Sixties and Seventies*. Berkeley: University of California Press, 2004.

Veterans History Project, American Folklife Center, Library of Congress. http://www.loc.gov/vets/.

Walker, William O., III. *Opium and Foreign Policy: The Anglo-American Search for Order in Asia, 1912–1954*. Chapel Hill: University of North Carolina Press, 1991.

Waterhouse, Larry G., and Mariann G. Wizard. *Turning the Guns Around: Notes on the GI Movement*. New York: Praeger, 1971.

Watts, Max. "US-Army-Europe: Von der Desertion zum Widerstand in der Kaserne oder wie die U-Bahn zur RITA fuhr." In *Widerstand in der US-Armee: Vom Krieg in Vietnam bis zum Golf*, 72–93. Berlin: Harald Kater, 2003.

Westmoreland, William C. "Facing Up to the External and Internal Challenges." *Armed Forces Journal* 108, no. 9 (January 4, 1971): 23–25, 42.

———. *A Soldier Reports*. Garden City NY: Doubleday, 1976.

Wiggers, Richard. "From Supreme Authority to Reserved Rights and Responsibilities." In *The United States and Germany in the Era of the Cold War, 1945–1968: A Handbook,* edited by Detlef Junker, 1:103–10. Cambridge: Cambridge University Press, 2004.

Willoughby, John. *Remaking the Conquering Heroes: The Social and Geopolitical Impact of the Post-War American Occupation of Germany*. New York: Palgrave, 2001.

Young, Alfred F. *Dissent: Explorations in the History of American Radicalism*. DeKalb: Northern Illinois University Press, 1968.

Zeiger, David, dir. *Sir! No Sir! The Suppressed Story of the GI Movement to End the Vietnam War*. Documentary. Displaced Films, Pangea Productions, 2005.

Zinn, Howard. *Disobedience and Democracy: Nine Fallacies on Law and Order*. Cambridge MA: South End, 2002.

INDEX

media, mainstream (*continued*)
26–27, 28–29, 33, 37, 53, 54–55, 65–66, 68–69, 73, 80, 233–34; depiction of black power movement, 23–24. *See also* underground newspapers

Mickleson, Donna, 100

militancy and black power movement, 23, 26–27, 32–33, 36–37, 38, 53, 73, 77–78, 253

military intelligence surveillance, 142–48

military justice system: civil rights in drug abuse cases, 140–41, 203–15; Darmstadt 53 incident, 70–74, 110, 131–32, 253; Fort Jackson 8 incident, 101, 107–8; as platform for activism, 98–99, 120, 132–34, 138–41; racial discrimination in, 26–28, 38–45, 85–86, 88; Ramstein 2 case, 60, 62, 63, 132, 235; reform efforts, 84–88

military police, 6–7, 12, 26

Mind Expander (periodic flyer), 185

Moratorium Day, 126–27, 129

Morris, Joe A., Jr., 73

Moskos, Charles C., 13, 47

Mulford, Ralph K., III, 72

NAACP, 35–36, 41–44, 50, 57–58, 64, 77–78

Narcotic Rehabilitation Act (1966), 165

narcotics. *See* drugs and drug abuse

National Mental Hygiene Division, 164

National Urban League, 77–78

Negro Newspaper Publishers Association (NNPA), 7

Nellingen Anti-Drug Movement, 141, 194–96, 206, 207–9

New Left (Germany), 231–32, 236–38

newspapers. *See* media, mainstream; underground newspapers

Newton, Huey P., 61, 62, 111

New York Times, 28, 29, 55, 98, 142, 144, 170, 171, 228, 249–51

Nixon, Richard M., 32, 77, 165–69, 171–72, 243

Nordlie, Peter G., 88–91

Now House (street clinic), 181

offset negotiations, 231, 242, 243; end with offset agreement, 244; payments for, 247, 254

oil corporations, 148–49

Olais, Raymond, 139, 140

Oleo Strut (coffeehouse), 102–4

opium, 162, 172. *See also* heroin

Overseas Weekly (newspaper), 26–27, 28–29, 33, 37, 53, 54–55, 118, 180

Pacific Counseling Service, 108

PACS (Paris American Committee to Stop-the-War), 116

Paris, as haven for deserters, 114–17

Pearson, Willard, 81, 185, 186, 191–92, 214–15

Perrin, Richard, 115–16

Persons, Wilton B.: on Darmstadt 53 incident, 71–72, 74; on dissent, 148; on Hobson case, 28; involvement in drug abuse special committee, 187, 207–9, 214, 222–23, 244, 245; military justice reform efforts, 84–88; on race relations improvement strategy, 78–80, 89; report on military justice discrimination, 44–45; selected as judge advocate, 68

Peterson, Bruce, 103

Polack, Randall, 118

police, military, 6–7, 12, 26

CPSIA information can be obtained
at www.ICGtesting.com
Printed in the USA
LVHW041919150819
627783LV00005B/38